The Courtroom Elite:
An Organizational Perspective
on Criminal Justice

The Courtroom Elite: An Organizational Perspective on Criminal Justice

by
Peter F. Nardulli
University of Illinois

Ballinger Publishing Company • Cambridge, Massachusetts
A Subsidiary of J.B. Lippincott Company

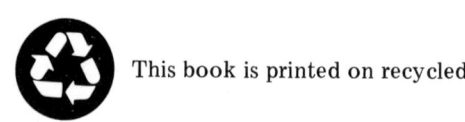 This book is printed on recycled paper.

Copyright © 1978 by Ballinger Publishing Company. All rights reserved. No part of this publication may be reproduced, stored in a retrieval system, or transmitted in any form or by any means, electronic mechanical photocopy, recording or otherwise, without the prior written consent of the publisher.

International Standard Book Number 0-88410-757-4

Library of Congress Catalog Card Number: 78-2358

Printed in the United States of America

Library of Congress Cataloging in Publication Data

Nardulli, Peter F.
   The courtroom elite.

   1. Criminal justice, Administration of—United States. 2. Criminal courts—United States. 3. Criminal courts—Illinois—Chicago. I. Title.
KF9223.N37   345'.73'05   78-2358
ISBN 0-88410-757-4

Dedication

For my Grandmother, my Mother and Father, and Ann

Contents

List of Figures	xi
List of Tables	xiii
Preface	xv
Acknowledgments	xvii

Part I
Approaches to the Study of Criminal Courts — 1

Chapter 1
The Study of Criminal Courts, Part I:
The Crime Survey Tradition — 3

Historical Factors and the Crime Survey Tradition	4
The Crime Survey Paradigm	5
Assumptions Underlying the Crime Survey Paradigm	19
The Crime Survey Researcher's Paradigm and Their Empirical Evidence	21
Summary	33

Chapter 2
The Study of Criminal Courts, Part II:
The Topical Tradition — 41

viii Contents

The Topical Paradigm 41
Works Within the Topical Tradition 45
Summary 56

**Chapter 3
The Study of Criminal Courts, Part III:
The Organizational Approach** 65

An Organizational Mode of Analysis and the Study
   of Criminal Courts 66
Dominant Modes of Activity 78
The Sentencing Decision in the Felony Trial Courts
   of Alphaville and Betaville 81
A Broader View 91
Summary 97

**Part II
Preliminaries to the Empirical Analysis** 103

**Chapter 4
The Organizational Perspective: An Extension** 105

The Setting of the Felony Courts of Chicago, 1972-73 105
Environmental Considerations 119

**Chapter 5
The Measurement of Organizational Phenomena** 125

Data Bases 126
Operationalization of Key Concepts 128

**Part III
The Empirical Analysis** 149

**Chapter 6
The Operations of Preliminary Hearing Courts** 151

Instrumental Activities 152
Screening 160

**Chapter 7
Dispositions in the Trial Courts** 179

Trial Court Operations: Gentlemanly Prerogatives 180

Factors Affecting the Attainment of Guilty Pleas   185
The Decision to Pursue a Case to Trial   190

Chapter 8
Sentencing in the Trial Courts   205
Sentencing: An Organizational Perspective   206
Data Analysis   210

Postscript   227

Index   241

About the Author   245

List of Figures

1-1	Crime Survey Researchers' Model of Factors Affecting the Efficiency of Criminal Courts	7
2-1	Topical Researchers' Input-Output Approach to the Study of Courtroom Phenomena	43
2-2	Bail Researchers' Approach to Assessing the Impact of Bail Status	47
2-3	Newman's Input-Output Approach to Factors Affecting Plea Bargaining	50
2-4	Sentencing Researchers' Approach to Assessing Disparities in Sentencing	54
3-1	Relationship Between Seriousness of Crime and Sentences in Alphaville	86
3-2	Relationship Between Seriousness of Crime and Sentences in Betaville	88
3-3	Relationship Between Seriousness of Crime and Sentence After a Guilty Plea in Alphaville and Betaville	89
3-4	Relationship Between Seriousness of Crime and Sentence in Alphaville and Betaville at Two Points in Time (guilty plea cases only)	90
3-5	Sentencing Decision Disaggregated by Type of Judge	94
3-6	Betaville Sentences Disaggregated by Judge and Conviction Mode	95
4-1	Formal Structure of the Felony Disposition Process in Chicago, 1972-73	107
4-2	Defense Counsel Responsiveness and Sentence Across Systems (guilty plea cases only)	121

List of Tables

1-1	Disposition of Criminal Cases in Cities and Counties Over 100,000 Population	24
1-2	Disposition of Criminal Cases in Cities and Counties Under 100,000 Population	26
1-3	Average Time Required to Dispose of Cases in Various Jurisdictions During the 1920s	28
1-4	Guilty Pleas in Selected Illinois Jurisdictions	30
1-5	Probation in Selected Illinois Jurisdictions	30
1-6	Definite Term Sentences in Selected Illinois Jurisdictions	31
1-7	Relationship Between Guilty Pleas and Probation in Selected Illinois Jurisdictions	31
1-8	Relationship Between Bail and Disposition in Trial Courts for Selected Illinois Jurisdictions	32
3-1	Differences Between Hypothetical Criminal Court Systems	83
4-1	Cases by Mode of Disposition in Chicago Felony Court System, 1972-73	118
5-1	Defendant-based Samples	127
5-2	Questionnaire Data on Nature of Law Practice for Different Types of Criminal Practitioners	139
6-1	Bail Information for Selected Offenses in the Preliminary Hearing Courts	154
6-2	Essential Data on the Dismissal Regression Analysis for the General Felony Courts	166
6-3	Essential Data on the Dismissal Regression Analysis for the Drug Courts	168

6-4	Cross-Tabulation of Disposition Mode by Discrete Version of Defense Counsel Responsiveness Scale (drug court cases only)	169
6-5	Essential Data on Revised Dismissal Regression Analysis for the Drug Courts	171
6-6	Predicted Dismissal Rates Across Different Confinement Periods	172
7-1	Essential Data on the Guilty Plea Regression Analysis	188
7-2	Essential Data on the Pursued Regression Analysis	194
7-3	Essential Data on Second Pursued Regression Analysis	197
7-4	Predicted Probabilities for Various Combinations of Session and Defense Counsel Variables	197
8-1	Essential Data on the Guilty Plea Sentencing Regression Analysis	210
8-2	Impact of Judge's Responsiveness Upon Predicted Sentence in Modal Armed Robbery Cases (in months)	212
8-3	Impact of Defense Counsel's Responsiveness Upon Predicted Sentence in Modal Armed Robbery Cases (in months)	212
8-4	Essential Data on the Trial Sentencing Regression Analysis	214
8-5	Impact of Mode of Disposition Upon Predicted Sentences in Modal Cases for Released Defendants (in months)	215
8-6	Impact of Confined Delay Variable Upon Predicted Sentence in Modal Armed Robbery Cases (in months)	217
8-7	Essential Data on the Second Trial Regression Analysis	218
8-8	Impact of Motions Variable Upon Predicted Sentence in Modal Armed Robbery Cases Across Categories of the Caseload Variable (in months)	219

Preface

This book presents a somewhat unique theoretical perspective on the operations of criminal courts. It has been developed after a thorough review of empirical studies of American criminal courts since the 1920s; a year's field work in the criminal courts of Chicago; and several years of contemplating, synthesizing, empirically examining, and refining notions acquired during the earlier phases of the project. Stated succinctly, this perspective holds that the fundamental problem with American criminal courts is merely one version, albeit unique, of the classical bureaucratic problem. That is, a small cadre of individuals—charged with the responsibility of performing a given task, vested with the power to perform it, and subjected to few external constraints—has utilized the resources under its control to pursue its self-interests.

In the Anglo-American system of criminal justice, power over the handling of criminal cases is vested almost exclusively in a small group of criminal justice officials: the judge, the prosecutor, and the defense counsel (the courtroom elite). Moreover, because many of the decisions made by the courtroom elite are of low visibility and are difficult to evaluate, external control over the actions of these officials is extremely limited. This, coupled with the fact that in many instances it is in the common interest of the judge, the defense counsel, and the prosecutor to dispose of cases expeditiously, has created a situation in which neither the dictates of due process nor the interests of the community or the defendant are of paramount importance in criminal court decision making. Rather, decisions often reflect the interests of those who control the dispositional process—the members of the courtroom elite.

Stated somewhat differently, the nature of the power and interest structure within Anglo-American criminal courts has enabled judges, prosecutors, and defense counsel to forge and maintain a coalition, the interests of which are reflected in the structure of the dispositional process. The fact that the courtroom elite has vested interests in how criminal cases are processed, as well as the power to effectuate those interests, has important implications for criminal court operations. A review of some historical bodies of work on criminal courts (Chapters 1 and 2) indicates that earlier researchers neglected to consider these implications in their analyses and that, in different ways, their works suffered. Chapter 3 argues that one consequence of the institutional structure of criminal courts, as described above (a monopolistic power structure and a tightly knit interest structure), is that important parallels exist between how they process their work loads and how other organizations handle theirs. It integrates several relevant notions in the literature on organizational behavior into a mode of analysis thought to be applicable to the study of criminal courts.

The remainder of the book (Parts II and III) extends the theoretical perspective developed in Chapter 3 to an examination of the felony court system in Chicago. The system's setting and environment are described in Chapter 4, and Chapter 5 describes the approaches used to operationalize some of the rather abstract concepts introduced earlier. The empirical chapters (6, 7, and 8) blend qualitative and quantitative data into a description of the court organization in Chicago. These data are also used to test some of the basic hypotheses derived from the organizational mode of analysis. The screening of cases in the preliminary hearing courts, conviction procurement in the trial courts, and trial court sentencing are all examined empirically.

Not all of the theoretical expectations are realized, and the empirical analyses indicate the need for various refinements in the mode of analysis suggested here. But the results of the empirical analyses support the assertion that, while there are significant external constraints upon criminal court operations, the interests of the courtroom elite have a significant impact upon the processing of criminal cases at various stages of the dispositional process. While these results are technically restricted to Chicago during the period of this study (1972-73), they do demonstrate that the application of the organizational mode of analysis developed here can lead to many insights into how criminal courts dispense justice.

Acknowledgments

I am indebted to a great number of people and institutions for their contributions to this work. Most of the data used in the empirical analyses resulted from my participation in the Comparative Study of Felony Dispositions Project. This project was headed by Herbert Jacob and James Eisenstein and was funded by the National Science Foundation. Most of the analysis was done at the Institute of Government and Public Affairs at the University of Illinois. I am deeply indebted to Samuel K. Gove, the director, for his unswerving support and patience during the preparation of this manuscript; without the financial and intangible support he provided I doubt I would have been able to complete it. The University of Illinois' Research Board and Program in Law and Society also provided me with valuable research support.

For their substantive contributions I am indebted to many people. The heaviest debt, of course, is to Herbert Jacob. He has seen the ideas embodied in this work develop, over the course of six years, from a seminar paper to a dissertation to a manuscript. He has dutifully read, commented, and critiqued each paragraph in each stage of development. In the end we differed in many regards; neither of us has been able to persuade the other on a number of important points. These differences notwithstanding, his contributions over the years have made this a better work. I am greatly indebted to Jeffrey Stonecash, who also bore the burden of reading the manuscript in its entirety. Like Herb, he has seen this work develop over the course of several years. His patient listening as I droned on about various problems contributed much; his cogent comments and criticisms contributed even more. One last person who was kind enough to have read the entire manuscript was James Gibson. Like the others his comments were well taken and contributed significantly to the final product. Heywood Sanders made invaluable contributions to the various statistical problems I encountered. He taught me much of what I know about applied statistical analysis, and for this I am very grateful. Wesley Skogan, Phillip Monypenny, Michael Preston, Marcus Felson, and Steven Seitz read various chapters and made valuable contributions. None of these individuals or institutions are, of course, responsible for any of the interpretations or shortcomings embodied in the following pages.

Stephanie Cole skillfully edited each chapter of this book and Jean Baker expeditiously shepherded it through the typing and duplication phases. Florence Edmison ably typed, retyped, and corrected several drafts of each chapter. Velma Sykes was saddled with the job of typing first drafts from illegible, handwritten copies and performed remarkably well. Lorena McClain also contributed her skills to the typing effort. Kathleen Proch, Marianne Guerini, Al Lizotte, and Terry Goodin all performed valuable services as research assistants.

On an intangible level I am indebted to Ann, Marc, and Beth Nardulli for their forbearance over the course of this work. Finally, I could not close without acknowledging my debt to Karl de Schweinitz, who encouraged me to begin the joint J.D.-Ph.D. program at Northwestern. I will not soon forget his efforts in guiding me through the joint program.

The Courtroom Elite:
An Organizational Perspective
on Criminal Justice

✳ *Part I*

Approaches to the Study of Criminal Courts

The ultimate objective of this work is to set forth, elaborate upon, and empirically examine one way of thinking about criminal courts, a view based upon various notions derived from the literature on organizational behavior. This organizational perspective is based upon the belief that there are important parallels between the operations of criminal courts and the operations of goal-oriented collectivities. More specifically, it is believed that it is in the common interests of the judge, prosecutor, and defense counsel (the courtroom elite) to process cases expeditiously. Because the structure of the Anglo-American criminal justice system vests these individuals with monopolistic power within the courtroom setting, considerations emanating from the shared interests of the courtroom elite affect criminal court operations. These considerations, as well as other organizationally relevant factors (external considerations, for example) are reflected in the informal procedures used to process work loads in criminal courts, much like parallel fac-factors affect the handling of work loads in other organizations.

While this basic notion is not original, it is a relatively recent observation. Earlier, empirically oriented students of criminal courts ignored the implications of these considerations for courtroom operations (as some contemporary students ignore them), with debilitating effects upon efforts to understand courtroom phenomena. To better understand the organizational mode of analysis to be developed here and to put it in intellectual and historical perspective, the first two chapters in this part outline, discuss, and critique earlier traditions in the empirical study of criminal courts. These reviews are included because of the belief that an understanding of where we have been enhances an understanding of where we are. The first chapter deals with what is termed "the crime survey tradition" in the study of criminal courts. It dominated thinking about criminal courts in the early part of the twentieth century. The next chapter outlines the "topical tradition," which spanned the early 1950s and the late 1960s. Chapter 3 outlines and elaborates upon the organizational mode of analysis to be used to direct the empirical analyses in the later sections of this work. It also contrasts this mode of analysis with earlier ones.

✻ *Chapter 1*

The Study of Criminal Courts, Part I: The Crime Survey Tradition

The Cleveland crime survey, the results of which were published in 1921, was the first large-scale attempt to empirically study the operations of American criminal courts.[1] Directed by two eminent legal scholars, Roscoe Pound and Felix Frankfurter, the survey was initiated by the Cleveland Foundation (a prominent civic organization) and jointly financed by business groups, bankers, labor organizations, the League of Women Voters, and other civic groups.[2] The Cleveland study was followed by crime surveys in Missouri, New York, Illinois, and many other states and cities.[3] These later projects were also the products of civic groups; they were closely patterned after the Cleveland study. These surveys, plus various other contemporary works, constitute what will be referred to as "the crime survey tradition" in the study of criminal courts.[4]

The crime survey tradition represents the first systematic, empirically based body of thought on the operations of American criminal courts. It is important to understand because much contemporary thinking about criminal courts has been influenced by these early works. This chapter will outline and critique this body of thought by first briefly discussing the historical context of the crime surveys. The historical context is important because various historical factors served as an impetus for the surveys and had a siginficant impact upon their orientation; an appreciation of them is essential to an understanding of the surveys. Second, the crime survey researchers' paradigm is outlined. This section discusses what they thought was important to study as well as what they thought affected the operations of criminal courts. Third, some important assumptions underlying the crime survey paradigm are identified and analyzed. Finally, the empirical data collected by the crime survey researchers are examined in light of their paradigm.

HISTORICAL FACTORS AND THE CRIME SURVEY TRADITION

The immediate impetus for several of the early crime surveys was a scandal involving a local criminal justice official,[5] but the surveys were really the result of several more fundamental historical factors. These factors included the "crime wave" which allegedly swept the country during the post-World War I era, the overly politicized nature of local criminal justice systems, reputed ties between organized crime and criminal justice officials, and dissatisfaction with the enforcement of Prohibition laws. One final factor that had a significant influence upon the crime surveys was the predominance of the municipal reform movement during this period.

These historical factors gave rise to a widespread dissatisfaction with the operations of local criminal justice systems during the period of the crime surveys.[6] To many the crime wave was evidence that the courts were not performing their deterrence function properly. Many attributed this ineffectiveness to the highly politicized nature of criminal justice systems. They claimed that urban criminal justice systems were little more than appendages of powerful political machines, a source of patronage jobs. Judgeships were awarded to party faithful on the basis of ethnicity and local prosecutors were political appointees often assigned to courts in their own wards.[7] Defense attorneys, policemen, bailiffs, and clerks were often accused of having political connections and of making contributions to the campaigns of criminal court judges. Even aldermen such as Michael "Hinky Dink" Kenna and John "Bathhouse" Coughlin were accused of tampering with criminal cases.[8]

Another widely cited cause of dysfunctioning in the criminal justice system was alleged ties between criminal justice officials and organized crime. Prohibition had led to an unprecedented consolidation and centralization of organized crime, and the enormous profits resulting from bootlegging operations were used to purchase protection which was easily acquired from the local officials. This situation heightened public indignation over the operations of criminal courts. It particularly infuriated those involved in the Prohibition movement. After many decades of struggle they felt their victory was being diluted by those in control of the criminal process who, for political as well as personal gain, refused to faithfully execute the Prohibition laws.[9]

The municipal reform movement, which was in its prime during this period, interacted with the abovementioned factors to heighten public disenchantment with the administration of criminal justice. It was an important factor because the movement had a significant impact upon people's perception of how local governments should operate.[10] In the view of municipal reformers there was no room for politics in municipal administration (i.e., there is no Republican or Democratic way to pave a street). The logic of the municipal reformers was easily extended into the realm of criminal justice. As Alfred Bettman, a prominent member of the Cleveland crime survey staff, once told members of the American Bar Association, "There is or should be no Republican method of trying a burglary case different from the Democratic method of trying a burglary case."[11] Given this orientation, it is not surprising that leaders in the municipal reform movement—and progressives in general—were appalled at the thought of a partisan system of criminal justice that maintained an unholy alliance with organized crime and operated in such a corrupt and inefficient manner so as to allow professional criminals to pass through it unscathed. In reality, the crime survey movement was an extension of the municipal reform movement into the area of criminal justice.

THE CRIME SURVEY PARADIGM

The crime survey researchers' progressive heritage had a significant impact upon the approach they used to study criminal courts. First, this heritage led them to a preoccupation with the notion of "efficiency." In fact, this notion was the dominant concern of the surveys. The primacy of this orientation toward efficiency is perhaps best captured in the words of John Henry Wigmore in the introduction to the Illinois crime survey report.

> Not everything is wrong, of course. But enough is wrong at every point to make the whole result a dismal and disconcerting picture. The main feature of what is wrong may be put into one word ... Inefficiency. No one part of the system of criminal justice works to maximum power, and most of them to less than moderate power ... Inefficiency everywhere. The Constitution's law is inefficient; the Legislature's law in inefficient; the Supreme Court's law is inefficient. The Trial Court's methods are inefficient; the Prosecuting Department is inefficient, and likewise the Police System. The Jury System is inefficient. The Probation and Parole Systems are inefficient; and with them the Prison System is inefficient.[12]

The crime survey researchers' reformist origins also led them to the belief that certain structural changes in American society (the shift from a rural, agricultural society to an urban, industrialized society) accounted for inefficiencies in local government agencies, including the criminal courts. These agencies were not functioning properly because they had not adapted to the changes in the environment within which they operated. Reginald Heber Smith reflects this orientation in his chapter entitled "The Fundamental Trouble" in the Cleveland survey report.

> Care must be taken not to ascribe the Cleveland failure to the evil work of individuals alone, although undoubtedly there has been exploitation by those whose elimination would have a salutary effect. Their removal, however, would not effect a cure. On the contrary, popular clamor for a victim diverts attention from the real difficulties, which are not capable of so easy and dramatic a solution. The conditions which made exploitation possible must be removed before permanent improvement can be effected.
>
> These conditions are first, the persistence of a system of criminal justice become obsolete and wholly inadequate through the rapid growth of urban population and modern industrial life; and second the unorganized, uninformed, and socially indifferent attitude of the more intelligent portion of the citizenship, brought about by concentration on material prosperity to the exclusion of civic life. The pages of this report tell the story, often in bare statistical form, of how an inadequate system is made use of to defeat the end of criminal justice in the absence of an informed and watchful social conscience.[13]

This municipal reformist orientation was extended to the study of criminal courts by the crime survey researchers in the form of an implicit model of factors posited to affect the operations of local criminal court systems. Within this model, efficiency was conceptualized in terms of disposition rates and delays. Systems that eliminated (failed to convict) a large proportion of cases were less efficient than those with higher conviction rates; systems with longer average processing times were considered less efficient than those with shorter average processing times. In a very crude sense, these two variables were the primary dependent variables in the crime survey model.

In their model the crime survey researchers also identified four factors that had an impact upon the efficiency of criminal courts. Three of these factors directly affected the operations of criminal courts; one had an indirect effect. The factors with direct effects were related to the administrative aspects of the process, the person-

Figure 1-1. Crime Survey Researchers' Model of Factors Affecting the Efficiency of Criminal Courts

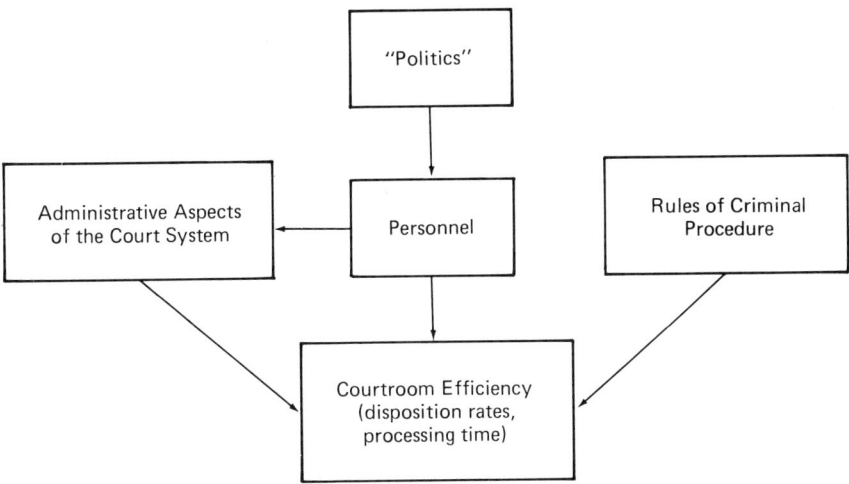

nel who manned the courts, and the rules of criminal procedure which governed the disposition of criminal cases. The indirect factor that was widely held to affect the efficiency of criminal courts was "politics"—a phantomlike phenomenon never defined by those who deplored its pervasiveness in the realm of criminal justice. The interrelationships among these factors are depicted in Figure 1-1.

Because of the importance of this model in the crime survey tradition, each of the factors hypothesized to have an effect upon the efficiency of criminal courts will be discussed in some detail. First, however, a few remarks concerning the model should be made. While the factors depicted in the model were those most commonly thought to affect efficiency, occasionally other factors were also mentioned, for example, the incompetency of American jurors, the unwillingness of juries to convict, the nature of the criminal law, and public apathy. Also, while the factors included in Figure 1-1 were the most frequently cited factors, it should be noted that not all commentators gave equal weight to each factor. Certain scholars tended to emphasize a given factor and to discount the importance of the others.

Perhaps the most extreme examples of this can be found in the case of two of the most prominent crime survey researchers—Raymond Moley and Alfred Bettman. Moley tended to dismiss the importance of administrative and procedural factors while emphasizing personnel.

> In the face of the great extent to which criminal law is subject to administrative discretion many well worn assumptions find their validity questioned. One of these is the contention that the way to improve criminal justice is to make procedures less technical and more favorable to the state. The rules, they say, are antiquated, cumbersome, overly favorable to the defendant. The remedy proposed is to sweep away the cobwebs, expedite proceedings and eliminate some of the restrictions upon the prosecution. But set procedural rules are in practice seldom invoked. As we have seen, a large majority of cases are decided before the "game" really begins. Trials are exceptional and the process of compromise is one in which formal rules do not operate to any important extent. . . .
>
> Much as procedure has been the favorite interest of lawyers the organization of courts has been the theme of the political scientist. Courts should be organized on a business basis, he says. There should be an executive head with large power. There should be integration of effort, specialization of cases. Our machine is cumbersome, based upon bygone conditions. In those few instances in which it has been tried, perfection of organization has failed to create marked difference in the net result. Good prosecutors and strong judges seem to do well in badly organized courts while, as we shall see, inferior persons do badly in the midst of structural perfection.[14]

Bettman, on the other hand, attacked those who placed so much emphasis on personnel and on criminal procedure. He even attacked the "politics" factor.

> The efficiency and quality of the administration are dependent, amongst other factors, upon the caliber—mental, educational, and moral—of the men who administer. That the prosecuting attorney should be able and honest requires no survey to demonstrate. That probation officials should know their business will be disputed by none.
>
> In connection with commonplaces such as these, there usually appears, in and out of the surveys, the much-used but never-defined word "politics." "Politics," whatever it may mean, is blamed for this or that quite freely. Indeed, parts of some of the surveys seem to be pieces of special pleading for blaming everything upon the connection between politics and the prosecutor or politics and the police. The American public surely knows that politics plays its part in fixing the quality of the administration of justice as in all other public organisms. If a case be prosecuted with dominatingly political (in the colloquial sense) motivations or conducted from the point of view of its "political" effect, the efficiency and quality of the result will, of course, be diminished.[15]

With these provisos set forth, it is now possible to discuss in more detail the nature of the factors depicted in Figure 1-1.[16]

"Politics" and Personnel[17]

In the view of the crime survey researchers, the "politics" factor and the personnel factor were closely connected. They believed that the vast majority of those involved in the processing of criminal cases were, at best, incompetent and, at worst, unscrupulous. This accounted for much of the inefficiency in criminal courts as reflected in low conviction rates and excessive delays. Moreover, the low caliber of criminal law practitioners (judges, prosecutors, defense counsel, clerks, etc.) was due to the ubiquity of politics. These practitioners were either political appointees or elected officials or had political connections. Hence they were susceptible to the influence of campaign contributors, big city bosses, or lower order politicos. The pervasiveness of politics not only attracted incompetents but also tended to bring criminal court practice into disrepute. In turn, this caused men of integrity and ability to maintain their distance from criminal courts.

It should also be indicated that, from the crime survey researchers' perspective, the "politics"-personnel problem had its roots in the structural changes in society. In rural systems where lawyers' reputations were well known, unscrupulous practitioners could be weeded out by local bar associations and by judges. This was not possible in metropolitan courts, however, given the anonymity of urban life. Moreover, judges and prosecutors—public officials well known to their rural constituents—were kept in line by the watchful rural citizenry. The crime survey researchers' view of "politics," personnel, and societal change is aptly reflected in Smith's discussion of the *nolle prosequi*.

> The motion *nolle prosequi* is another example of the decay of an institution which flourished successfully under the rural conditions of its origin, but which threatens to become a menace in a great modern city. Where the few criminal cases furnish diversion for the town, where the prosecutor is a marked man among his fellow-citizens, where interest in the crime and the criminals lightens the harvest and shortens the winter evenings, there can be little abuse of the motion *nolle prosequi*. Such checks are lost, however, in the rush and roar of a great city, especially the typical American metropolis, with its mounting crime rate, its lack of a tradition of disinterested public service, and the insidious ramifications of political influence.[18]

Specific examples of the "politics"-personnel factor abound in the surveys. Perhaps the most succinct treatment of the relationship between "politics" and the police can be found in Healy's chapter on prosecution in the Illinois crime survey report. Commenting upon the effectiveness of the police, he said:

> Numerically, our police force may have kept pace with crime, but in matters of efficiency and intelligent methods of crime detection we seem to have learned little and done less....
>
> The reason for this condition is recognized by every student of the question. Instead of being a purely crime detecting and apprehending agency, the police force of Chicago has been, through all the history of our City, the adjunct of whatever political faction happened to be in power. Its activities have been limited to the policy of the administration, instead of being governed and controlled by the letter of the law. Handicapped by the varying and vacillating policies of the administration, it is always a matter of police uncertainty as to which law shall be enforced and which violation shall go unchallenged. For many years there has been fastened upon the police department an active or a tolerant attitude on the part of the city administration toward vice and gambling. Responding to this attitude the police department has been demoralized and individual members have resorted to grafting and the levy of tribute, without which vice and gambling would soon be suppressed. Every sophisticated observer knows that these resorts would not be tolerated if it were not for the financial tribute which they pay to the public officials or their political satellites for protection.[19]

Healy attempted to document this by noting that during the fifty years which preceded the survey (1879-1929) Chicago had twenty-five police commissioners, while Scotland Yard had six in eighty-five years and Berlin had ten in sixty years. Healy concluded that because of this rapid turnover the average citizen saw the police commissioner as an integral part of the machine.[20]

In the view of the authors of the Wickersham report, prosecutors suffered from some of the same problems as the police, and this affected their performance adversely:

> Thus the prosecutor's office, with its enormous power of preventing prosecutions from getting to trial, its lack of organization, its freedom from central control, and its ill-defined responsibility, is a great political prize. Under the political conditions which obtain in large cities, except for occasional outbursts of popular indignation, prosecutors are likely to be selected with reference to the exigencies of political organizations rather than with reference to the tasks of law enforcement. The system of prosecutors elected for short terms, with assistants chosen on the basis of political patronage, with no assured tenure yet charged with wide undefined powers, is ideally adapted to misgovernment. It has happened frequently that the prosecuting attorney withdraws wholly from the courts and

devotes himself to the political side and sensational investigatory functions of his office, leaving the work of prosecution wholly to his assistants. The "responsibility to the people" contemplated by the system of frequent elections does not so much require that the work of the prosecutor be carried out efficiently as that it be carried out conspicuously. Between the desire for publicity and the fear of offending those who control local politics, the temptation is strong to fall into an effective perfunctory routine for everyday cases with spectacular treatment of sensational cases.[21]

Healy's observation of assistant state's attorneys in the municipal court of Chicago seems to affirm the conclusion of the members of the Wickersham commission.

The assistant state's attorneys in charge of these preliminary hearings are usually drawn from the lower ranges of the salary grades in the state's attorney's office. Their salaries run from two to three hundred dollars a month. They are, therefore, the less experienced and confident members of the staff. Oftentimes, especially in the outlying branches of the court they are selected with reference to their own political bailiwicks. This assistant seems chiefly interested in filling out a form report which he mails to the state's attorney's office at the end of the day's work. . . . An examination of these sheets indicates that some of the assistants scarcely rise above the literacy grade, and, added to this, are so meager in the information which they record that the reports are scarcely usable at all.

In observing the conduct of cases in the Municipal Court, it requires careful observation to determine whether the assistant state's attorney is there as a clerk, reporter, prosecutor, or casual visitor. He is usually seen lounging against the bench engaged in conversation with every passerby, careless, unimposing, undignified, and indolent—surely a sorry way for the peace, honor and dignity of the State of Illinois to be represented in court.[22]

In the Cleveland survey, Smith focused very heavily upon private defense counsel, political influences, and the operations of criminal courts. In Smith's view the source of this problem lay with the "professional criminal lawyer":

Another factor to be considered, partly the result of the foregoing and partly the result of many other causes, is the professional criminal lawyer. A poll of the bar of Cleveland shows that most lawyers dislike criminal practice, partly because of a feeling that it is detrimental to civil practice and partly because of professional ignorance or dislike of the required technique. The result is that a large part of the lucrative practice in the criminal courts goes to a small number of specialists.

> ... Moreover, many of this small group of professional criminal lawyers are in politics. Were the system as invulnerable as Achilles, these political criminal lawyers would find the penetrable heel.[23]

Smith reserved most of his contempt for a small segment of the criminal bar—the Police Court Ring—a group which dominated Cleveland's police courts.

> Owing to the fact that no record is kept of attorneys in cases before the criminal branch of the Municipal Court, no statistical data can be submitted of the attorneys practising in this court. It is common knowledge, however, that certain attorneys monopolize most of the business, and in a rough fashion divide the practice among themselves. Thus one group represents prostitutes, another pickpockets, another suspicious persons, etc. Anyone connected with the court knows the names of these attorneys.
> Theoretically, there is no objection to a limited group practising in a particular court. Indeed, under wholly different conditions a limited group of advocates would serve to facilitate the administration of justice by focusing responsibility for the ethical conduct of cases on a definite group. In the "police court" of Cleveland exactly the opposite has resulted. Men of ability as lawyers, or of fine sensibilities, shun this court, so that there is a tendency for men of less refinement to drift into the practice. The activities of these men are nowhere spread upon the record; they involve people who dare not or do not know how to complain. Some of these lawyers were formerly police prosecutors, in which capacity they made the acquaintance of habitual offenders and professional crooks; some are city councilmen with a voice as to the salaries of certain court attendants and a control over votes, which a weak judge cannot entirely overlook; others are connected in various ways with people of political importance.[24]

Smith's basic objection to these professional criminal lawyers was, of course, that they monopolized criminal practice and perverted the criminal process. He charged that the regulars received a disproportionate number of assigned cases from criminal court judges.[25] He even alleged that these attorneys had arrangements with the police whereby, when things were slow, the police would raid a house of ill repute.[26] In his report on Chicago's municipal court, Moley concurred with many of Smith's observations. Regulars, Moley noted, are in every branch court and they obtained referrals from policemen and bailiffs—for a price. Court officials even sell positions as regulars. The position is accompanied by referrals and a promise that the referrals will not be prosecuted vigorously by the state.[27]

In an effort to document the deleterious effect which these political criminal attorneys had upon the dispositional process, Smith analyzed the cases in which they participated. He found that "Even during a period in which judges were stiffening in the matter of 'bench paroles', the political criminal lawyer has been able to snatch some advantage for his clients...."[28] He found that these attorneys were able to secure more *nolles*, had higher acquittal rates, lower guilty plea rates, and a greater percentage of suspended sentences. Hence, for Smith, the connection between the professional criminal lawyer and criminal court inefficiency was established empirically.

In terms of competency, judges—particularly trial court judges— fared much better in the eyes of the crime survey researchers than did other participants in the process. Smith, for instance, made the following comments with regard to the judges on Cleveland's court of common pleas:

> In respect of legal ability it [the bench] consists of two judges who, by reason of long experience on the bench, have acquired a wide knowledge of the law and practice; five judges of fair native ability, some of whom need experience to become good judges; two judges of mediocre ability; one judge not tried out sufficiently to afford a basis for judging legal qualifications; one judge of practically no juristic qualifications, and one whose unusual legal gifts make his presence on the bench a decided asset. In respect of faithfulness to duties, the list includes one judge who is notoriously unpunctual, several others designated as somewhat "lazy," and one who is occasionally guilty of gross neglect of his duties. Two judges possess considerable dignity of character, but others are characterized as "playing politics," "weak before popular clamor," "publicity getters," etc. One judge is remarkable for social-mindedness, which makes him fertile in constructive ideas, but sentimental in dealing with criminals. The personal habits of all but one of the judges seem to be above serious criticism.[29]

The police court judges, however, did not fare so well:

> The Municipal Court bench is characterized as follows:
> In respect of legal ability the court contains four judges who might be said to measure up to the requirements of the office. ... Two of the others are credited with fair ability, three are mediocre, and one apparently has no qualifications worth mentioning. The list includes two judges characterized as "playing politics," and two others designated as "gallery players."
> On the whole, the personnel of the municipal bench is inferior in quality and ineffectual in character.[30]

While the judges tended to be somewhat more competent than the other participants this did not mean they were above "politics," as Moley noted.

> In the last analysis a court is as good as the ability, the courage, and the political independence of its judges make it. We have shown how sadly these qualities have diminished during the past ten years of the court's

existence. We should, therefore, be inviting a very serious trifling with our problem if we should insist upon the accomplishment of secondary objectives when the main objective remains untouched. Such civic interest as is possible in Chicago, and there are apparently definite reasons for hope in a renaissance of activity, should direct itself to delivering, so far as it is humanly possibly, the Municipal Court from the blighting influence of machine politics. . . . It is not stretching the truth to say that positions on the municipal bench have become to some extent semi-sinecures for the retainers of the feudal lords of Chicago politics. Considering this, and also considering the fact that there is a definitely established relationship between the underworld and some feudal lords, it is not strange that there should be extended to the lords of the underworld privileges and favors by the judiciary of the city. This, of course, constitutes a condition which no self-governing community can long endure.[31]

Smith noted that the political ties of the judge required that he cater to party chieftains, petty politicians, and associates from his earlier political days. The judge was also required to bid for the support of different interest groups.

More important in its effect on the bench than the tendency to respond occasionally to political influence is the bid for support which many judges make to different groups and factions in the city. This is almost entirely a new influence upon the judiciary. "In order properly to play the game," observes one of the more sophisticated judges, "it is necessary for a judge to attend weddings, funerals, christenings, banquets, barbecues, dances, clam-bakes, holiday celebrations, dedications of buildings, receptions, opening nights, first showings of films, prize-fights, bowling matches, lodge entertainments, church festivals, and every conceivable function given by any group, national, social, or religious." Several of the judges have a reputation for "handshaking" nearly every night in the week. One judge of fine, simple nature is reported to have been inveigled into making a speech on the educational and moral value of motion pictures at the first showing of a particularly salacious film. The judge, of course, had not seen the picture. Another judge is said to have refereed a prize-fight. In the past the saloon, as the neighborhood center, has been assiduously courted. Three judges of unquestioned character campaigned by visiting the saloons in the different foreign sections of the city, and were presented to long lines of foreign-speaking voters with the aid of an interpreter. No drinks were bought, not a cent was spent, only handshakes were exchanged, yet this was deemed essential campaigning. All were reelected.[32]

Finally, because he was a politician the judge had to cater to the media. According to Smith, he had to do something to gain coverage since even bad publicity is better than none.[33] In Cleveland, the need for notoriety had even led to a practice whereby judges who were up for reelection were assigned to police court, where they could attract the attention of the newspapers.[34]

Administrative Factors

As lineal descendants of the municipal reformers, the crime survey researchers placed a great deal of emphasis upon administrative factors. In this regard they included problems relating to resources, operating procedures, and formal structures. Speaking of Detroit's newly created recorder's court, a commentator in the highly prestigious *Journal of the American Judicature Society* contended:

> Detroit has reached the end of its worry about crime. It has created a machinery for reinforcing law which will speedily raise it far above every other city in the country. From this time there will be steady improvement in conditions, which probably are already better than in any other large city. Detroit has been redeemed by her vigilant police and her model criminal court in such swift and dramatic manner that many of her own citizens are hardly aware yet that there has been a great transformation.
>
> There has been a vast amount of vague and meaningless moralizing about crime in this country. The problem is in some respects simpler than many persons seek to make it. There can be improvement anywhere when police and court efficiency join hands.[35]

While perhaps this is an extreme view, it does emphasize the importance which the crime survey researchers place upon administrative factors.[36] These facets were important because, as the authors of the Wickersham report note,

> In forming any judgment with respect to criminal prosecution, we must bear in mind the numerous and very serious difficulties with which the American prosecutor is beset in seeking to enforce the law in the urban industrial community of today with the machinery set up for the typically rural and usually pioneer community of from 150 to 100 years ago.[37]

Bettman concurred, contending that,

> Some of the inefficiencies in American administration of criminal justice are attributed to the fact that a system devised for rural conditions has had industrial and metropolitan conditions thrown upon its machinery.[38]

Hence, in the view of the crime survey researchers the administrative problems that plagued criminal courts, like the personnel problems, had their roots in the structural changes occurring in American society at the end of the nineteenth century.

Resources. The crime survey researchers were really concerned with two things when they discussed the resources aspect of the administrative problems of local criminal justice systems. First, they were concerned with manpower. Smith noted that the large caseloads in the municipal court in Cleveland (150 to 300 per day) gave rise to haste in the dispositional process.[39] This, in turn, led to unnecessary eliminations and even to convictions of the innocent. Lashley noted that overworked Missouri prosecutors were unable to prepare their cases properly, and could not even adequately perform such basic functions as preparing written instructions for juries, interviewing witnesses, and attending coroner's inquests.[40] Bettman contended that the lack of a stenographer in Cleveland's municipal court induced perjury and led to unwarranted dismissals.[41]

A second concern related to the resources problem had to do with the physical facilities available to those charged with the administration of criminal justice. Moley, for instance, observed that the physical conditions in the municipal court of Chicago were such that the efficient administration of criminal justice was seriously impeded. Speaking of the Harrison Street court, he said,

> It is housed most inadequately considering the amount of business that it must dispose of. When the court is in session in the morning the room is crowded almost to suffocation. The noise is very great. On one side of the room is a runway fenced in by wire which, in a very inadequate way, separates the prisoners coming from their cells from the people in the room. There is no reason why communication cannot be carried on between prisoners and visitors and articles passed through from the latter to the former. The section before the bench is jammed with policemen, lawyers, bondsmen, reporters, detectives, visitors, curious and genuinely interested—men, women, and children, young and old, rich and poor, vicious and innocent. The bailiffs during the entire session of the court go through ineffective motions of seeking a better order. They are constantly rapping for order and pleading with the mob to move back from the bench and open the way to the bull pen.
>
> Benches are provided for those who have legitimate business in court but usually no one is sitting on them. For self protection and in order to see and hear better, people prefer to stand. The smoke is always thick. There is much laughing, loud talking, whispering and expectorating. At times the noise rises to almost deafening proportions, due to the shuffling about and the loud shouts of the bailiff and the pounding of the gavel and the remarks of the bystanders and the efforts of the judges to elicit information from reluctant witnesses. It is probable that many cases are dismissed for want of prosecution because the complaining witness fails to hear the case called.[42]

Smith found similar conditions in both the municipal and common pleas courts of Cleveland. He quotes a former judge who suggested that "the place should have a hose turned on it."[43] Besides expressing concern over the physical facilities of the court, the crime survey researchers contended that the facilities made available to the prosecutor[44] and to support personnel in such agencies as the clerk's office and the probation department[45] were also inadequate.

Operating Procedures. The second major aspect of the administrative problems plaguing local criminal justice systems related to the internal procedures (or lack thereof) used in courts and prosecutors' offices. The procedures that received most comment were the mechanics of scheduling and record keeping in municipal courts. With regard to scheduling, most observers contended that misdemeanors, quasi-criminal offenses, and cases involving women should not be on the same docket as preliminary hearings in felony cases. In the crime survey researchers' opinions prosecutors were not needed for the less serious types of offenses and their energies would be better spent if they were to focus exclusively upon felony cases.[46] Another scheduling problem that received a good deal of criticism was that the "call" was controlled by the clerks, who frequently manipulated it for their own purposes. Smith charged that this allowed professional criminal attorneys to have their cases heard at convenient times in front of favorable judges.[47] Moley also observed that clerks would occasionally manipulate the call sheets so that a case would be called a day early. When no complainant arrived, the case would be dismissed for want of prosecution.[48]

The record-keeping systems of municipal courts, as well as trial courts and prosecutors' offices, were also criticized severely. A failure to keep adequate records made any type of internal or external evaluation impossible. It also permitted graft.[49] After reviewing the incredibly complex nature of the lower court record-keeping system in Cleveland, Smith observed,

> We regard the question of record keeping as one of first importance. The activities of police court hangers-on are to a large extent dependent upon the assurance that they will leave no tracks behind them, and the watchful interest of the press and the public is baffled into inaction by obstacles which make vigilance too difficult. Moreover, the failure of the system to meet modern needs makes for informal action on the part of some of the judges, and informality in the court breeds suspicion and disrespect.[50]

Structure. The third facet of the administrative problems with local criminal justice systems related to their general structure. Most of the crime survey researchers were of the opinion that the dispositional process was too complex and disjointed to be effective. Smith goes into great detail outlining the opportunities for "escape"[51] and Bettman concurs in Smith's contention that the process is too complex.[52] In the case of the courts, this situation was aggravated by the lack of an administrative head who could coordinate and supervise the activities of the various judges as well as channel cases in an intelligent manner to the judges who could best handle them.[53]

The structure of prosecutors' offices was also criticized by the crime survey researchers. These offices were cited for failing to coordinate the prosecutorial effort adequately and for failing to implement any rational division of labor.[54] In Cleveland, for example, the preliminary hearing in a felony case was conducted by an office different from that which prosecuted the case at trial. Hence, the prosecutor who initially handled the case usually did very little work on it. Much valuable information was lost and many leads were not followed.[55]

Criminal Procedure

Criminal procedure concerns the legal rules governing the applicability of the criminal law to specific cases. In commenting upon this factor in the Missouri crime survey report, Hadley and Barrett contended:

> The principal defect, at least in the work of actual prosecution, that makes for an inefficient administration of justice, is our cumbersome, archaic and inefficient system of criminal procedure with the glorification of technicality and formalism which it fosters and maintains. The effect of this system, with its apparently inevitable delays and defeats of justice, is also to create a flabby as compared with a stern and vigorous sense of justice on the part of public officials and the public generally.[56]

These rules, largely developed in England during the Stuart period, were cumbersome and archaic. The society then was predominantly agrarian. Moreover, during this period the criminal laws were overly oppressive and the Stuart monarchs used them as a political weapon.

> Most of the provisions governing criminal procedure have come down to us as an inheritance from English law established in a period when, as a French writer has well said, almost every line of the substantive and procedural law of crimes was dripping with blood. The necessity of protecting political offenders against oppressions and all offenders against the severity

and barbarity of punishment then provided for, resulted in a conspiracy of mercy on the part of courts and lawyers through hypertechnical constructions of indictments and all matters of law and procedure. The decisions expressing this technical attitude have become a part of our law and their effect has been to hamper and in many instances to nullify the power of the state in its efforts to enforce its laws.[57]

In support of the position that American criminal procedure was outmoded and cumbersome, the crime survey researchers noted that by 1850 the English had effectively reformed the system of rules which America inherited from them and was still using.[58]

While many of the crime survey researchers were quite critical of the rules of criminal procedure, none took the position that these rules should be abolished totally. Hence, one of the major tasks that they set for themselves was the identification of those aspects of criminal procedure that were impediments to the effective prosecution of criminals.[59] The most basic procedural guarantees identified as impediments were such things as the exclusion of illegally seized evidence; the privilege against self-incrimination; the requirement of an indictment by the grand jury in felony cases; an unwaivable right to a jury trial in felony cases; the requirement of unanimous consent of the jury in order to convict a defendant of a felony; the writ of habeas corpus; and an overly technical interpretation of double jeopardy.[60] Most of the criticisms, however, were reserved for less fundamental aspects of criminal procedure such as defective pleadings, negative averments, invalid jury instructions, and the number of peremptory challenges.[61]

ASSUMPTIONS UNDERLYING THE CRIME SURVEY PARADIGM

In order to understand the crime survey researchers' model, one must appreciate the crucial role of two assumptions embodied in it. The first is the "ideal system" assumption—the belief that the basic structure of Anglo-American criminal justice is an optimal one (i.e., it provides the best possible means for administering criminal justice). More specifically, this assumption holds that it is an ideal arrangement to vest in a tripartite body—the judge (a neutral referee), the prosecutor (the people's advocate), and the defense counsel (the defendant's advocate)—all of the important functions and powers (to initiate charges, set bail, determine guilt or innocence, impose sentences, make motions, etc.) relating to the disposition of criminal cases.

The relationship between this assumption and the model set forth in Figure 1-1 is quite direct. Because of their adherence to the ideal system assumption, the crime survey researchers failed to examine critically the basic foundations of American criminal justice as a source of dysfunctioning. They did not consider that low conviction rates and long delays were, at least in part, the result of a rational strategy pursued by those who were vested with control of the process by virtue of the basic structure of American criminal justice. It did not occur to the crime survey researchers that the judges, prosecutors, and defense counsels might pool their resources in pursuit of common interests (dispose of cases informally, work less diligently, go home early more frequently, etc.) that were inconsistent with the attainment of a fair and efficient system of criminal justice. Instead, in their paradigm they focused on factors that they considered to be external to the basic structure of American criminal justice. The antiquated rules of criminal procedure, the overly complex, unorganized structure of criminal courts, and the political influences emanating from urban political machines were not integral parts of American criminal justice. Rather, they were external factors that impeded criminal law practitioners from performing the tasks assigned to them by the ideal system in an optimal manner.[62]

It is important to understand the relationship between the ideal system assumption and the crime survey researchers' model because this assumption had a significant effect upon their approach to criminal justice reform. Within this paradigm, the source of criminal justice dysfunctioning is external to the ideal system. Hence, when devising criminal justice reforms one does not tamper with the basic structure of American criminal justice. Rather, criminal justice problems are resolved by making such changes as streamlining criminal procedure, insulating criminal justice officials from political pressures, and by organizing the administrative aspects of court operations along businesslike principles of efficiency. Once these changes were made, criminal justice officials would be free to exercise the powers granted to them and to perform their designated tasks in a manner consistent with the ideals embodied in Anglo-American jurisprudence. These types of changes were the key to the crime survey researchers' hopes of reforming American criminal courts, but their efficacy was based upon a second assumption—the "legal man" assumption.

The legal man assumption is the belief that the legal profession develops people who are socialized to respond, in their official capacities, to legal norms and professional canons of ethics. They are, in fact, officers of the court. Unlike economic man, legal man is not an omniscient being motivated by his own self-interest. There were such men in the legal profession, the crime survey researchers believed, but they did not generally practice in the criminal courts, nor did they preside over criminal trials. This was, of course, because the highly politicized nature of the criminal justice system made criminal practice distasteful to them. Moreover, the crime survey researchers contended, legal men who did work in the criminal realm were often frustrated by the procedural and administrative factors cited earlier.[63]

The legal man assumption was a key tenet of the crime survey paradigm because the validity of the ideal system assumption was dependent upon it, as was the crime survey researchers' program for criminal justice reform. If the legal man assumption were not valid, then one could not assume that criminal justice practitioners, unencumbered by political, procedural, and administrative constraints, would not use the powers vested in them to pursue their own self-interests. For example, once a prosecutor is given a tenured position, a manageable caseload, and a streamlined set of procedural rules, he may still decide to use his discretionary powers in a manner inconsistent with the just and efficient administration of criminal justice. He may, for example, manipulate his charging and dismissal powers to induce guilty pleas and alleviate the need to try cases. This was not a problem for the crime survey researchers, however, because of the legal man assumption. Legal men existed; they merely had to be recruited.

THE CRIME SURVEY RESEARCHERS' PARADIGM AND THEIR EMPIRICAL EVIDENCE

In conducting their surveys, the crime survey researchers collected an immense amount of data relating to many facets of the dispositional process. The type of data that were collected, as well as the research design used to collect them, reflected the crime survey model as depicted in Figure 1-1.

While various authors administered questionnaires to prosecutors (Missouri) and judges (Illinois, Cleveland), did empirical analyses of appellate court decisions (Illinois), and engaged in other types of tangential quantitative work, the basic types of data collected in the crime surveys were dispositional and delay data. The dispositional data, in particular, set forth in what the crime survey researchers called mortality tables, constituted the main thrust of the quantitative work in the surveys. These two types of data were, of course, the focus of the quantitative work in the surveys because they were the crime survey researchers' operational equivalents of efficiency—the dependent variable in their model.[64]

In collecting the dispositional and delay data the directors of several of the major surveys (Missouri, New York, Illinois) made a conscious effort to sample from criminal justice systems located in fundamentally different types of counties (urban, less urban, lesser urban, and rural).[65] The crime survey model provided the rationale for this research strategy. Urban counties were plagued by political machines that corrupted personnel and by overwhelming caseloads that aggravated the problems caused by inefficient administrative structures and antiquated rules of procedure. Moreover, less urban and rural areas were closer to the type of environment in which the present system of criminal justice was designed to operate. Hence, while the crime survey researchers did not attempt to operationalize such phenomena as administrative efficiency, caliber of personnel, and significance of political influence, their research design allowed them to test the validity of their model in an indirect manner.

In order to evaluate the utility of the crime survey researchers' approach, the data that they collected will be analyzed in light of the expectations implicit in their model (i.e., nonurban systems should be characterized by fundamentally different processes and should be more efficient than urban systems). In order to do this the disposition and delay statistics collected in all the major surveys, and compiled by Alfred Bettman in his comprehensive review of the surveys, are analyzed. Then some within systems relationships analyzed in one of the surveys (Illinois) is compared across systems (urban and nonurban).

Dispositions, Delays, and the Crime Survey Paradigm

Tables 1-1 through 1-3 contain the disposition and delay statistics for the major surveys. If the crime survey paradigm is of much value, the nonurban systems should be more efficient (higher conviction rates, shorter processing times) than the urban systems. But, as Tables 1-1 and 1-2 reveal, the average conviction rate for urban systems was 33.9, while the average for the nonurban systems was 35.9. A t-test was performed on the difference between the means and it was not significant at the .05 level. Similar tests were performed on the urban and nonurban means for each of the processing intervals in Table 1-3. All differences were insignificant at the .05 level, except that the mean processing time for cases eliminated at the grand jury level in urban jurisdictions (twenty-seven days) was significantly shorter than the time in nonurban jurisdictions (fifty days), an unexpected finding.

While the results of the above analysis indicate that outputs in urban criminal courts do not differ significantly from those in nonurban areas, they should be viewed cautiously. They tend to cast doubt upon some fundamental aspects of the crime survey paradigm because the low conviction rates and long delays in rural areas were not anticipated. But, on the other hand, there are significant problems with using the macro level data compiled by the crime survey researchers to test hypotheses concerning efficiency.

First, because of differences in the screening process across jurisdictions (police department arrest policies, prosecutor screening mechanisms) it is not valid to compare outputs. Some data contained in the Missouri survey aptly illustrate this point. When only cases input in to the system are considered, St. Louis has a conviction rate of 46.6 percent, while Kanses City has a conviction rate of only 23.4 percent (see Table 1-1). In St. Louis, however, prosecutors refused to issue warrants in 39.29 percent of the cases in which the police requested them, while Kansas City prosecutors refused warrants in only 17.55 percent of all cases. If conviction rates are based upon the total number of warrants applied for by police, the conviction rate in St. Louis drops to about 28 percent; in Kansas City it drops to about 19 percent.[66] The 23 percent differential is reduced to a 9 percent differential.

A second reason that outputs alone cannot be used to evaluate efficiency is that, even if one could control for inputs, one would have to know the determinants of dispositions within each system. System A, for example, may have a conviction rate comparable to System B. But, within System A the primary determinant of conviction (conceptualized as a dummy variable, convicted/not convicted) might be the defendant's bail status, while in System B the primary determinant might be the strength of the state's evidence. Hence, in order to meaningfully evaluate outputs in terms of efficiency across systems, one must know the determinants of disposition within each system and be able to evaluate those determinants in the light of efficiency.

Within System Relationships

Because of the considerations just discussed within system analyses would have provided the crime survey researchers with a much more rigorous examination of their ideas. Unfortunately, given the technology of the day, such analyses were much more tedious than the aggregate analyses which dominated the surveys. There were, however, some within system analyses which were conducted. In a crude way they can be used to shed some light on the question: Does the dispositional process in urban areas differ in fundamental ways

Table 1-1. Disposition of Criminal Cases in Cities and Counties Over 100,000 Population

	N.Y. City (1925)	4 N.Y. Cities (1926)	4 Pa. Cities (1926)	Cook Co. (Chicago) (1926)	Cleveland (1919)	St. Louis (1923–24)	Baltimore (1927)	Milwaukee (1926)	Cincinnati (1925–26)	Jackson Co. (Kansas City) (1923–24)	Multnomah Co. (Portland) (1928)
Total cases (percent)	19,084 (100)	1,603 (100)	31,439 (100)	13,117 (100)	3,927 (100)	1,492 (100)	2,311 (100)	1,838 (100)	1,445 (100)	1,697 (100)	818 (100)
Preliminary hearing stage											
Dismissed	.4	—	.4	25.6	11.2	7.2	—	3.1	10.1	30.8	10.9
Discharged	40.6	33.1	61.7	18.2	12.3	8.0	17.2	12.8	16.5	15.2	3.0
Disposed of as misdemeanors	16.2	22.2	3.7	.1	2.1	7.4	6.0	—	26.2	1.4	36.8
Miscellaneous disposition	.8	2.8	8.6	4.6	.6	5.4	4.5	1.5	1.8	3.2	4.2
Total	58.0	58.1	74.4	48.5	26.2	28.0	27.7	17.4	54.6	50.6	54.9
Grand jury stage											
Cases entering	42.0	41.9	25.6	51.5	73.8	72.0	72.3	N.A.	45.4	49.4	45.1
No true bill	11.9	5.6	2.8	10.6	15.9	.4	4.6	N.A.	12.1	—	6.7
Miscellaneous disposition	.6	1.6	.2	.8	—	4.6	1.2	N.A.	.2	2.1	1.5
Total	12.5	7.2	3.0	11.4	15.9	5.0	5.8	N.A.	12.3	2.1	8.2
Trial stage											
Total entering	29.5	34.7	22.6	40.1	57.9	67.0	66.5	82.6	33.1	47.3	36.9
Dismissed	4.4	2.3	2.4	12.7	12.1	9.3	2.1	14.0	2.1	16.5	7.0
Acquitted	2.6	1.3	6.8	4.4	5.2	5.6	11.3	3.9	2.8	2.9	1.2

Miscellaneous disposition (nonconviction)	1.5	2.8	1.1	3.3	4.2	5.5	3.3	1.2	2.8	4.5	5.6
Total nonconvictions	8.5	6.4	10.3	20.4	21.5	20.4	16.7	19.1	7.7	23.9	13.8
Guilty pleas	18.5	24.7	—	16.0	27.7	39.2	—	38.2	16.6	17.0	20.5
Convicted after trial	2.5	3.6	—	3.6	8.7	7.4	—	25.3	9.8	6.4	2.6
Total convictions	21.0	28.3	12.3	19.7	36.4	46.6	49.8	63.5	25.4	23.4	23.1

Source: Adapted from Alfred Bettman, "Criminal Justice Surveys Analysis," in U.S. Commission on Law Observance and Enforcement, *Report on Prosecution* (Washington, D.C.: Government Printing Office), pp. 190–91.

26 Approaches to the Study of Criminal Courts

Table 1-2. Disposition of Criminal Cases in Cities and Counties Under 100,000 Population

	N.Y. Cities (5,000–100,000) (1926)	Buchanan Co.; St. Joseph, Mo. (1923–24)	8 Ill. Urban Cos. (1926)	7 Ill. Less Urban Cos. (1926)	7 Mo. More Urban Cos. (1922–24)	11 Mo. Less Urban Cos. (1922–24)	18 Mo. Rural Cos. (1922–24)	N.Y. Rural Areas (1925)	2 Ill. Rural Cos. (1926)
Total cases (percent)	1,088 (100)	300 (100)	2,293 (100)	904 (100)	1,080 (100)	1,223 (100)	1,240 (100)	1,312 (100)	33 (100)
Preliminary hearing stage									
Dismissed	—	27.2	14.3	7.5	5.8	5.7	2.1	9.5	15.2
Discharged	27.8	18.00	11.9	10.0	3.1	7.7	1.4	4.6	—
Disposed of as misdemeanors	12.7	10.0	.8	.5	1.2	1.5	.1	.2	—
Miscellaneous disposition	2.9	4.7	2.1	10.1	2.0	1.1	.6	1.4	9.1
Total	43.4	60.4	29.1	28.1	12.1	16.0	4.2	15.7	24.3
Grand jury stage									
Cases entering	56.6	39.6	70.9	71.9	87.9	84.0	95.8	84.3	75.7
No true bill	7.9	—	7.7	6.8	—	—	.2	16.1	6.1
Miscellaneous disposition	1.5	—	8.0	5.7	2.4	1.3	6.0	2.1	9.1
Total	9.4	—	15.7	12.5	2.4	1.3	6.2	18.2	15.2
Trial stage									
Total entering	47.2	39.6	55.2	59.4	85.5	82.7	89.6	66.1	60.5
Dismissed	2.6	16.3	15.0	14.1	25.8	22.8	26.7	4.6	—
Acquitted	2.2	1.3	2.0	3.2	4.8	4.4	6.5	3.9	—
Miscellaneous disposition (non-conviction)	6.0	.7	14.2	14.2	12.6	11.9	13.4	8.5	24.2

Total nonconvictions	10.8	18.3	31.2	32.5	43.2	39.1	46.6	17.0	24.2
Guilty pleas	31.9	19.7	20.7	22.0	33.3	34.6	35.5	42.3	30.2
Convicted after trial	4.5	1.6	3.3	4.9	9.0	7.0	7.5	6.8	6.1
Total convictions	36.4	21.3	24.0	26.9	42.3	43.6	43.0	49.1	36.3

Source: Adapted from Alfred Bettman, "Criminal Justice Surveys Analysis," in U.S. Commission on Law Observance and Enforcement, *Report on Prosecution* (Washington, D.C.: Government Printing Office), pp. 195–98.

Table 1-3. Average Time Required to Dispose of Cases in Various Jurisdictions During the 1920s[a]

	Eliminated in Preliminary Hearing		Eliminated in Grand Jury		Eliminated in Trial Court		Guilt established	
	No. of Cases	Median Days	No. of Cases	Median Days	No. of Cases	Median Days	No. of Cases	Median Days
New York City (1925)								
New York County	—	—	1,406	28	906	72	2,333	36
Kings County	—	—	691	19	246	82	861	47
Bronx County	—	—	103	20	78	67	370	46
Queens County	—	—	108	55	124	153	204	91
Richmond County	—	—	35	23	29	143	89	57
New York City (1926)	4,778	3	844	16	1,634	53	888	51
Chicago and Cook County (1926)	5,857	11	1,348	19	2,332	113	2,569	74
New York upstate cities over 100,000 (1926)	931	2	116	35	172	83	384	65
Buffalo (1925)	—	—	65	22	67	102	282	61
Rochester (1925)	—	—	31	27	16	90	149	46
Syracuse (1925)	—	—	19	36	4	70	125	80
St. Louis (1923-24)	401	20	—	—	258	95	654	52
Milwaukee (1926)	292	17	—	—	350	57	1,149	17
Jackson County (Kansas City) (1923-24)	818	30	—	—	341	70	321	31
Buchanan County (St. Joseph) (1923-24)	162	19	—	—	54	200	60	48
New York cities under 100,000 (1925)	—	—	234	61	116	85	786	67
New York cities under 100,000 (1926)	472	8	102	67	161	89	353	58
8 urban Illinois counties (1926)	660	8	190	45	379	82	543	66
7 urban Illinois counties (1926)	154	4	40	7	122	110	226	48
36 rural and partially urban Missouri counties (1922-24)	269	11	—	—	1,109	147	1,397	53
Rural New York (1925)	—	—	230	72	69	83	609	67
Rural New York (1926)	206	1	238	46	298	71	570	55

Source: Adapted from Alfred Bettman, "Criminal Justice Surveys Analysis," in U.S. Commission on Law Observance and Enforcement, *Report on Prosecution* (Washington, D.C.: Government Printing Office), p. 214.

[a] In median days from initiation of charges to final disposition.

from the dispositional process in nonurban areas? Because of limited resources and data a comprehensive analysis of this question is not possible. Therefore, only selected relationships examined in the Illinois survey will be compared across jurisdictions.

In the Illinois survey report, Gehlke examined several within system relationships. Perhaps the most important of these were the role of the guilty plea within each system, the relationship between probation and guilty pleas, and the relationship between bail and disposition. Each of these relationships was important to the crime survey researchers. Where guilty pleas accounted for a large proportion of all convictions, it is probable that a good deal of informal bargaining took place behind the scene. Where probation was related to a plea of guilty, there were culpable defendants being "let off the hook." Where defendants who were released on bail were eliminated at a higher rate than were confined defendants, there was evidence of an inefficient process being manipulated by defendants in a position to manipulate it. Hence, within the crime survey paradigm it would be expected that guilty plea rates would be greatest in urban systems. Moreover, in urban systems it would be expected that probation would be positively related to having pleaded guilty, and being eliminated (not convicted) would be positively related to being released on bail. Similar relationships would not be expected in nonurban jurisdictions.

Before these relationships are examined a few comments are in order concerning Gehlke's sampling design. He selected Cook County (Chicago) as the urban jurisdiction in Illinois and then selected two rural counties, seven less urban counties, and eight more urban counties. He also selected two downstate counties—Williamson and Franklin—because "they have attracted much attention in recent years because of certain conditions amounting almost to civil warfare."[67] For this reason these counties were equated with corrupt urban counties and their process was expected to be closer to that of Cook County than to those of the nonurban jurisdictions.

Table 1-4 contains the guilty plea rates for all of the Illinois jurisdictions. As row two shows, guilty plea rates do not differ markedly across jursidictions except in "corrupt" Williamson and Franklin counties, where they are much lower—an unexpected finding. Ignoring Williamson and Franklin counties, Gehlke places much emphasis on the fact that in Cook County most guilty pleas are to a reduced charge (row three)—unlike the situation in the nonurban counties.[68] What Gehlke failed to note, however, is that the stark differences in row three appear to be merely reflective of a difference in the style of bargaining.

Table 1-4. Guilty Pleas in Selected Illinois Jurisdictions

	Cook County	Williamson and Franklin Counties	Eight More Urban Counties	Seven Less Urban Counties	Two Rural Counties
Percentage of all trial court cases resulting in guilty pleas	39.71 (n = 5,253)	12.75 (n = 361)	37.25 (n = 1,267)	36.87 (n = 537)	50.0 (n = 20)
Guilty pleas as a percentage of all convictions $\left(\dfrac{\text{Guilty Pleas}}{\text{Convictions}}\right)$	81 (n = 2,582)	61 (n = 75)	86 (n = 549)	81 (n = 243)	83 (n = 12)
Guilty pleas to a lesser offense as a proportion of all guilty pleas $\left(\dfrac{\text{GPs-Lesser Offense}}{\text{Total GPs}}\right)$	75	30	30	30	8.3

Source: *The Illinois Crime Survey* (Chicago: Blakely, 1929), pp. 48-52).

Table 1-5. Probation in Selected Illinois Jurisdictions

	Cook County	Williamson and Franklin Counties	Eight More Urban Counties	Seven Less Urban Counties	Two Rural Counties
Percentage of convicted defendants given probation	21.46 (n = 2,582)	2.67 (n = 75)	32.06 (n = 549)	20.16 (n = 243)	8.32 (n = 12)

Source: *The Illinois Crime Survey* (Chicago: Blakely, 1929), p. 53.

To argue that these differences reflect a fundamental difference in the dispositional process, one would have to contend that the charge reductions resulted in lower sentences. If this were true, since plea bargained cases account for the vast majority of convictions, this would be reflected in lower sentencing patterns in Cook County than in the downstate counties. Two observations indicate this is not the case. First, as Table 1-5 shows, Cook County did not release defendants on probation at a rate greater than the eight more urban counties and the seven less urban counties. The probation rate was much lower in Williamson and Franklin counties but, again, this was not an expected result, given their allegedly corrupt nature. The

Table 1-6. Definite Term Sentences in Selected Illinois Jurisdictions

	Cook County	Williamson and Franklin Counties	Eight More Urban Counties	Seven Less Urban Counties	Two Rural Counties
Percentage of definite term sentences	50.45 ($n = 1,994$)	11.27 ($n = 71$)	24.18 ($n = 304$)	27.57 ($n = 185$)	9.09 ($n = 11$)
Percentage of definite term sentences under 1 year	49.8 ($n = 1,006$)	25.0 ($n = 8$)	84.09 ($n = 88$)	86.28 ($n = 51$)	100.0 ($n = 1$)
Percentage of definite term sentences from 1-4 years	45.03 ($n = 1,006$)	25.0 ($n = 8$)	9.09 ($n = 88$)	7.84 ($n = 51$)	—

Source: *The Illinois Crime Survey* (Chicago: Blakely, 1929), pp. 67-69.

Table 1-7. Relationship Between Guilty Pleas and Probation in Selected Illinois Jurisdictions

	Cook County	Williamson and Franklin Counties	Eight More Urban Counties	Seven Less Urban Counties
Percentage of cases given probation after conviction by trial	7.62	60.42	1.53	1.12
Percentage of cases given probation after guilty plea	22.32	100.0	39.5	23.06
Ratio of percentage given probation in guilty plea cases to percentage given probation in cases resulting in conviction after trial (row 2 ÷ row 1)	2.93 ($n = 554$)	1.65 ($n = 75$)	25.82 ($n = 176$)	20.59 ($n = 49$)

Source: *The Illinois Crime Survey* (Chicago, Blakely, 1929), pp. 78-80.

number of cases in the two rural counties was too low to yield reliable information.

The data that Gehlke presents on sentencing also demonstrate that while Cook County tended to reduce charges more frequently than did other jurisdictions, it gave at least as severe penalties. As Table 1-6 shows, Cook County gave a greater percentage of definite term sentences, a practice considered to be more severe than indefinite term sentences because it leaves the parole board no leeway. Moreover, the average length of the definite term sentences in Cook County appears to be longer than in downstate jurisdictions.[69] Hence, given these data it does not appear that the different style of plea bargaining in Cook County reflects any meaningful difference between the dispositional process there and in downstate Illinois.[70]

Table 1-7 contains some crude statistics on the relationship between being given probation and pleading guilty. Row three shows that one is much more likely to obtain probation after pleading guilty in counties other than Cook, Williamson, and Franklin—in direct contradiction to the crime survey researchers' expectations. Table 1-8 also shows that there is a positive relationship between being eliminated and being released on bail in all Illinois jurisdictions where there were enough cases to analyze the relationship. The relationship was more consistent across jurisdictions at the trial level, however, than at the preliminary hearing level. These findings are, again, contrary to what one would expect given the thrust of the crime survey paradigm.

Table 1-8. Relationship Between Bail and Disposition in Trial Courts for Selected Illinois Jurisdictions

	Cook County	Williamson and Franklin Counties	Eight More Urban Counties	Seven Less Urban Counties
Percentage of cases eliminated at preliminary hearing level (defendant free on bail)	64.40 ($n = 2,245$)	—	36.82 ($n = 262$)	28.72 ($n = 32$)
Percentage of all cases eliminated at preliminary hearing level	48.49 ($n = 6,361$)	—	29.09 ($n = 667$)	28.10 ($n = 254$)
Differential (row 1 minus row 2)	15.91	—	7.73	.62
Percentage of cases eliminated at trial court (defendant free on bail)	68.96 ($n = 1,595$)	92.11 ($n = 114$)	73.16 ($n = 421$)	67.97 ($n = 153$)
Percentage of all cases eliminated at trial court	50.85 ($n = 2,671$)	79.22 ($n = 286$)	56.67 ($n = 718$)	54.75 ($n = 294$)
Differential (row 4 minus row 5)	18.11	12.89	16.49	13.22

Source: *The Illinois Crime Survey* (Chicago: Blakely, 1929), Table E, pp. 87-88.

SUMMARY

In light of the empirical evidence gathered by crime survey researchers, their view of criminal court operations seems rather deficient. Indeed, one might surmise, on the basis of the similarities observed across types of court systems, that the sources of what the crime survey researchers viewed as dysfunctioning and inefficiency were related to certain institutional characteristics of criminal courts that were invariant across jurisdictions. That is, such things as high dismissal rates, high guilty plea rates, the relationship between guilty pleas and probation, and so forth, may be reflecting certain structural features inherent in the basic structure of criminal courts. That these deficiencies may have been due to certain factors inherent in the basic structure of the Anglo-American criminal court system was never considered by the crime survey researchers. Indeed, such a proposition is directly contrary to the crime survey paradigm and the assumptions upon which it was based.

The basic structure of the Anglo-American criminal court system can be viewed as a tripartite body composed of a neutral arbiter, the community's advocate, and the defendant's advocate. These individuals are charged with the responsibility and given the power to process criminal cases in accordance with several basic principles of fundamental fairness. If the work of the crime survey researchers is viewed in light of this basic structure, it can be seen that their analyses did not dwell upon factors that were inherent components of it. The crime survey researchers did not, for example, critically examine the role structure within the criminal court setting, or the delegation of powers, or the assignment of tasks—facets of criminal courts that are inherent in this basic structure and invariant across systems. Rather, analyses in the crime surveys focused upon tangential factors (politics, inept personnel, cumbersome procedures, etc.) that varied across systems and purportedly impeded criminal court practitioners in urban jurisdictions from effectively performing the tasks assigned to them.

The crime survey researchers may have failed to critically examine the basic structure of Anglo-American criminal courts as a source of dysfunctioning because of their establishment biases or because they were prominant and well socialized members of the legal profession. Whatever the cause of this failure, it hampered their understanding of criminal court operations, as was painfully evident in their empirical analyses. The results of these analyses are consistent with the notion that what the crime survey researchers perceived as criminal court dysfunctioning was at least partly due to certain institutional characteristics inherent in the basic structure of criminal courts. This proposition has received some support in recent years and has much appeal. Indeed, it is at the heart of the organizational perspective to be developed here, and will be extended upon and refined in Chapter 3.

NOTES

1. The Cleveland Foundation, *Criminal Justice in Cleveland* (Cleveland: The Cleveland Foundation, 1921).

2. This survey, like those that followed it, was handsomely financed and well staffed. In Cleveland $50,000 was raised for the survey. This money was used to employ thirty-five researchers and a large number of staff members and directors.

3. Citations to the individual studies will not be given here. They can be found along with a fairly comprehensive bibliography by Julian Leavitt in the Wickersham Report. See National Commission on Law Observance and Enforcement, *Report on Prosecution*, Vol, 4 (Washington, D.C.: Government Printing Office, 1931). Other bibliographies of criminal justice studies during the 1920s include Esther Conner, "Crime Commissions and Criminal Procedure in the United States since 1920: A Bibliography," *The Journal of the American Institute of Criminal Law and Criminology* (May 1930):129-44; Dorothy Culver, *Bibliography of Crime and Criminal Justice 1927-1931* (New York: H.W. Wilson, 1934); and Augustus Kuhlman and Raymond Moley, *A Guide to Materials on Crime and Criminal Justice* (New York: H.W. Wilson, 1929). In addition to the survey reports themselves there were also several good synopses. See Raymond Moley, *Politics and Criminal Prosecution* (New York: Minton, Balch, 1929); Raymond Moley, *Our Criminal Courts* (New York: Minton, Balch, 1930); and Alfred Bettman, "Criminal Justice Surveys Analysis," in U.S. National Commission on Law Observance and Enforcement, *Report on Prosecution*, Vol. 4 (Washington, D.C.: Government Printing Office, 1931), pp.39-221.

A review of these works reveals some interesting insights into the people that conducted them. First, the surveys were dominated by a small group of scholars; Raymond Moley, for instance, participated in the Cleveland, Missouri, New York, and Illinois studies as well as in seven other studies. C.E. Gehlke did the statistical analysis for the four surveys mentioned above. Bruce Smith, Arthur Lashley, Alfred Bettman, and others participated in more than one survey. It can also be said that the crime survey researchers were men of public affairs. Staff reports were prepared by former governors, state's attorneys, university presidents, judges, and prominent bar officials. As will be demonstrated, the dominant role played by this establishment-oriented elite led to the adoption of a common methodology and the development of a unity of perspective which had a constraining effect upon their ability to understand and analyze the operations of criminal courts.

4. It should be noted from the outset that the crime surveys were very comprehensive studies that went far beyond the study of criminal courts. Indeed, it would be misleading to imply that the courts were the primary focus

of the surveys. Rather, the surveys focused upon the problem of crime and how it could be deterred and controlled. The crime survey researchers recognized the complexities of this problem and its relationship to personal, societal, and governmental factors. Hence the surveys included reports on such diverse topics as police, psychiatry, prosecution, judicial administration, penal treatment, and the social nature of crime. The present analysis, however, will necessarily be restricted to those aspects of the surveys which pertain to criminal courts.

5. The Cleveland crime survey was a reaction to a case in which the chief judge of the municipal court was charged with murder. The Illinois survey was a response to the assassination of an assistant state's attorney in the presence of several well-known gangsters.

6. Just how widespread this dissatisfaction was is a matter of some dispute. Haller, for instance, in an article on urban crime in Chicago during the 1920s, contends that the criminal justice system was deeply rooted in the ethnic cultures of the city. Crime was a means of social mobility for the immigrants, and their ambitions required a rather loosely knit court system controlled by people who understood their needs and who could identify with their aspirations. Hence the criminal justice system played a role not dissimilar from that of the political machine. It was, in fact, an extension of the machine which existed and persisted because it fulfilled a need.

Most of the discontent, Haller argues, was among the Protestant native American establishment, which could not identify with the values and life experiences of the immigrants. The crime survey researchers were recruited from the establishment segment of the population and, while they had little contact with the everyday operations of the criminal justice system, they spearheaded the drive for reform. See Mark Haller, "Urban Crime and Criminal Justice: The Chicago Case," *The Journal of American History* 57 (1970):619.

7. Moley relates an interesting experience in Chicago when a group of twenty-five foreign defendants were herded into the courtroom. After the charges against the defendants were dropped, "The arresting officer looked toward the assistant state's attorney who gave him a meaningful smile in reply while the judge was questioning one of the witnesses. As if uttering the thought that was foremost in the minds of all those present the officer grunted, 'There isn't a vote in the whole damn crowd!'" (Raymond Moley, "The Municipal Court of Chicago," in Illinois Association for Criminal Justice, *The Illinois Crime Survey* (Chicago: Blakely, 1929), p. 408.)

8. For an excellent recounting of the relationship between urban crime and urban politics during this period, see Haller, "Urban Crime and Criminal Justice," and the references therein. See also selected sections of Harold Gosnell, *Machine Politics Chicago Model*, 2d ed. (Chicago: University of Chicago Press, 1968), pp. 13, 70, 79, 126, 188.

9. Prohibition was such a potent contemporary issue that one of the major themes in Herbert Hoover's successful 1928 presidential campaign was a promise to institute a study of the enforcement of the Prohibition laws. The resulting report was, of course, the Wickersham Commission report.

10. The municipal reform movement also had a significant impact upon how people thought local government could be changed to operate "properly." Pro-

gressives placed a great deal of confidence in the efficacy of structural reforms (recall, referendum, city manager or commission government, nonpartisan elections, etc.) and this greatly influenced the thinking of crime survey researchers in their analysis of criminal justice problems and their development of criminal justice reforms.

11. Alfred Bettman, "Criminal Justice in America," *American Bar Association Journal* 11 (July 1925):458.

12. John Henry Wigmore, in *Illinois*, p. 5. For an interesting historical perspective on the notion of efficiency and the role it played in the progressive movement during this period, see Martin J. Schiesl, *The Politics of Efficiency: Municipal Administration and Reform in America 1800-1920* (Berkeley: University of California Press, 1977).

13. Reginald Heber Smith, in *Cleveland*, p. 1.

14. Moley, *Our Criminal Courts*, pp. xiii-xiv.

15. Bettman, in *Prosecution*, pp. 175-76.

16. While it appears from the above quotations that both Bettman and Moley discount the relevance of all factors in the model other than the one that they perceive to be of most significance, it should be remembered that these quotations represent extreme positions. Moreover, both citations are from summary works. A careful examination of Bettman's and Moley's analyses in the surveys reveals that they gave far more credence to other factors than these quotations indicate. See especially Bettman, "Prosecution," in *Cleveland*; Moley, "The Municipal Court of Chicago," in *Illinois*; and Moley, Introduction, *Missouri Crime Survey*.

17. In this section and the others discussing and elaborating upon the crime survey model extensive use will be made of rather lengthy quotations. While some may find this distracting, I was unable to adequately capture the flavor and richness of the crime survey researchers' thoughts without the extensive use of quotations.

18. Smith, in *Cleveland*, p. 100.

19. Healy, "The Prosecutor in Chicago in Felony Cases," in *Illinois*, pp. 289-90.

20. Ibid., p. 290.

21. *Report on Prosecution*, p. 15.

22. Healy, "The Prosecutor," p. 306. Other evaluations of prosecutors can be found in Healy, "The Prosecutor," pp. 329-30, and Bettman, "Prosecution," pp. 92-93, 100.

23. Smith, in *Cleveland*, pp. 5-6.

24. Ibid., pp. 58-59.

25. Ibid., p. 82.

26. Ibid., pp. 59-60.

27. Moley, "The Municipal Court of Chicago," pp. 408-10.

28. Smith, in *Cleveland*, p. 17.

29. Ibid., p. 25.

30. Ibid., p. 26

31. Moley, "The Municipal Court of Chicago," pp. 418-19.

32. Smith, in *Cleveland*, p. 35.

33. Ibid., p. 41.
34. Ibid., p. 43.
35. *Journal of the American Judicature Society* 4 (April 1921):189.
36. This view is all the more extreme when considered in relation to Moley's analysis of the recorder's court a decade later. He showed that in the long run great expectations of the reformers had not been realized. See Moley, *Our Criminal Courts*, pp. 83-90.
37. *Report on Prosecution*, p. 20.
38. Bettman, in *Prosecution*, p. 60.
39. Smith, in *Cleveland*, p. 55.
40. Arthur V. Lashley, "Preparation and Presentation of the State's Case," in *The Missouri Crime Survey* (New York: MacMillan, 1926), pp. 136-43.
41. Bettman, in *Cleveland*, p. 117.
42. Moley, "The Municipal Court of Chicago," p. 405.
43. Smith, in *Cleveland*, p. 51.
44. Bettman, in *Cleveland*, p. 34.
45. Smith, in *Cleveland*, p. 51.
46. Ibid., p. 52 and Bettman, in *Prosecution*, pp. 94, 115-16.
47. Smith, in *Cleveland*, p. 52.
48. Moley, "The Municipal Court of Chicago," p. 414.
49. Ibid., pp. 413-14.
50. Smith, in *Cleveland*, p. 67.
51. Ibid., pp. 6-17.
52. Bettman, in *Prosecution*, p. 155.
53. Smith, in *Cleveland*, pp. 71-82.
54. Bettman, in *Cleveland*, p. 34.
55. Ibid., p. 54.
56. Herbert S. Hadley and Jessee W. Barrett, "Necessary Changes in Criminal Procedure," in *Missouri*, p. 350. Despite this rather extreme position, it should be said that the procedure factor was probably given less credence by many of the crime survey researchers than the ones discussed earlier. Moley, *Our Criminal Courts*, p. xiii, and Healy, in *Illinois*, p. 286, take the position that procedure is unimportant. Bettman tries to shed some empirical evidence on the question by examining federal criminal cases. Although they operate with the same rules as local courts, they are much more efficient (Bettman, in *Prosecution*, pp. 66-69). Bettman also cites evidence showing that appellate courts are not overly technical in their interpretation of procedural matters.
57. Hadley and Barrett, "Necessary Changes in Criminal Procedure," p. 353. For another good discussion of the origins of American criminal procedure with citations to early works see Moley, *Our Criminal Courts*, p. 91ff.
58. Hadley and Barrett, "Necessary Changes in Criminal Procedure," p. 351, and Moley, *Our Criminal Courts*, p. 93.
59. The best examples of such analyses of criminal procedure in the surveys are: J. Hugo Grimm, "Ten Years of Supreme Court Decisions," in *Missouri*; Hadley and Barett, "Necessary Changes in Criminal Procedure"; Albert J. Harno, "The Supreme Court in Felony Cases," in *Illinois*; E.W. Hinton, "The Trial Courts in Felony Cases," in *Illinois*. A summary of some other work can be

found in Moley, *Our Criminal Courts*, Chap. 6, and Marcus Kavanaugh, "Improvement of Administration of Criminal Justice by Exercise of Judicial Power," *American Law Review* 59 (July 1925):481-501.

60. Harno, "The Supreme Court in Felony Cases," p. 121; Grimm, "Ten Years of Supreme Court Decisions," pp. 264, 225; and Hinton, "The Trial Courts in Felony Cases," pp. 218, 219.

61. See references in note 59.

62. The crime survey researchers persisted in this belief even in the face of evidence indicating that, rather than being constrained by external factors, members of the courtroom elite were able to manipulate internal processes to respond to external pressures, without really changing fundamental relationships. Two examples will illustrate this point. Smith notes that public pressure on judges to reduce bench paroles led to a reduction in such paroles by 25 percent; nolles, however, increased by over 15 percent. The use of other dismissal techniques also increased. See Smith, in *Cleveland*, pp. 14-15. Moley notes a similar occurrence in the municipal court of Chicago. Nolles came under increased scrutiny by the press; between 1912 and 1927 they declined by 18 percent. During the same period, however, cases dismissed for want of prosecution increased by 26 percent.

63. One point concerning the legal man assumption should be clarified: legal men may differ on ideological grounds. Because of these ideological differences they may interpret the law differently and may even sentence a given defendant differently. What legal men do not do, however, is manipulate their interpretation of the law or their judicial powers in order to maximize their own self-interest. For example, Judge A may always sentence defendants more severely than does Judge B. But, if Judge A conforms to the crime survey researchers' concept of a legal man, he would not adopt a sentencing policy aimed at inducing guilty pleas (i.e., sentence more severely after trial) *merely* because he finds it tiresome to preside over trials.

64. For a brief discussion of these data as indicators of efficiency see Bettman, in *Prosecution*, p. 52.

65. The most explicit discussion of this research strategy can be found in Gehlke, in *Illinois*, p. 31ff.

66. Gehlke, in *Missouri*, pp. 290-91.

67. Gehlke, in *Illinois*, p. 32. It should also be noted that Gehlke selected Milwaukee because of its reputation for being an "efficient" system (i.e., it had high conviction rates). Milwaukee will be excluded from this analysis because it was selected solely on the basis of its score on the dependent variable. Gehlke does not document any differences in Milwaukee that would theoretically account for the different outputs.

68. Ibid., p. 49.

69. Indefinite term sentences are difficult to evaluate because of varying ranges, but Table C-2 (*Illinois*, p. 69) shows no markedly different patterns in Cook County.

70. It should be emphasized that this analysis of the severity of sentencing across these jurisdictions is merely suggestive. It may well be that the types of cases convicted in Chicago are much more serious than those convicted in down-

state Illinois and are deserving of more severe punishment. In that case a finding of similar sentencing structures would indicate that Chicago judges in fact sentence more leniently. Without case-level data, however, a more valid analysis of sentencing cannot be undertaken. The only argument that can be made in support of the position that judges across Illinois jurisdictions are sentencing roughly similar types of cases is that, according to Table B-1, page 59 of the Illinois report, the different jurisdictions handle fairly similar types of offenses (i.e., the proportion of their caseload accounted for by murder cases, rape cases, etc., is roughly similar). This is, however, a very crude indicator.

Chapter 2

The Study of Criminal Courts, Part II: The Topical Tradition

In 1955 the American Bar Foundation, led by former U.S. Attorney General and Supreme Court Justice Robert H. Jackson, embarked upon a large-scale study of American criminal justice.[1] This study symbolized the beginning of a renewed interest in criminal justice research after decades of neglect during the Great Depression and World War II. It also gave rise to a new tradition in the study of criminal courts, the "topical tradition." Within this framework a significant number of works on various aspects of the dispositional process were conducted, including studies of charging, bail, the prosecutorial function, plea bargaining, and sentencing. Most were conducted between the mid-1950s and the late 1960s.

This discussion of the topical tradition will be presented in two parts. The first will contrast the work of the topical researchers with that of the crime survey researchers, outline the dominant mode of analysis within the topical tradition, and note some of its basic shortcomings. The second section of this chapter will deal with selected works within the topical tradition. It will illustrate the role of the topical paradigm in this body of research as well as document some of the shortcomings discussed in the first section.

THE TOPICAL PARADIGM

The topical tradition differed from the crime survey traditional in several significant ways. For example, the topical tradition was not dominated by an elite of scholars with public affairs backgrounds who shared a common ideological orientation. Rather, topical researchers spanned the ideological spectrum. They tended to be law professors, young idealistic lawyers, or legally oriented social scientists.

A more fundamental difference concerned the historical factors that affected the researchers in each tradition. The crime survey researchers, it will be remembered, labored during a period plagued by sensationalized crime waves and widespread suspicion of the linkages among politics, organized crime, and criminal justice officials. These gave rise to much antidefendant sentiment as well as to considerable dissatisfaction with the criminal justice system and the personnel who controlled it. This dissatisfaction was exacerbated by the prevalence of the municipal reform movement. Researchers within the topical tradition were affected by a radically different set of historical factors. The impetus for the renewed interest in criminal justice research during the 1950s can be traced to the heightened social consciousness characteristic of certain segments of postwar American society. This heightened consciousness was manifested in other contemporary phenomena such as the civil rights movement, the revolution in criminal procedure initiated by the Warren Court, and the concern for the welfare of the impoverished.

The widespread dissatisfaction with the criminal justice system perceived by the crime survey researchers led to their interest in implementing their perception of dominant community values and concerns in local court systems. In turn, this led to their efficiency orientation. The historical factors that affected researchers within the topical tradition, on the other hand, led them to be more concerned with implementing values embodied in the notion of due process than with implementing dominant community values.[2] Correspondingly, the dominant concern of the topical researchers was the divergence between legal theory and reality within the criminal justice system (i.e., the extent to which legally irrelevant factors affected the handling of criminal cases.)[3]

The Mode of Analysis in Topical Research

In examining the divergence between legal theory and reality, the topical researchers adopted a legalistic perspective: that is, their theoretical analyses were aimed at delineating legal theory relevant to the performance of a given task within the dispositional process (admitting a defendant to bail, for example). This led the topical researchers to view courtroom phenomena in light of an input-output model of the dispositional process (see Figure 2-1).[4] On the basis of their legal analysis, they could determine whether a given factor— such as sex, race, prior criminal record, and number of charges—was

Figure 2-1. Topical Researchers' Input-Output Approach to the Study of Courtroom Phenomena

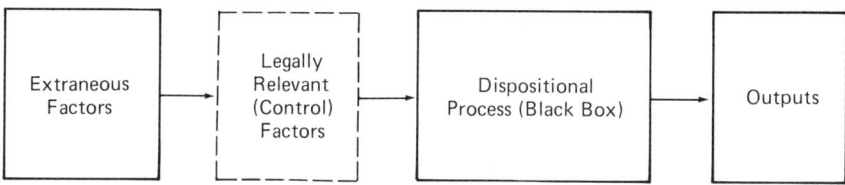

an extraneous or a legally relevant factor.[5] The quantitative analyses which were performed were designed to examine the impact of a given extraneous factor upon one or more facets of the dispositional process (disposition of the case, sentence, etc.). In general, they used some form of correlation analysis or examined differences in means or proportions. The extent to which the criminal process was consistent with legal theory was determined by the impact which extraneous factors had upon a given aspect of courtroom operations.

An example will illustrate this approach. If a topical researcher were interested in assessing the impact of a given extraneous variable —such as race—upon sentencing, he would merely correlate race with sentence length or compare the proportion of whites with the proportion of blacks given probation. If he were especially industrious he would attempt to control for some legally relevant variables such as type of offense, number of charges, or prior criminal record. The introduction of such controls, however, was not the norm in the topical tradition. Evaluation of the sentencing process (i.e., the extent to which the sentencing function was performed in a manner consistent with legal theory) was based upon whether or not race made a difference.

Shortcomings

As this brief review indicates, despite the differences in the approaches and concerns of the crime survey researchers and the topical researchers, both were ultimately concerned with evaluating and reforming the operations of criminal courts in light of some predetermined criteria (efficiency, legal theory). Unfortunately, despite their differences the topical researchers efforts were frustrated by the same basic shortcomings that plagued the efforts of the crime survey researchers: In their analyses, the topical researchers failed to take into account the unique institutional characteristics of criminal courts. Because of the differences in these two approaches, this shortcoming had different ramifications in the work of the topical researchers.

The topical researchers conducted largely within system analyses of various aspects of the dispositional process. These analyses were structured in light of legal theory, not with reference to any empirically grounded, theoretical understanding of how criminal courts process their work loads. Legally the different stages of the dispositional process are wholly separate proceedings. The criteria relevant to setting bail are different from those appropriate for accepting guilty pleas, and the latter are different from those pertinent to sentencing. This legalistic perspective led the topical researchers to view the various components of the dispositional process in isolation from one another.

If the topical researchers had not viewed the dispositional process as a black box (as depicted in Figure 2-1), they would have been more sensitive to some of the important interrelationships among its various facets. What happens at one stage of the process often has implications for what happens later, and the interconnections are not mere happenstances. Indeed, it will be argued later that criminal cases are processed in light of an overall, integrated dispositional strategy reflecting various types of considerations.

The term "dispositional strategy" can best be conceptualized as a plan or design for handling work loads in criminal courts (i.e., for disposing of cases).[6] Similar plans operate in most organizations. Their role is to foster the transformation of inputs into outputs. They specify what tasks to perform on what inputs in order to produce the desired type and mix of outputs. They also specify how the various tasks are to be performed. In order to understand how and why various tasks are performed it is often necessary to view them in light of the entire design or plan. Such is the case in criminal courts. Many of the shortcomings in the work of the topical tradition can be traced to the failure to view the operations of criminal courts in light of this overall design. Because of this failure, the topical researchers were often not able to formulate meaningful questions, nor validly answer the questions they raised. Often their isolative tendencies even impeded their efforts to interpret the results they obtained. This frustrated their evaluative efforts.

In an attempt to illustrate, document, and elaborate upon some of the observations made concerning the nature of the topical tradition and its shortcomings, an in-depth analysis of several groups of works within it will be undertaken. Here, as in Chapter 1, an exhaustive treatment of the literature was impossible. Rather, a sampling of major areas was selected for illustrative analyses: the bail literature, the plea bargaining studies, and works dealing with judicial sentencing behavior. These areas were chosen because they are representative of the topical tradition and because they constitute the major thrusts of research within it. Even within these restricted bodies of literature, an exhaustive treatment was neither possible nor particularly worthwhile. Therefore, areas within each of these bodies of work were selected for analysis either because they illustrate the topical paradigm or because they demonstrate the shortcomings of works within it.

WORKS WITHIN THE TOPICAL TRADITION

Bail Studies

Of all the stages in the dispositional process examined by the topical researchers, the bail system was perhaps the most thoroughly analyzed. In large part, the significant amount of interest in the bail system during the 1950s and the 1960s was due to the pioneering efforts of Caleb Foote and of the participants in the Manhattan Bail Project.[7] Years before his contemporaries, Foote was decrying and outlining defects in the bail system, advocating and directing empirical research into its operations, and constructing legal arguments challenging the constitutionality of monetarily based bail systems.[8] The directors of the Manhattan Bail Project, on the other hand, verified some of Foote's earlier findings and demonstrated how the bail process could be reformed.[9] The results of the project spurred the bail reform movement of the 1960s, as well as a significant amount of research on the bail system.[10]

Bail researchers within the topical tradition addressed many aspects of the bail system, but they focused upon three facets of it: (1) the legal aspects of the right to bail, (2) the realities of the bail system, and (3) the consequences of disparities. An analysis of these primary concerns will reveal the impact of the topical paradigm upon the work of the bail researchers.

Legal Theory. When viewed in light of the primary concerns of the topical researchers, a delineation of the legal aspects of the right to bail was essential to the work of the bail researchers. In order to assess the functioning of the bail system in terms of its deviation from legal theory and in order to differentiate between legal and extraneous factors, the legal underpinnings of bail had to be articulated. This analysis provided the bail researchers with their substantive orientation to the bail process.

In outlining the legal aspects of bail, the topical researchers discussed the origins and nature of the right to bail,[11] as well as the purposes of bail (to allow the defendant to prepare his defense, to prevent pretrial incarceration, and to assure the defendant's presence at his trial).[12] The amount of bail, they concluded, should be no more than the amount required to assure the defendant's presence at his trial.[13] Thus the factors which the judge should consider in setting bail include such matters as the nature of the offense, the circumstances surrounding it, the weight of the evidence, the defendant's financial status, the defendant's character, the character of the surety, and previous bail forfeitures.[14]

Realities. In examining bail practices the topical researchers were primarily concerned with the extent to which bail practices were consistent with legal theory. To examine this question they observed bail hearings and collected quantitative data on the operations of bail systems in several American jurisdictions. Much of the quantitative analysis, however, was merely undirected data manipulation roughly aimed at delineating the structure of the bail system. Average bail amounts and detention periods were computed, bail amount was broken down by offense, and release rates were broken down by offense, bail amount, and so forth.[15] From this morass of data, the bail researchers concluded that the bail system was not functioning in a manner consistent with legal dictates. Insufficient weight was given to the defendant's personal traits and community ties, and the average length of pretrial incarceration was held to be too long.[16] In some cases pretrial incarceration exceeded the average sentence given to convicted defendants.[17] In the opinion of the bail researchers, this state of affairs existed because judges gave too much weight to the offense with which the defendant was charged[18] and to the recommendation of the prosecutor.[19] Moreover, they failed to make sufficient use of nonmonetary release mechanisms such as release on personal recognizance.[20]

The crude analyses cited above provided the bail researchers with indirect evidence that the bail system was not functioning in a manner consistent with legal dictates. More direct evidence, however, came from their analysis of the results of pretrial release projects.[21] They determined that the forfeiture rates for defendants released on their own recognizance were comparable to or lower than forfeiture rates for defendants who posted a monetary bond.[22] The rearrest rate of defendants released on pretrial parole was also adjudged to be satisfactory.[23] These findings confirmed the bail researchers' belief that many indigent but trustworthy defendants were being subjected needlessly to pretrial incarceration and that the bail system was not functioning properly.

Consequences. After having established through their legal and empirical analyses that there was a significant divergence between legal theory and contemporary American bail practices, the bail researchers attempted to determine the costs of the divergence. They identified two types of costs: costs to the community and costs to the defendant. The costs to the community were primarily economic. They included the costs of detaining reliable defendants; of providing welfare payments to their families; of providing legal counsel to those who, if released, could have retained an attorney; the loss of tax revenues; and the loss of spending power.[24] The costs to the defendant were personal, economic, and legal.[25] Prolonged incarceration caused both physical and psychological harm to defendants and injured familial relations. The economic costs were basically related to loss of income. Legally, incarceration hampered the defendant's ability to prepare his defense properly. An incarcerated defendant does not have adequate access to his attorney and he is not available to contact witnesses and run down leads. Moreover, the bail researchers contended, prolonged detention lowered morale and made defendants more likely to enter guilty pleas.

The bail researchers devoted a great deal of attention to the legal costs to defendants of pretrial incarceration. Their empirical analyses consistently showed that an extraneous factor—bail status—affected both disposition and sentence. Incarcerated defendants were convicted more frequently and were more apt to receive prison sentences than were defendants who were released before trial.[26] These were some of the central findings of the bail studies; the manner in which they were derived illustrates the topical researchers' legalistic, input-output approach to the analysis of courtroom phenomena. In analyzing the effects of pretrial detention upon conviction and sentence, most bail researchers merely compared conviction rates and the proportion of jail sentences among incarcerated defendants with those released on bail. Some researchers did, however, attempt to control for intervening variables; they found that the relationships were essentially unchanged.[27] Figure 2-2, an elaboration of Figure 2-1, illustrates the bail researchers' approach.

Figure 2-2. Bail Researchers' Approach to Assessing the Impact of Bail Status

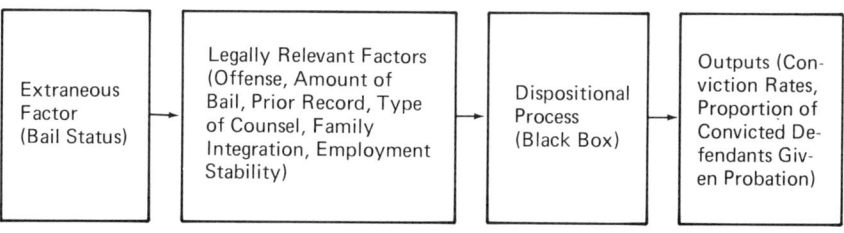

Shortcomings. The bail researchers' analyses of the impact of pretrial incarceration at later stages of the dispositional process also illustrates the deficiencies of the topical researchers' input-output mode of analysis. These analyses suffered from the bail researchers' tendency to view bail as an isolated process. Although they examined the impact of bail status upon later stages of the process, they failed to view bail as an integral part of that process. If they had they may well have found similarities in decision-making criteria across various types of decisions. More specifically, factors such as seriousness of the offense and strength of the evidence may be important in the bail decision as well as in the conviction and sentencing decisions.[28] If so, the reported relationship between incarceration, conviction, and sentence may well be spurious.[29]

Even if the relationships between bail status and conviction, and bail status and sentence, had not disappeared with the introduction of the above mentioned variables, the bail researchers may well have interpreted their findings differently if they had adopted a less isolated view of the bail process. As it were, the topical researchers' input-output mode of analysis led to some rather dubious explanations of their findings.

Caleb Foote, for example, cited two reasons for the relationship between incarceration and conviction.[30] Incarcerated defendants, he noted, are not as able as released defendants to settle their disputes out of court. Hence, the dismissal rates for the latter are higher. A second factor leading to a higher dismissal rate for released defendants is related to courtroom delay. Cases involving confined defendants were disposed of in an average of one month; those involving released defendants took an average of nine months. Foote contended that this longer period resulted in the loss of valuable evidence, which forced prosecutors to dismiss cases involving released defendants more frequently. Patricia Wald, in "Pretrial Detention and Ultimate Freedom," also attempted to explain the impact of pretrial incarceration upon later stages in the dispositional process.[31] She viewed the higher conviction rates as a result of the defendant's diminished ability to prepare his defense. He cannot track down leads, contact witnesses, and communicate with his attorney freely. Wald attributed the more severe sentences given incarcerated defendants to factors such as the defendant's physical appearance and demeanor. In addition, the incarcerated defendant is not given the opportunity to demonstrate his rehabilitation by staying out of trouble during the pretrial period.

These explanations may have some validity, but both are somewhat naive. They ignore the possibility that bail can be used by criminal justice officials as a management tool to help them handle their work loads efficiently. It might well be, for example, that the judge and prosecutor follow a conscious strategy—unchallenged by many defense counsel—to incarcerate a goodly proportion of all defendants. This strategy would enable them to process their work loads effectively because it enhances their control over them. Such a view of bail would yield many insights into the bail process and its role within the larger dispositional process.[32]

This integrated view of bail would also yield ideas on bail reform quite different from those advocated by topical researchers. Many of the bail reforms suggested by topical researchers were devised to provide judges with more complete information on the background of the defendant. Others were aimed at offering special training sessions for judges and probation officers. The purpose of the training sessions, in Wald's terms, would be to "give them a greater understanding of the effects of prior detention, so they could *consciously counteract its subconscious influence*" (emphasis added).[33] The shortcomings of such proposals are quite evident if bail is seen as a tool consciously manipulated by criminal justice officials in an effort to enhance their control over their work loads.

Plea Bargaining Studies

Although there was some early work on plea bargaining,[34] most topical researchers did not evidence an interest in it until the 1960s.[35] Then, because of its prevalence and its potential for abuse, plea bargaining became a highly controversial and widely discussed topic. To some, bargaining epitomized everything that was wrong with contemporary American criminal justice. To others, it was a necessary expedient that, if used properly, could be a valuable administrative tool. Of paramount concern to the topical researchers, of course, was the extent to which plea bargaining was or could be made consistent with contemporary notions of due process. The way the plea bargaining researchers addressed this issue and others was heavily influenced by the narrow, legalistic nature of the topical paradigm.

Topical Analyses of Plea Bargaining. Unlike the bail researchers, who almost universally condemned the bail system, the plea bargaining researchers disagreed about the merits of the bargaining process.[36] This debate is illustrative of the effects which the topical paradigm had upon the plea bargaining researchers: the legitimacy of plea bargaining was approached almost exclusively from a legalistic perspective.[37] The plea bargaining researchers' examination of legal concepts such as "voluntarily entered" and "knowingly made" led to a concern with the reliability of bargained pleas. This concern gave rise to such questions as, Do promises by prosecutors constitute coercion? Are trials necessarily more reliable methods of determining culpability than are negotiations?, and Are there situations in which a plea is a more meaningful and effective disposition than a trial?

Unfortunately, with one exception, the plea bargaining researchers' legalistic approach never led them to address more fundamental, empirical questions.[38] For example, What are the characteristics of cases that are most apt to result in guilty pleas? What are the pressures and influences upon a defendant to "cop a plea"? When are they most effective? It is unfortunate that the plea bargaining researchers did not focus more of their resources upon such empirical questions, because their views on the merits of bargaining were influenced in part by their perceptions of certain empirical phenomena.[39] For instance, advocates of plea bargaining tended to argue that most guilty pleas occurred in cases where the state's evidence was very strong,[40] while opponents tended to see it occurring most frequently in evidentially weak cases.[41] Also, proponents tended to see the plea package as a reflection of an experienced defense counsel's perception of the likely result of a trial.[42] Opponents were inclined to see the package as a result of tactical strategies and inherent biases in the system.[43]

Quantitative Work. Perhaps only one quantitative work within the plea bargaining studies focused upon factors affecting the bargaining process, Donald Newman's early, frequently cited article, "Pleading Guilty for Consideration: A Study of Bargain Justice."[44] In that article, Newman's implicit attempt was to assess the fairness of the bargaining process by examining the relationships between guilty plea rates and the retention of an attorney, and guilty plea rates and the defendant's status as a recidivist. As illustrated in Figure 2-3, his analysis reveals the topical traditions' input-output approach to courtroom phenomena.

Figure 2-3. Newman's Input-Output Approach to Factors Affecting Plea Bargaining

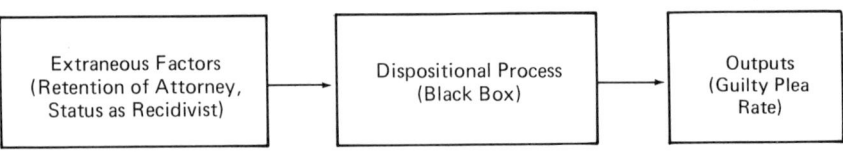

Analyzing a sample of ninety-seven convicted defendants, Newman found that while most convicted defendants (93.8 percent) eventually plead guilty, more than one-third (38.1 percent) initially enter a plea of not guilty.[45] Defendants originally pleading not guilty were more likely to have an attorney; those originally pleading guilty were more likely to be recidivists. This finding raises some doubts about the legitimacy of the factors that influence the bargaining process. Newman goes on to report, however, that there were no differences in the guilty plea rates of defendants who retained counsel and those who did not. Nor were there any differences in the probation rates among those who pleaded guilty initially and those who changed their plea to guilty at a later stage. One important difference, however, was that defendants represented by defense counsel were more apt to plead guilty in exchange for a concession such as a reduced charge or a fixed sentence.[46]

While Newman's statistical depiction of the plea bargaining process seems to indicate that it functions in a fairly evenhanded manner, serious shortcomings make this inference questionable. Moreover, they are related to his tendency to view the bargaining process in isolation from the other facets of the dispositional process and its role within the court's overall dispositional strategy. One shortcoming relates to his faulty conception of guilty plea rates. Instead of computing these rates in terms of all cases $\left(\frac{\text{guilty pleas}}{\text{total cases}}\right)$, he computed them only in terms of convicted cases $\left(\frac{\text{guilty pleas}}{\text{convicted cases}}\right)$. The difficulties with this conception of guilty plea rate can be seen if the bargaining process is viewed in light of the screening mechanism, so well documented by the crime survey researchers, which operates at various stages in the dispositional process. When viewed from this systemic perspective, the finding that defendants represented by defense counsels have the same guilty pleas rate $\left(\frac{\text{guilty pleas}}{\text{convictions}}\right)$ as do unrepresented defendants is almost meaningless. Represented defendants may have lower conviction rates and, hence, lower real guilty plea rates $\left(\frac{\text{guilty pleas}}{\text{total cases}}\right)$. This would have uncovered by a more realistic conception of guilty plea rates.

A second shortcoming in Newman's analysis would have made his findings invalid even if he had used a more meaningful conception of guilty plea rates. This shortcoming is his failure to introduce any controls into his analysis—such as the weight of the evidence and the seriousness of the offense. If, for example, defendants charged with very serious offenses or confronted with strong cases are more inclined to retain attorneys, then the lack of a difference in guilty plea rates may suggest the presence of inequities in the bargaining process (i.e., that a certain class of defendants was more susceptible to certain types of pressures, other things held equal).

Finally, Newman can be faulted for not having asked very relevant questions. He examines the relationship between the presence of an attorney and a guilty plea. But he does not examine the relationship between different types of attorneys and the submission of a guilty plea, an important question given the crime survey researchers' concern with politically connected attorneys and members of the "police court ring." Also, while Newman compares probation rates for defendants who pleaded guilty at different stages of the process, he does not compare sentences of those who did not plead guilty with those who did. Nor does he analyze the determinants of sentence in guilty plea cases.[47]

Interpretational Shortcomings. As in the case of the bail researchers, the plea bargaining researchers' failure to analyze the bargaining process as an integral part of the dispositional process led to some questionable explanations of certain phenomena. Perhaps the best example of this is their explanations of the causes of the predominance of bargain justice. The most frequently cited explanation relates to the administrative crisis in modern urban criminal courts caused by the large volume of cases. Albert Alschuler expanded upon this explanation somewhat. He noted that the administrative crisis has occurred because of (1) an overall increase in crime, (2) an increase in the scope of criminal law, and (3) an increase in the length and complexity of trials due to the constitutional revolution in criminal procedure.[48] A second, supplementary, explanation was made by Donald Newman and by the President's Commission on Law Enforcement and Administration of Criminal Justice. They contended that an important factor in the emergence of bargain justice is the effort by criminal justice officials to individualize justice and the treatment of offenders.[49] In support of their argument they note that, because many urban criminal justice systems are not highly dependent upon guilty pleas, administrative concerns cannot be the sole cause of bargain justice.

What is interesting about this aspect of the plea bargaining researchers' analysis is that, in their view, criminal justice officials are *forced* to plea bargain either because of their heavy case loads or because of their desire to individualize justice. They never suggested that plea bargaining persists because it is consistent with the interests of those who dominate the dispositional process (judges, prosecutors, and defense counsel). That is, they failed to note that plea bargaining may be ubiquitous because it provides these individuals with an informal, expedient way to handle light as well as heavy case loads (i.e., it is an integral part of the dispositional strategy employed by criminal court practitioners to manage work loads).

Their failure to consider such an explanation is all the more remarkable when viewed in light of two other observations. First, their reliance upon the significance of the relationship between plea bargaining and the "administrative crisis" in American criminal courts ignored the work of the crime survey researchers. The latter found that plea bargaining was as prevalent in low-volume rural court systems as in urban systems during the 1920s—before the increases in the crime rate, the enhanced scope of the criminal law, and the revolution in criminal procedure.[50] The plea bargaining researchers also ignored the fact that efforts to individualize justice—let the punishment fit the individual, not the crime—do not require an abrogation of all rights at the fact-finding stage of the proceedings. These efforts could be focused at the sentencing stage, after a finding of guilty.

As was the case in the bail studies, the plea bargaining researchers' interpretational shortcomings were not merely academic. These shortcomings had a marked effect upon their proposals for reform of the bargaining process. Both Vetri and the members of the President's Commission placed much emphasis upon increasing judicial control over the bargaining process (allowing the judge to scrutinize charging practices and to assess the evidentiary basis of the plea).[51] They would also require the presence of the defense counsel at all bargaining sessions. To heighten the effectiveness of judicial supervision, members of the President's Commission also recommended formalizing the negotiating session and requiring that a written or oral report of the proceedings be made in open court. On the basis of this report, the judge would perform his arbitrating function. To make the negotiating sessions meaningful the report recommended full and frank disclosure of all relevant information, including a presentencing report.

Several points should be made about these reform proposals. First, those dealing with the roles of the judge and defense counsel reveal the plea bargaining researchers' naive conception of these officials' motivations; they view the defense counsel and the prosecutor as adversaries and the judge as a disinterested third party. They ignore the fact that, in many cases, it may be in the personal interests not only of the judge and the prosecutor but also of the defense counsel to dispose of a case expeditiously by using informal mechanisms such as plea bargaining. If it is acknowledged that factors other than those emanating from their formal roles affect the behavior of these participants, the futility of the proposed reforms can be seen.

The proposed reforms dealing with the conduct and control of the bargaining session can be criticized on similar grounds. If, for instance, the immediate, personal interests of the defense counsel and of the prosecutor were not involved in the outcome of the negotiations, then a presentencing report might have a dominant influence upon the plea package. If the defense counsel and prosecutor were adversaries, then their report on the content of the negotiations might reflect what actually transpired. And finally, if in reality the judge were a disinterested third party, then he might make a meaningful inquiry into the report. But, to the extent that these participants pursue common interests, these expectations are not justified.

Sentencing Studies

Criminal justice scholars who focused upon judicial sentencing during the 1950s and 1960s were influenced greatly by the topical paradigm.[52] Because they were primarily concerned with the extent to which judicial sanctioning power was exercised in a manner consistent with legal theory, they focused their empirical work almost solely upon disparities in sentencing.[53] In a manner similar to that of the bail researchers and, to a lesser extent, Newman, they identified extraneous and legal factors plausibly relevant to the sentencing decision. These factors are indicated in Figure 2-4.

There was little disagreement among the sentencing researchers about the existence of disparities. There was, however, a significant amount of disagreement over whether the disparities that did exist could be accounted for by legal or extraneous factors.[54] Edward Green was perhaps the leading advocate of the position that legal factors were predominant. He concluded his book *Judicial Attitudes*

Figure 2-4. Sentencing Researchers' Approach to Assessing Disparities in Sentencing

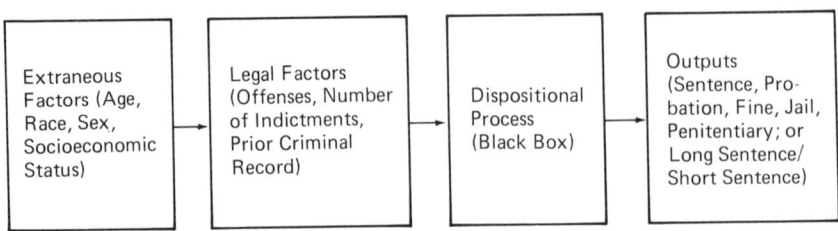

in Sentencing by noting: "The findings of the statistical analysis summarized above yield a picture of certain orderly processes underlying the application of the criteria for sentencing ... the results provide assurances that the deliberation of the sentencing judge are not at the mercy of his passions or prejudices but comply with the mandate of the law."[55] Bullock and others disagreed. Bullock contended, "Certain factors other than those specified in the law were found significantly associated with the length of sentences imposed by a jury upon an offender. ... Those who enforce the law conform to the norms of the local society concerning racial prejudice, thus denying equality before the law."[56]

What was perhaps most interesting about this controversy was that so much was made of so little. The incredibly insignificant nature of the researchers' findings was made painfully evident by John Hagan in a recent article.[57] Hagen performed a secondary analysis on twenty earlier sentencing studies in which he compared the strength of the measures of association between various socioeconomic characteristics of defendants and sentencing. The highest measure obtained (tau_b) was .08, but the average was only .015.[58]

Shortcomings. Even if the sentencing researchers had uncovered much more significant relationships between extraneous factors and sentencing, their findings would have been of limited value in assessing the legitimacy of disparities in judicial sentencing. Their input-output mode of analysis led them to view sentencing in isolation from other stages in the dispositional process and to ignore its role within the court's overall dispositional strategy. This impeded their ability to validly assess the role of extraneous factors in criminal court sentencing. It also hampered their ability to identify sources of disparities in sentencing.

Without exception, the sentencing researchers used samples of only convicted defendants in analyzing the effects of extraneous factors upon sentencing. Such an analysis may not yield valid results because when "all other factors" are controlled, black defendants or defendants of low socioeconomic status may well have higher conviction rates than do other defendants. Many whites or persons of high socioeconomic status charged with comparable crimes may never be subjected to any type of sentence. Given the magnitude of the screening process, as documented by the crime survey researchers, this might be an important confounding factor in the analysis of extraneous considerations. The effects of extraneous factors at earlier stages of the dispositional process may mitigate their impact at later stages. Thus, an assessment restricted to one phase of the process may be inadequate. Several examples of this will be seen in Chapters 7 and 8.

The topical researchers' failure to view sentencing in light of its role within the court's overall dispositional strategy also inhibited their analysis of sentencing disparities. It impeded their ability to identify sources of disparities. Most of the extraneous factors examined concerned social characteristics of the defendant (race, sex, socioeconomic status); almost none concerned their actions within the courtroom setting. This is a significant omission because criminal courts, like other organizations, have established informal operating procedures to handle their work loads. Moreover, sentencing is one of the most potent tools available to criminal court officials to enforce compliance with informal norms. Defendants who resist informal processing may be sentenced more severely than others. Thus, by failing to view sentencing in light of its role within this larger design the topical researchers may well have neglected a major source of disparities. Chapter 8 will present some empirical evidence to support this proposition.[59]

SUMMARY

Works in the topical tradition differed from those in the crime survey tradition in several ways. They were conducted by different types of researchers who evidenced different concerns and who used a different approach to the study of courtroom phenomena. But, while there were differences between the two bodies of literature there were also similarities. Both traditions were oriented toward the evaluation of courtroom operations, although they used fundamentally different criteria in assessing those operations. Moreover, the evaluative efforts of both were frustrated because of their failure to recognize certain rather unique institutional characteristics of criminal courts and integrate them into their analyses. Chapter 3 suggests and illustrates an organizational mode of analysis that attempts to take such factors into account and integrate them with other important considerations. This perspective will hopefully remedy many of the shortcomings in earlier studies of criminal courts.

NOTES

1. For more background information on the foundation's study see Wayne LaFave, *Arrest: The Decision to Take a Suspect Into Custody* (Boston: Little, Brown, 1965), p. ix.

2. The differences in the orientations of these two groups of researchers can be roughly illustrated by referring to Herbert Packer's classic depiction of two models of the criminal process. See Herbert Packer, *The Limits of the Criminal Sanction* (Stanford: Stanford University Press, 1968), Chapter 8. Most crime survey researchers would have identified with the values underlying Packer's crime control model, with its presumption of guilt and its emphasis upon efficiency and the need to protect the community at large. But a proviso is necessary here: while informal proceedings are an integral part of Packer's crime control model, the crime survey researchers abhorred the informal nature of the criminal proceedings that they observed; they felt that this informality permitted external factors, such as politics, to impede criminal court operations. It is doubtful, however, that they would have objected to informalities that led to increased efficiency.

Unlike the crime survey researchers, most topical researchers would have identified with the values underlying Packer's due process model. (On page 243 Packer explicitly recognizes this.) They agreed with the model's emphasis upon individual liberties and the efficacy of formal fact-finding procedures. Unlike most crime survey researchers, most topical researchers would have sacrificed efficiency for enhanced reliability. Perhaps the prime exceptions to this were some of the plea bargaining researchers who advocated plea bargaining as a dispositional technique (see note 37 below).

3. The term "legal theory" will be used throughout this chapter in a rather general, loose sense. It refers to the vast body of literature, including court decisions, law review articles, and legal treatises, which attempts to specify the legal principles underlying various aspects of the criminal process. Examples of legal theory include analyses of the acceptable standards governing arrests, criteria for the acceptance of waivers, and principles underlying search and seizure restrictions. It is recognized that within this body of literature there are various types of legal theories (such as theories related to arrest, bail, and confessions). Moreover, there are several interpretations of each theory. For the purposes of this analysis, however, these distinctions are largely irrelevant. What is important to note about the term "legal theory," as it is used here, is that it refers to a set of *normative* principles relevant to the performance of a given criminal justice function. The value of this set of principles is determined by the rigor of the legal research and analysis that underlie it. The extent to which these principles are adhered to in practice is irrelevant to their validity.

4. Both John Hogarth and John Hagan use a somewhat similar input-output model to describe sentencing studies. However, neither suggests that the model is applicable to other areas of criminal justice research. See Hogarth, *Sentencing as a Human Process* (Toronto: University of Toronto Press, 1971), and Hagan, "Extra Legal Attributes and Criminal Sentencing," *Law and Society Review* 8 (1974):557-83.

5. It should be noted that the source of most of the extraneous factors employed in the topical researchers' analyses was some vaguely defined conflict model of the dispositional process. Not all topical researchers were adherents of conflict theory, of course, but most of the controversy among them centered around the impact of class related factors (such as race, socioeconomic status,

indigency, and bail status) upon various facets of the dispositional process. The legal factors employed in the topical researchers' analyses generally came from their review of relevant legal theory.

6. This notion of dispositional strategy will be elaborated upon in Chapter 3. Its applicability to and utility in the study of criminal courts will be demonstrated in the empirical chapters (6, 7, and 8).

7. The intellectual predecessor of these pioneers was, of course, Arthur Beeley. Beeley wrote *The Bail System in Chicago* (Chicago: University of Chicago Press, 1927) almost thirty years before the next significant empirical study on bail appeared. His basic thesis was that the bail system was not properly administered because too many defendants with stable backgrounds were being incarcerated before trial. The later works on bail were merely attempts to verify this proposition and to outline its legal and practical implications.

8. Caleb Foote, "Compelling Appearance in Court: Administration of Bail in Philadelphia," *University of Pennsylvania Law Review* 102 (1954): 1030-79; "Foreword: Comment on the New York Bail Study," *University of Pennsylvania Law Review* 106 (1958):685-92; "Introduction: The Comparative Study of Conditional Release," *University of Pennsylvania Law Review* 108 (1960): 290-304; and "The Coming Constitutional Crisis in Bail: Parts I and II," *University of Pennsylvania Law Review* 113 (1965): 959-89, 1125-85.

9. The results of the Manhattan Bail Project, as well as its history and mode of operations, can be found in Chares Ares, Ann Rankin, and Herbert Sturz, "The Manhattan Bail Project: An Interim Report of the Use of Pretrial Parole," *New York University Law Review* 38 (1963):67-95; Bernard Botein, "The Manhattan Bail Project: Its Impact on Criminology and the Criminal Law Process," *Texas Law Review* 43 (1965):319-31; and Daniel Freed and Patricia Wald, *Bail in the United States: 1964* (Washington, D.C.: National Conference on Bail and Criminal Justice, 1964), Chapter 6.

10. For a retrospective view of the bail reform movement during the 1960s see Patricia Wald, "The Right to Bail Revisited: A Decade of Promise Without Fulfillment," in *The Rights of the Accused*, ed. Stuart S. Nagel (Beverly Hills, Calif.: Sage, 1972), pp. 175-85.

11. For a review of the origins and legal history of bail, see Foote, "The Coming Constitutional Crisis"; Ares et al., "The Manhattan Bail Project," pp. 68-70; Botein, "The Manhattan Bail Project," p. 321; and Freed and Wald, "Bail in the United States," pp. 1-9.

12. Foote, "Compelling Appearance in Court," p. 1031; Ares et al., "The Manhattan Bail Project," p. 69; and Freed and Wald, "Bail in the United States," p. 4; and "Bail: An Ancient Practice Reexamined," Note, *Yale Law Journal* 70 (1961):469.

13. Foote, "Compelling Appearance in Court," p. 1033; Ares et al., "The Manhattan Bail Project," p. 70; and "Bail: An Ancient Practice," p. 970. The bail researchers also concluded that other facets of the bail system should be considered when evaluating its fairness. For instance, bail should be set swiftly, officials should help the defendant contact a bondsman, bondsmen's practices should be regulated to prevent them from taking advantage of defendants, and procedures governing the bail system should be straightforward. On these

matters see Foote, "Compelling Appearance in Court," p. 1032, and Note, "A Study of the Administration of Bail in New York City," *University of Pennsylvania Law Review* 106 (1958):700.

14. Foote, p. 1034; "A Study of the Administration of Bail in New York City," p. 706; Ares et al., "The Manhattan Bail Project," p. 70; "Bail: An Ancient Practice," p. 974; and Freed and Wald, "Bail in the United States," p. 6.

15. For examples of these quantitative analyses see David McCarthy and Jeanne J. Wahl, "District of Columbia Bail Project: Illustration of Experimentation and a Brief for a Change," *Georgetown Law Review* 53 (1965):682-92; Ares et al., "The Manhattan Bail Project," pp. 79-85; and "Administration of Bail in New York City," pp. 711-29.

16. Ares et al., "The Manhattan Bail Project," pp. 82-84; and McCarthy and Wahl, "District of Columbia Bail Project," pp. 686-89.

17. William Brockett, "Presumed Guilty, The Pretrial Detainee," *Yale Review of Law and Social Action* 1 (1971):11.

18. Foote, "Compelling Appearance in Court," p. 1035; Freed and Wald, "Bail in the United States," p. 12; and "Bail: An Ancient Practice," p. 974.

19. Botein, "The Manhattan Bail Project," p. 324; Foote, "Compelling Appearance in Court," p. 1041; Freed and Wald, "Bail in the United States," p. 16; and Frederic Suffet, "Bail Setting: A Study of Courtroom Interaction," in *Crime and Justice in Society*, ed. Richard Quinney (Boston: Little, Brown, 1969), p. 300.

20. "Administration of Bail in New York City," p. 717.

21. Ares et al., "The Manhattan Bail Project," p 86; and McCarthy and Wahl, "District of Columbia Bail Project," pp. 712-18. For a summary of the forfeiture rates in forty-three pretrial release projects, see *Bail and Summons: 1965* (New York: Institute on the Operation of Pretrial Release Projects, October 1965), p. 9.

22. Ares et al., "The Manhattan Bail Project," p. 86; and McCarthy and Wahl, "District of Columbia Bail Project," pp. 712-14.

23. McCarthy and Wahl, "District of Columbia Bail Project," pp. 715-21, 731-32.

24. "Administration of Bail in New York City," p. 723; McCarthy and Wahl, "District of Columbia Bail Project," p. 721 et seq.; Botein, p. 325; Brockett, "Presumed Guilty," p. 18.

25. "Administration of Bail in New York City," p. 725; Brockett, "Presumed Guilty," p. 16; Botein, "The Manhattan Bail Project," p. 325; and McCarthy and Wahl, "District of Columbia Bail Project," p. 693.

26. Foote, "Compelling Appearance in Court," pp. 1050-51; "The Administration of Bail in New York City," pp. 726-27; Ares et al., "The Manhattan Bail Project," pp. 84-85; McCarthy and Wahl, "District of Columbia Bail Project," pp. 693, 699; Brockett, "Presumed Guilty," p. 20; Ann Rankin, "The Effects of Pretrial Detention," *New York University Law Review* 39 (1964):642-43.

27. McCarthy and Wahl, for instance, controlled for the type of offense when analyzing the relationship between incarceration and conviction, and controlled for the type of offense and the mode of disposition when examining the relationship between incarceration and sentence. The relationships still hold but the

n is so small that the comparisons are largely meaningless. (See McCarthy and Wahl, "District of Columbia Bail Project," pp. 693-700.) Brockett controlled for the amount of bail (he analyzed only cases with $500 or $1,000 bail); he found that incarceration still affects conviction and sentence. (See Brockett, "Presumed Guilty," p. 20.) In perhaps the most refined attempt to control for intervening variables, Rankin controlled for the defendant's criminal background, the amount of bail, the type of counsel, the defendant's family integration, and his employment stability. (See Rankin, "The Effects of Pretrial Detention," p. 644.) Like the others, however, Rankin dealt with all of these variables as dichotomies and methodologically her analysis is quite crude.

28. An approach to the operationalization of these two concepts is presented below in Chapter 6. More rigorous definitions are provided at that point.

29. A recent, more sophisticated study has shown that, when many of the complexities of the dispositional process are controlled, in some systems the relationship between pretrial incarceration and disposition and sentence becomes very slight. See James Eisenstein and Herbert Jacob, *Felony Justice: An Organizational Analysis of Criminal Courts,* (Boston: Little, Brown, 1977), Chapters 9 and 10.

30. Foote, "Compelling Appearance in Court," p. 1052.

31. Wald, "Pretrial Detention and Ultimate Freedom," p. 632.

32. More will be said of this in Chapter 6.

33. Wald, "Pretrial Detention and Ultimate Freedom," p. 638.

34. Some of the most frequently cited early works include Ruth Weintraub and Rosalind Tough, "Lesser Pleas Considered," *Journal of Criminal Law and Criminology* 32 (1941-42):502-29; Samuel Dash, "Cracks in the Foundation of Criminal Justice," *Illinois Law Review* 46 (1951):385-406; Donald Newman, "Pleading Guilty for Consideration: A Study of Bargain Justice," *Journal of Criminal Law, Criminology and Police Science* 46 (1956):780-90; and "The Influence of Defendant's Plea on Judicial Determination of Sentence," Note, *Yale Law Review* 66 (1956):204-22.

35. The primary later works include Donald Newman, *Conviction: The Determination of Guilt or Innocence Without Trial* (Boston: Little, Brown, 1966); President's Commission on Law Enforcement and Administration of Criminal Justice, *Task Force Report: The Courts* (Washington, D.C.: Government Printing Office, 1967); Arnold Enker "Perspectives on Plea Bargaining," Appendix A, *Task Force Report: The Courts,* President's Commission on Law Enforcement and Administration of Criminal Justice (Washington, D.C.: Government Printing Office, 1967); Arthur Rosett, "The Negotiated Guilty Plea," *The Annals* 374 (1967):70-81; Albert Alschuler, "The Prosecutor's Role in Plea Bargaining," *University of Chicago Law Review* 50 (1968):50-112; David Sudnow, "Normal Crimes: Sociological Features of the Penal Code in a Public Defense Office," *Social Problems* 12 (1965): 255-76; Dominick Vetri, "Guilty Plea Bargaining: Compromises by Prosecutors to Secure Guilty Pleas," *Pennsylvania Law Review* 112 (1964):865-908; Arnold Trebach, *The Rationing of Justice* (New Brunswick, N.J.: Rutgers University Press, 1964); Note, "Official Inducements to Plead Guilty: Suggested Morals for a Marketplace," *University of Chicago Law Review* 32 (1964):167-87.

36. Arguments in defense of plea bargaining can be found in Newman, *Conviction;* Enker, "Perspectives on Plea Bargaining"; Vetri, "Guilty Plea Bargaining"; and Rosett, "The Negotiated Guilty Plea." Arguments opposed to it can be found in Dash, "Cracks in the Foundation"; Alschuler, "The Prosecutor's Role"; and Trebach, *The Rationing of Justice.* Those who support plea bargaining usually cite its administrative advantages and note that while such a system has drawbacks, a trial is also not a totally reliable method of determining culpability. Moreover, a trial-oriented system would tax criminal justice resources inordinately. Supporters of plea bargaining also note that it has penological advantages because (1) an admission of guilt is the first step toward rehabilitation, and (2) it allows for greater flexibility in the determination of sentence. Finally, Enker argues that in some cases plea bargaining is a more rational dispositional technique than is a trial because it acknowledges that guilt is often a relative concept, not an absolute one. He also notes that while plea bargaining is less amenable than a trial to external scrutiny, it is more visible and more meaningful to those most directly affected by it.

Those who oppose a bargaining-oriented system of criminal justice contend that it brings improper pressures to bear upon a defendant and that they are often punished for exercising their constitutional rights. Moreover, the ultimate bargain is affected by so many tactical and extraneous factors that sentences are penologically irrelevant and often unfair. Opponents also contend that the assertion that plea bargaining is an expression of remorse is a sham. A final disadvantage often cited is that the bargaining process often frustrates the enforcement of constitutional policies governing the operation of the criminal process. This makes it difficult to regulate the actions of criminal justice officials.

37. The best legal analyses of plea bargaining can be found in Vetri, "Guilty Plea Bargaining," and "Official Inducements to Plead Guilty."

38. To say that the plea bargaining researchers seldom addressed these empirical questions is not to say that they never contemplated them. Alschuler, Sudnow, and others devoted a considerable amount of effort to describing the bargaining process. The criticism is that their thoughts were never operationalized and examined empirically.

39. It should be emphasized that, while their perception of certain empirical matters played an important role in the plea bargaining researchers' assessment of plea bargaining, this assessment was also heavily influenced by their value judgments on such questions as: Do the interests of the defendant or the society deserve more protection in the criminal justice system? The opponents of plea bargaining came down on the side of the defendant. This led them to evaluate the fairness of the bargaining process in terms of the coercive pressures applied to the defendant. The proponents of plea bargaining, however, were more responsive to society's interests. They tended to view fairness in terms of equal opportunity to bargain, the availability of defense counsel, time to reflect upon the offer, knowledge of judicial sentencing practices, and so forth. Hence, these differences in the perception of fairness may well have resulted in different assessments of plea bargaining even if more empirical data on its correlates were available.

40. This is implicit in Enker, "Perspectives on Plea Bargaining," P. 117.
41. Alschuler, "The Prosecutor's Role," p. 59 et seq.
42. Enker, "Perspectives on Plea Bargaining," p. 113.
43. Alschuler, "The Prosecutor's Role," pp. 57, 112.
44. Newman, "Pleading Guilty for Consideration." Herbert Jacob's early article, "Politics and Criminal Prosecution in New Orleans" (*Tulane Studies in Political Science* 8 (1963):77-98) could be viewed as a quantitative examination of factors affecting plea bargaining, but it fits more neatly in the crime survey tradition than in the topical tradition. That is, Jacob's approach and the factors he considers seem to be similar to those employed by the crime survey researchers.
45. Newman, "Pleading Guilty for Consideration," p. 782.
46. Ibid., pp. 785-86.
47. In one sense, these last criticisms are unfair in that Newman's work did not set out to answer these types of questions. The point is, however, that it was the constraining effect of the topical paradigm that led him to ignore these types of considerations.
48. Alschuler, "The Prosecutor's Role," p. 50.
49. Newman, *Conviction*, p. 76; *Task Force Report: The Courts*, p. 4. See Chapters 7 and 8 of *Conviction* for examples of "individualizing justice."
50. Several more recent studies have also called into question the relationship between workload and guilty pleas. See Milton Heumann, "A Note on Plea Bargaining and Case Pressure," *Law and Society Review* 9 (1975): 515-28; Malcolm Feeley, "The Effects of Heavy Caseloads," paper presented at the Annual Meeting of the American Political Science Association, San Francisco, California, September 5, 1975; and Peter F. Nardulli with Kathleen Proch, "The Caseload Controversy and the Study of Criminal Courts" (unpublished mimeograph).
51. Vetri, pp. 883-84; *Task Force Report: The Courts*, pp. 12-13.
52. One significant exception is an early work by Lloyd Ohlin and Frank Remington, "Sentencing Structure: Its Effect upon Systems for the Administration of Criminal Justice," *Law and Contemporary Problems* 23 (1958): 495-507. Ohlin and Remington discuss certain "accommodative factors" emanating from the nature of the dispositional process that have to be considered when analyzing the sentencing function. However, they do not introduce these accommodative factors into any empirical examination of sentencing, nor do any of the later sentencing researchers follow up on their insights.
53. Examples of these studies include Edward Green, *Judicial Attitudes in Sentencing* (London: MacMillan, 1961); Henry Bullock, "Significance of the Racial Factor in Sentencing," *The Journal of Criminal Law, Criminology, and Police Science* 52 (1961):411-41; and Stuart Nagel, "Disparities in Criminal Procedure," *UCLA Law Review* 14 (1967):1272-1305. A good review, which includes a more comprehensive listing of the case-oriented studies, is Hagan, "Extra Legal Attributes and Criminal Sentencing," *Law and Society Review* 8 (1974): 557-83.

It should be mentioned that a second body of literature on disparities in judicial sentencing also exists. It focuses upon differences across judges. The most prominent works include Frederick Gaudet et al., "Individual Differences in the Sentencing Tendencies of Judges," *Journal of Criminal Law, Criminology, and Police Science* 23 (1933):811-18; Frederick Gaudet et al., "The Differences between Judges in the Granting of Probation" *Temple Law Quarterly* 19 (1945):471-84; Alfred Somit, Joseph Tanenhaus, and Walter Wilke, "Aspects of Judicial Sentencing Behavior," *University of Pittsburgh Law Review* 21 (1960):613-20; and Green, *Judicial Attitudes*, Chapter 6. With the exception of *Judicial Attitudes*, all of these works deal with aggregate data but largely conform with the input-output approach of the topical researchers. Since many of the same criticisms made below with regard to the case-oriented studies apply to the judge-oriented studies, for the sake of brevity these works will not be systematically reviewed in this section. Suffice it to say that, if these studies were included in the analysis, Figure 2-4 would have to be modified by adding "identity of judge" to the list of extraneous factors.

54. The nature of the debate can be understood by reading Green, *Judicial Attitudes*, Chapter 1.

55. Ibid., pp. 100 and 102, respectively.

56. Henry Bullock, "The Significance of the Racial Factor in Sentencing," in *Crime and Justice in Society*, ed. Richard Quinney (Boston: Little, Brown, 1969), pp. 428 and 429, respectively.

57. Hagan, "Extra Legal Attributes."

58. These figures include only the results of studies that focused upon sentences in state cases with fairly general samples (i.e., not capital cases alone).

59. Actually the empirical analyses reveal a second important benefit of viewing sentencing in light of its role within the court's overall dispositional strategy: the types of factors affecting sentence vary depending upon whether the case was formally or informally processed. Thus, by combining all types of cases (guilty plea, slow plea, bench trial, jury trial) in a sentencing analysis, the topical researchers' efforts to assess the role of extraneous factors may well have been frustrated. More will be said of this in Chapters 3 and 8.

✳ *Chapter 3*

The Study of Criminal Courts, Part III: The Organizational Approach

The purpose of this chapter, as in Chapters 1 and 2, is to identify and discuss a distinct way of thinking about criminal courts. In this chapter an organizational approach is analyzed. The first two chapters attempted to delineate earlier traditions by reviewing relevant bodies of literature and outlining and critiquing rough models of common thought patterns embodied in them. Such an approach is not feasible in this chapter for two reasons. First, if there is a distinct organizational tradition in the study of criminal courts it is in its embryonic stages. A careful review of works that are commonly cited as organizational approaches to the study of criminal courts simply does not reveal a distinct set of common thought patterns.[1] While these studies are loosely organized around a common theme they evidence a myriad of focuses, concerns, and methodologies. This may be a healthy state of affairs in the developmental stages of a tradition, but it does not lend itself to the format used in earlier chapters.

A second reason for adopting a different format here is that this chapter is designed to function as a bridge between this section and the empirical section of this work, which is an organizational analysis of the felony court system in Chicago. Ideally, this chapter will facilitate an understanding not only of how the empirical analyses performed here differ from those done in earlier traditions, but also of how they fit into a much broader perspective on the operations of criminal courts. This requires more than just a review of relevant studies written in the developmental stages of that perspective. It requires considerable license to abstract from and expand upon what has been done and to speculate on what can be done.

To meet these objectives, this chapter first outlines and elaborates upon an organizational mode of analysis considered useful in viewing criminal courts. This suggested organizational perspective integrates three types of considerations—internal factors, external factors, and setting—that are important in understanding how criminal courts operate. After a discussion of the predominant type of work-related activity in criminal courts, some hypothetical examples are given to illustrate the types of insights that such an approach can produce. Finally, some rather basic questions are addressed pertaining to the role of this mode of analysis within the study of criminal courts.

AN ORGANIZATIONAL MODE OF ANALYSIS AND THE STUDY OF CRIMINAL COURTS

While the works that are commonly acknowledged as organizationally oriented studies of criminal courts constitute a rather disparate body of literature, common to them is at least one thesis that justifies characterizing them as an organizational tradition. Their general contention is that factors emanating from the collective efforts of judges, prosecutors, and defense counsel (the courtroom elite) to pursue common interests have important consequences for the processing of criminal cases.[2] These collective efforts are manifested in the cooperative patterns of behavior reported by many observers of criminal courts. Further, to abstract a bit from what has been argued in these studies, these common interests can be defined as the shared desire to process cases expeditiously.[3] It is this contention—that is in the interests of the courtroom elite to process cases expeditiously—that makes this tradition organizational in nature and that forms the basic premise in the mode of analysis to be proposed here.

The notion of shared concerns is crucial in the linkage between the study of courts and the study of organizations because much of the organizational literature revolves around the notion of collective efforts to achieve common ends. This is reflected in many often-cited definitions of organizations. Etzioni, for example, says that organizations "are social units (or social groupings) deliberately constructed and reconstructed to seek specific goals."[4] Simon calls them "systems of interdependent activity, encompassing at least several primary groups and usually characterized, at the level of consciousness of participants, by a high degree of rational direction of behavior toward ends that are objects of common acknowledgement and expectation."[5] Selznick says, "Organization is the arrangement of personnel for facilitating the accomplishment of some agreed purpose through the allocation of functions and authority."[6] Blau and Scott contend that this concern with goal orientation is the factor that distinguishes the study of formal organizations from the study of social organizations.[7]

This overall concern in the organizational literature with the study of collective efforts to pursue common ends makes an organizational perspective an attractive conceptual device in the study of criminal courts. It should be emphasized, however, that the literature on organizations is not useful in the study of criminal courts merely because it leads to a consideration of how the interests of an intraorganizational coalition are manifested in courtroom operations. The organizational literature is also useful because it leads one to consider the effect of external constraints upon the coalition's pursuit of its common ends and sensitizes one to the fact that the implications of these collective efforts may be different in different settings. All three factors—the interests of the courtroom elite, external (environmental) considerations, and the court's setting—are essential in viewing courts from an organizational perspective. Indeed, perhaps the most significant contribution that an organizational mode of analysis could make to the study of criminal courts would be an understanding of how the courtroom elite's efforts to pursue common interests are manifested in different settings and how this coalition responds to changes in environmental constraints.[8]

How the three types of factors discussed above can be meshed into an integrated perspective on the operations of criminal courts, and the types of contributions that such a perspective might make, will be discussed shortly. First, each of the three components of this mode of analysis must be discussed in more detail.

Internal Considerations: The Common Interests of the Courtroom Elite

As is evident from what has already been said, a crucial notion in this analysis is that it is in the interests of the judge, prosecutor, and defense counsel to process cases expeditiously. This is the basic premise underlying this approach; its centrality makes an examination of its viability and a discussion of its significance essential. In this regard, several questions must be addressed. Perhaps the most important is, What justification is there for arguing that it is in the mutual interests of the courtroom elite to process cases expeditiously? While several strong arguments can be made in support of this premise, even if one accepts them, other problems arise concerning the centrality of this premise in any conceptual device appropriate for the study of criminal courts. The most serious of these problems can be stated succinctly: Why focus on only one facet of a complex set of motivations, attitudes, values, and beliefs of only three participants in the dispositional process? There are other participants (victims, defendants, policemen, clerks), some of whom do not share the same concerns as the judge, prosecutor, and defense counsel. Also, while a judge, prosecutor, or defense counsel may have an interest in processing cases expeditiously, his behavior may also be influenced by his role perceptions, attitudes, or background, or other idiosyncratic predilections.

Arguments in Support of the Premise. Various arguments can be offered to support the view that it is in the interests of each member of the courtroom elite to process cases expeditiously. These arguments are grounded in the nature and structure of work within criminal courts, although they vary somewhat for private defense counsel, who are not members of a semi-permanent courtroom work group, and other members of the courtroom elite, who are. With regard to private defense counsel, certain financial considerations make it in their economic self-interest to expeditiously process cases. These individuals get paid on a case-by-case basis. But because most criminal defendants cannot afford even moderate legal expenses, average fees in such cases tend to be quite low. Thus, in order to maintain a lucrative criminal practice most private attorneys need to be able to process a large volume of work units (criminal cases) with a minimal expenditure of effort.[9] To do this they are dependent upon the availability of informal dispositional procedures as well as the cooperation of other members of the courtroom work group.

While the argument with regard to the other participants—judges, prosecutors, and public defenders—is somewhat different, it also revolves around the nature of work in criminal courts. It does not, however, hinge upon the amount of work these individuals must do (the case load pressure argument).[10] Rather, it focuses upon the structure of their work loads. As Feeley notes, work in criminal courts is structured in a distinct if not unique way.[11] When the cases on their respective calls are completed in a given day, normally the formal work requirements of the judge, public defender, and prosecutor are fulfilled. Thus, it is in their mutual self-interest to process expeditiously the cases on the call for a given day, regardless of how many cases are scheduled. The significance of this structure should not be underestimated. Its impact upon courtroom operations is reinforced by participants' perceptions of their work loads and the social setting of work in criminal courts.

Perception of Work Loads. In order to understand the role that participants' perceptions of their work loads play in this argument, it is necessary to introduce the notion of the presumption of guilt. As developed in the work of Packer[12] and Blumberg,[13] as well as elsewhere, the presumption of guilt is "a complex of attitudes, a mood . . . a prediction of outcome,"[14] based upon the participants' belief that weak cases are screened out at an earlier stage of the proceedings by police or prosecutors. Its consequences for the participants' perceptions of their work are best stated by Edward L. Barrett: "Most of the cases left to be dealt with by the system then are those in which there is no serious dispute over the guilt or innocence of the defendant. This fact sets the tone for the process . . . . Everyone concerned—the defense lawyer, the prosecutor, the judge, the probation officer—becomes aware of the fact that he is involved in a process where the primary focus is on deciding what to do with people who are in fact guilty."[15]

Thus, the presumption of guilt leads to a rather mundane and routinized definition of work within the criminal court setting. The more glamourous, ultimate question of guilt or innocence, which courts were originally designed to resolve, is seldom seriously considered. What this means is that there is seldom any motivation derived from professional considerations to engage in formal adversary proceedings. Such proceedings are designed to resolve another type of question entirely—guilt or innocence. Informal, truncated proceedings are more appropriate to resolve the types of problems routinely handled in criminal courts; they are also more desirable given the structure of criminal court work.

Social Setting. Various aspects of the social setting that surrounds work in criminal courts also reinforce the impact that the structure of work has upon the participants' motivations. First, as professionals, judges, prosecutors, and public defenders do not receive overtime pay for courtroom work. Thus, there are neither professional *nor* financial incentives to engage in formal, adversary proceedings as a matter of course. Second, no one desires extended courtroom proceedings because everyone has somewhere else to be. A free afternoon allows a judge time to catch up on his legal reading, play golf, be with his family, or prepare for a civic engagement later in the day. Indeed, many judges expect such benefits to accompany a seat on the bench. In some jurisdictions, a judgeship is the traditional reward for faithful party or public service, an early retirement with full benefits.[16] A free afternoon allows prosecutors and public defenders time to prepare for the next day's calendar. It can also give them time to devote to private practice—common in smaller jurisdictions, and not unheard of in urban ones (Baltimore, for example). A third, related point is that while all participants have somewhere else to go, no one can leave until everyone is done.[17] This is important to note because each has the ability to communicate his concern to others. As in any work setting where individuals interact on a continuing basis, criminal court actors who are not sensitive to the concerns of others will find it difficult to perform their own duties effectively. Thus, there are limits on the ability of individuals to consistently ignore the desires of others.

Significance of the Premise. An answer to the question of why this discussion focuses upon the judge, prosecutor, and defense counsel can be found in the elitist nature of the criminal court power structure. Within the courtroom setting these three individuals enjoy a virtual monopoly of power. Legally they are vested with the power to initiate and dismiss charges, sentence defendants, rule on guilt or innocence, make and rule on legal motions—in short, they are responsible for the performance of most vital tasks involved in the disposition of criminal cases. The formal structure does not give the victim, the arresting officer, or any other participant legal resources that compare with these. Hence, the latters' power to affect the nature of the proceedings is very limited. The defendant is vested with legal resources in the form of guaranteed rights, but normally he has access to these rights and privileges only through his attorney. Most defendants do not have the expertise to recognize and assert their rights.

Thus, the shared interests of the *courtroom elite* are emphasized in this perspective because members of this elite, unlike others in the courtroom setting, have the power to effectuate their concerns. The *shared interests* of the courtroom elite—as opposed to some other facet of these individuals' motivational, attitudinal, value, or belief structure—are focused upon in this perspective because of some other characteristics of the power structure in criminal courts. Most of the power exercised by members of the courtroom elite is derived from the wide discretion vested in them. Also, while the discretionary power in the court system is almost entirely vested in the courtroom elite, it is distributed among the various members in such a manner that none can dominate criminal court operations. This is, of course, not an uncommon situation in organizations. Moreover, according to James Thompson, such a situation is conducive to the development of a coalition that then can exercise a good deal of control within the organization. This is, indeed, what has occurred in criminal courts.

In discussing discretionary power and coalition formation,

Thompson states: "When the power of an individual in a highly discretionary job is less than his dependence, he will seek a coalition. ... We are thus viewing coalitions as linkages of competences or abilities which occur when two or more individuals in discretionary positions believe that their abilities to satisfy organizational dependencies are greater in combination than singly, *and where the results of increased power can be shared.*"[18] These observations make it clear why one aspect of these powerful participants' admittedly complex psyches—their mutual desire to expeditiously process cases—has been isolated and used as a basis for developing a theoretical perspective on the operations of criminal courts: These shared concerns form the basis for the coalition that determines much of what happens within the dispositional process.[19] Stated differently, the structure of the informal, cooperative relations—which so many researchers have contended actually determine how criminal cases are handled—is largely shaped by the mutual interests of the courtroom elite. These interests define the common ground upon which cooperative relations can be based and are reflected in the court's dispositional strategy. If the interests of these powerful individuals were not reflected in this strategy there would be little incentive or basis for modifying the formal adversary relationships embodied in traditional notions of due process. Extending Thompson's thoughts, if the results of increased power could not be shared, there would be little to foster or maintain the coalition.

Environmental Considerations

While the interests of the dominant coalition are important to consider when attempting to understand the operations of criminal courts, external constraints upon the ability of these individuals to pursue their own interests cannot be ignored. Environmental considerations must play an integral role in any organizational analysis of criminal courts. The importance and role of environmental considerations in the operations of organizations is perhaps best stated by Thompson:

> We and others have emphasized the coalitional nature of complex organizations, but always in terms of agreements among individual members, each having something to contribute and each receiving something in exchange. There is, however, a larger sense of configuration, which we will refer to as *co-alignment.*
>
> Perpetuation of the complex organization rests on an appropriate co-alignment in time and space not simply of human individuals but of streams of institutionalized action. Survival rests on the co-alignment of technology and task environment. . . .[20]

In Thompson's analysis, the concept of technology is a very broad term, referring to the means by which inputs are converted to outputs in an organizational setting. It is analogous to the concept of dispositional strategy as defined in Chapter 2.

One of the basic contentions in Thompson's work, captured in the above quotation, is that in order to understand an organization's technology, it is insufficient to merely consider the role of the organization's dominant coalition. Rather, one must also consider the role that relevant environmental considerations play. Environmental considerations affect the structure of an organization's technology because of the existence of various boundary-spanning mechanisms (environmental control devices) that monitor an organization's operations and have some control over its inputs and outputs. Environmental control devices can be mechanisms (such as competition and public opinion) or entities (such as government watchdog agencies). The type of control they exercise can be direct or indirect, and is often specialized (concerned with only certain facets of organizational operations). Also, control can relate to the flow of resources into an organization or to the utilization of resources within it.

Several rather general types of environmental control devices relevant to the operations of criminal courts will be discussed. First, however, two distinct types of environmental concerns must be differentiated. Each is related to the role played by criminal courts within the societal division of labor—processing suspects apprehended by police and charged with criminal transgressions.

Relevant Types of Environmental Expectations. Processing individuals charged with crimes entails such things as setting bail, arraigning defendants, ruling on legal motions, determining guilt or innocence, and sentencing convicted defendants. While there are many ways the performance of these various tasks might be structured in an overall dispositional strategy, criminal court officials are not free to structure them in any way they see fit. Rather, they operate under certain constraints, one important set of which can be labeled "qualitative." Anglo-American criminal justice is formally governed by contemporary notions of due process. While definitions of due process fluctuate somewhat, traditionally this notion has been held to require a specific forum in which cases must be heard. Also, it defines the relationship between participants in the dispositional process and grants certain rights to the accused. Practices that flagrantly violate accepted notions of due process would be inconsistent with societal expectations of how courts should operate, and could activate environmental control devices. Hence, the courtroom elite is forced to structure its behavior patterns around the essential requirements dictated by due process considerations.

A second set of constraints can be labeled "quantitative." It concerns the composition of the court's output—aggregate figures on acquittals, convictions, dismissals, sentences, and so forth. Regardless of how scrupulously criminal courts adhere to the ideals embodied in notions of due process, they may not be performing their societal role properly if their outputs are not roughly consistent with societal expectations. A series of meticulously executed murder and rape trials followed by sentences of probation would not satisfy such expectations in most communities, nor would consistently and notoriously low conviction rates in felony cases. Rather, they would result in such things as editorial condemnations, recall elections, primary challenges, and the like.

Environmental Control Devices. With these two distinct dimensions of environmental concerns clarified, the various types of environmental control devices relevant to the operations of criminal courts can be discussed. Input regulators and output regulators are the two basic types of such devices. Input regulators determine the magnitude and mix of cases that flow into the court system, and thus affect court operations only indirectly. Output regulators, the most important type of environmental control devices, perform two functions: communication and control. They convey to the court organization the content of societal demands and expectations, and they monitor and influence court operations to ensure that they are responsive to societal demands and expectations.

Input Regulators. There are at least three significant sets of input regulators in the courts' environment. The first is the citizen victim-witness. These individuals can affect inputs significantly because they generally make the initial decision to report a crime. A change in the attitudes or the distribution of attitudes in the citizenry could drastically affect the court's inputs. Actions taken by women's groups, for example, have probably led to an attitudinal change toward rape. More women than a decade ago are probably inclined to report rapes, and this affects the mix of cases flowing into criminal courts. "Turn in the pusher" campaigns by local community groups and police department attempts to improve community relations are other examples of factors that could affect community attitudes toward the criminal justice system and, indirectly, court inputs.

The police patrolman is a second significant input regulator. The patrolman investigates reports of criminal acts and uncovers some himself; he is responsible for most arrests made by a police department. While a patrolman's ability to uncover criminal activity and effectuate "good" arrests is highly dependent upon cooperation from citizens, the level of police resources and technology, and so forth, he enjoys wide discretion in making the decision to arrest. The shift from a traditional to a professional orientation in a department, changes in recruitment practices (affirmative action guidelines, psychological screening, degree requirements), or changes in training could affect the exercise of this discretion. Such changes may bring about differences in the quality of case preparation, as well as the nature and levels of cases considered by criminal courts.

One last important input regulator is the chief of police. As administrative head of the police department, he is an important entity in the court's organization. He is the chief liaison between the department and city, state, and federal agencies. His skills as a politician and grant seeker influence the department's share of the city budget as well as outside law enforcement funds. This affects the level of police resources and technology within the department and directly and indirectly could affect the nature and level of cases flowing into the courts. The police chief is also the focal point for political pressure from the community. In this capacity he considers inputs from the mayor, city council, local business interests, and other community groups concerned with law enforcement activities. Pressures from these groups can lead him, as the administrative head of the police department, to issue various policies and directives to patrolmen. While such proclamations seldom eliminate patrolmen's discretion on arrest encounters, they could lead them to be more sensitive to certain types of crimes or to activity in certain areas of the city. Thus, they could affect the composition of the court's inputs indirectly.

Output Regulators. There is a certain amount of specialization among the several entities that monitor criminal court outputs and internal operations. These entities can be thought of as predominantly oriented either toward the quantitative aspects of the organization's operations or toward the qualitative aspects of its operations. These entities can also be thought of as direct or indirect. Direct entities have the power to affect the internal operations of the organization directly, while indirect entities monitor the court organization's activities but cannot directly affect it. They can only bring pressure to bear upon entities that can affect the court's operations directly.

One important output regulator that can be considered direct and quantitatively oriented is the administrative head of the local court system, often referred to as the chief judge. The chief judge is the most visible judge and, as such, a focal point for community pressure. Often he is an elected official. Usually he has control over the assignment of judges and can transfer them at his discretion. The chief judge is oriented to the quantitative aspects of the court organization's output because he is an administrative figure with no review powers. Moreover, in his role as a local politico he is more concerned with the quantitative than the qualitative aspects of the court's output; usually these are the most politically salient aspects.

A second direct, quantitatively oriented environmental control agent is the head of the state's attorney's office. This official can introduce changes into the court organization because he has a good deal of control over the dismissal of cases, plea bargaining policies, and sentence recommendations. Moreover, he can transfer or fire his assistants at his discretion. He is amenable to pressure because he is an elected official in a highly visible county office. His position makes him a top official in his local party, and often he has higher political ambitions. The state's attorney is oriented toward the quantitative aspects of the court organizations operations because he, like the chief judge, is an administrative official and a local political figure.

The state legislature, while further removed from the courtroom than the chief judge and the state's attorney, can also be considered a direct and quantitatively oriented control agent. It has the power to pass criminal codes, provide for minimum sentences for certain crimes, and enact other laws relevant to the functioning of the court system. As elected officials, members are susceptible to pressure from various groups within the society. The legislature has, however, generally left the qualitative aspects of the court's operations to the judicial branch. Like the chief judge and state's attorney, the legislature's interests lie with the quantitative aspects of the court organization's operations.

There are several indirect, quantitatively oriented control devices. One is the county board, which usually determines the level of support for the prosecutor's office, indigent defense services, and support personnel (bailiffs, clerks, stenographers). The county board also provides the criminal court with physical facilities. Thus, members of the criminal court system cannot be indifferent to the dominant views of the county board. Local media can also be considered as quantitatively oriented, indirect environmental control agents. Because of the salience of the crime issue, newspapers and television stations often do special reports on the court's operations. Other examples of such environmental entities are local political parties, civic reform groups, and quasi-governmental watchdog agencies.

Only two types of control mechanisms monitor the qualitative aspects of the court organization's operations: appellate courts and professional groups such as the American Civil Liberties Union, the NAACP, and bar associations. Appellate courts are direct mechanisms because they have the power to review. They can introduce sweeping changes into the court organization, as evidenced by such rulings as *Gideon* and *Miranda*. The professional groups do not have the power of review, but can crusade for isolated causes concerning due process. These crusades take place in courtrooms, in the media, and in professional journals.

Limitations. Although the general significance of environmental considerations must be stressed, it should be noted that there are important limits upon the extent to which criminal court operations can be influenced by external factors. Several reasons account for these limits. First, the very abstract, intangible nature of "justice" and the low visibility of most criminal court decisions make it difficult to determine when criminal courts are failing to conform to societal expectations. It is generally much easier, for example, to determine whether one likes the taste of a candy bar, or whether a certain line of cars meets mileage standards, than it is to determine whether justice has been served in a series of criminal cases, whether a given sentence was too low, or whether a dismissal was warranted. The essentially conflicting nature of the qualitative and quantitative dimensions of environmental concerns also limits the extent to which external factors can influence the court's operations. Environmental entities cannot effectively stress the one aspect of the court's operations (qualitative or quantitative) because pursuit of one is limited by the existence of the other.

Finally, the public nature of criminal courts and the vital function that they perform for society inhibit effective environmental control. Many regulatory mechanisms that are effective in controlling the operations of other types of organizations—such as competition and threats to curtail or eliminate the flow of resources—are not applicable to criminal courts. While alternate systems of criminal justice exist on a limited scale in the United States (state system, local system, juvenile system, federal system, etc.), the notion of competing systems of criminal justice in which victims or defendants choose the forum of their preference is antithetic to Anglo-American criminal justice. Also, as presently constituted, American society could not exist without formal institutions to maintain internal order; this eliminates environmental regulation through the restriction or elimination of societal resources allocated to the criminal court system. Indeed, community dissatisfaction with the operations of criminal courts has often led to enhanced flows of resources into the court system!

Setting

By an organization's setting is meant such things as its physical plant, available labor force, the state of technological innovation, and other relevant phenomena that are relatively fixed in the short run. While the notion of setting is not as central to the thinking of most organization theorists as are internal and environmental considerations, it is important nonetheless. As Thompson points out, "The fact that we expect all organizations to seek the same state—self-control—does not mean that we expect all of them to attain it in the same way, with identical design, structures or behavior.... Appropriateness of design, structure, and assessments can be judged only in light of the conditions, variables, and uncertainties present for the organization."[21]

In other words, similarly oriented organizations facing similar kinds of environmental constraints may structure their operations in significantly different ways. Sensitivity to the "givens" that an organization must operate around can help one to understand otherwise inexplicable facets of its operations. Examples of some important "givens" to which criminal courts must adapt include differences in prosecutor screening practices, differences in case assignment procedures, differences in indigent defense systems, differences in available legal procedures, and differences in type of jurisdiction (felony-misdemeanor, specialized-general).

Summary

It is believed that an organizational mode of analysis integrating the three types of factors discussed here—internal factors, environmental factors, and setting—can yield significant and unique contributions to the study of criminal courts. This mode of analysis explicitly deals with the unique institutional characteristics of criminal courts neglected in earlier approaches. More specifically, it recognizes the important implications that the elitist power structure and tightly knit interest structure in criminal courts have for internal operations, while not ignoring external considerations. It also recognizes that the interplay of these two factors may have different ramifications in different settings.

Thus this perspective begins by explicitly contravening one of the most bothersome implicit presumptions underlying earlier analyses: the legal man assumption. Instead of viewing criminal justice officials as being responsive only to professional norms and ethics, this perspective is premised on the view that these individuals have a vested interest in the procedures used to handle cases as well as the inclination and power to effectuate those interests. This premise is then built upon by seeking to outline how these interests affect the operations of criminal courts in different settings and how external considerations are handled. It leads one to focus on the impact that these factors have upon the strategy used by criminal court practitioners to handle their work loads. Different stages of the dispositional process are not treated in isolation from other stages; they are viewed as integral parts of the criminal court's technology.

A substantive, though hypothetical, example will clarify some of the potential contributions this theoretical perspective can make. First, however, some comments are necessary concerning the predominant type of activity engaged in by line personnel in criminal courts, since the type of activity they engage in, while not unique, is different from that engaged in by their counterparts in many organizations. This has important implications for how we must structure our thinking about criminal courts when viewing them in light of the mode of analysis suggested above.

DOMINANT MODES OF ACTIVITY

To understand how the activity of line personnel in criminal courts differs from that in some other types of organizations, as well as the implications of these differences for examining criminal courts from an organizational perspective, it will be useful to contrast the operations of criminal courts with an organization whose line personnel engage in more conventional types of activity. Consider, for illustrative purposes, a car company. It produces a line of cars. There are, of course, a multitude of tasks that must be performed in order to produce any given model. Bodies must be constructed, undercoated, and painted; engines must be built, tested, and attached to the body; interiors must be installed; bumpers and doors must be affixed; and so forth. Moreover, while there may be a set number of tasks involved in producing a car, each task can be performed in a number of different ways.

Despite the fact that the matrix of possible ways to assemble a car is overwhelming, the actual production of a car is highly routinized: each is produced in light of a predetermined plan or strategy. The reason for this is that the production process is structured in light of a set of goals and constraints. The car company does not simply want to produce cars; it wants to produce them so as to maximize the return on its investment. The company also wants to produce cars meeting relevant safety, environmental, and energy regulations, as well as consumer preferences. Finally, at least in the short run, the car production process is constrained by the organization's physical plant, the level of technological innovation, the available labor force, and other "givens." Each of these considerations is reflected in one way or another in the overall plan used to produce cars.

The significance of these three types of considerations (internal, external, setting) in the car production process makes the structure of activity within it amenable to the approach suggested here. An analysis of the implications that each factor has for the production of a car may lead to a better understanding of the overall design of the car company's production plan as well as the structure of individual tasks within it. This perspective may, for example, shed some light on why seat belts are affixed, why a certain quality of material is used, why so many different styles of cars are produced, or why certain requirements are adhered to in producing engines.

There are significant parallels between the car production process and the dispositional process that suggest that the mode of analysis used for the former may also lend some order to the latter. Criminal courts, like car companies and other formal organizations, perform a task for society: they process criminal cases. Their output primarily consists of terminated criminal cases. As with the production of a car, the disposition of a criminal case requires that a series of tasks be performed. Charges must be initiated, bail must be determined, a preliminary hearing may have to be conducted, guilt or innocence may have to be determined, a sentence may have to be set, and so forth.

Despite these parallels, one significant difference exists between these tasks and those that must be performed to produce a car. While most of the tasks involved in producing a car involve physical activity by line personnel vested with little discretion, most of the tasks involved in processing a criminal case involve decision-making activity by line personnel vested with a good deal of discretion.[22] Although this difference calls for a somewhat different focus in the application of the mode of analysis suggested here, it does not mitigate its value in the court setting. While line personnel in criminal courts engage in predominantly decision-making activity, much of it is as routinized as the physical activity engaged in by car company operatives. When a judge sets bail in ten cases a day, five days a week, for six months, he develops decision rules, incorporating various criteria (if the case is an armed robbery set bond at X dollars, if it is a first offense reduce it Y dollars, if the defendant is steadily employed reduce it Z dollars) to assist him in making routine bond decisions. He does not reexamine the foundation of his bases for setting bail in every case any more than a car company employee reassesses his techniques for affixing bumpers with every car.[23]

What this difference in dominant types of activity means in terms of applying this mode of analysis to the study of criminal courts is that the primary focus of inquiry must be upon the criteria embodied in various criminal court decisions as well as upon the overall structure of tasks that are performed. Just as there are many ways to perform individual tasks in a car company, many different types of criteria can be embodied in a given criminal court decision. Consider just the sentencing decision. A judge can take into consideration the offense committed, various situational factors surrounding its occurrence, the penological needs of the defendant, the defendant's age, sex, or race, the mode of disposition (guilty plea or trial), the defense counsel, and so forth. Moreover, there are many different ways in which these various criteria can be integrated and weighted in the derivation of a sentence.[24]

The similarities as well as the differences between the car production process and the dispositional process clarify the potential contribution that the organizational mode of analysis proposed here can make to the study of criminal courts. Earlier it was argued that an understanding of the implications that each of the three factors discussed above had for the production of a car would lend some insights into the overall design of the car company's production plan as well as to the structure of individual tasks within it. Likewise, an understanding of the implications that these factors have for the disposition of criminal cases will give some insights into the court's dispositional strategy and the criteria embodied in criminal court decisions.

It has been argued that it is in the interests of the courtroom elite to expeditiously dispose of cases. This factor has direct implications for the criteria to be used in many of the decisions involved in the processing of criminal cases as well as for the structure of the court's dispositional strategy. Moreover, while the interests of the elite may be invariant across court systems, the implications of these interests for courtroom operations may vary across systems because of differences in the setting. Finally, relevant environmental factors, which may vary over time and across systems, may have direct implications for the structure of courtroom activity; these external considerations may also place constraints upon the impact of internal factors.

By itself, an understanding of how these three factors are reflected in criminal court operations will not lead to a complete understanding of the dispositional process. The application of this mode of analysis can yield many insights, however, into the operations of criminal courts, which could lead to the development of more refined and powerful models of the process. To illustrate in more concrete terms the types of insights that this mode of anlaysis may yield, an example of its application to one criminal court decision—the sentencing decision—in two hypothetical jurisdictions will be discussed.

THE SENTENCING DECISION IN THE FELONY TRIAL COURTS OF ALPHAVILLE AND BETAVILLE

Alphaville and Betaville are two hypothetical American cities. Similar in many respects, they also differ in important ways. Both are large cities (population one million) with similar aggregate socioeconomic characteristics, as well as similar crime rates for most major categories of offenses. Alphaville, however, is in the Northeast and is dominated by a Democratic political machine, while Betaville is in the Midwest and has a very competitive political system. Major elective city offices turn over quite frequently in Betaville, but do not in Alphaville. In Alphaville, being slated by the Democratic machine for a judgeship is tantamount to being elected; in Betaville, judicial elections are more competitive.

Another significant difference between the two cities lies with public concern over the crime problem. Crime rates in both cities are similar, but public opinion surveys have consistently shown that people in Betaville regard crime as a much more serious problem than do people in Alphaville. These surveys also show that Betaville residents place much more faith in punishment as a deterrent to crime than do Alphaville residents. Partly in response to this concern with crime and partly because it can have a significant impact upon policy in Betaville's competitive political process, the local media in Betaville devote a good deal of attention to the criminal justice system. In addition to the usual coverage of extraordinary crime and occasional exposés, Betaville newspapers report on ordinary street crimes. They interview prosecutors and defense counsel and frequently report sentences. While the media in Alphaville also report on extraordinary crimes and do occasional exposés, they very seldom get involved with ordinary cases.

The criminal justice systems in Alphaville and Betaville, like the cities in general, are similar in some respects and differ in others. Their police departments are of comparable size and orientation, and they have equivalent technological capabilities. They also have comparable clearance rates for most major categories of offenses. Each police department initiates felony charges by filing a preliminary hearing complaint form with the preliminary hearing court. In both cities these lower level courts screen weak or nonserious cases before they are sent to the grand jury. About 60 percent of all felony cases in each system are dismissed by these courts; the remaining 40 percent are sent to the grand jury. The grand jury in both cities does very little screening—over 99.5 percent of the cases referred to it receive true bills. Hence, the criminal trial courts in both cities receive comparable numbers and types of cases. To deal with these cases, both cities employ sixteen full-time judges, bailiffs, clerks, and stenographers. There are also thirty-two full-time prosecutors assigned to the criminal trial court division in each city, as well as several more in administrative capacities.

One difference between the two criminal justice systems lies in case assignment procedures. In Alphaville, cases are assigned by the chief judge to each of the sixteen courtrooms immediately after an indictment is returned. Except under highly unusual circumstances, the judge to whom the case is initially assigned will ultimately dispose of it. Moreover, because prosecutors are assigned semi-permanently to each courtroom, it is customary to have a preliminary conference involving all the participants. This is especially true if the defense counsel is a public defender or well-known private courtroom regular. In Betaville, case assignment is done somewhat differently. Cases are randomly assigned to each of the sixteen judges, but no one knows who the judge will be until a month before the case is set down for trial. Even then, if the initial assignee is busy with another case when the trial date comes, the case can be sent to an empty courtroom and heard before a different judge. Because of these uncertainties, extensive pretrial discussions of a case are infrequent.

Another significant difference between the trial court systems in Alphaville and Betaville concerns procedures for providing legal services for indigents. Alphaville has a public defender's office that employs twenty-five attorneys in administrative and trial capacities. They provide legal services for an indeterminate number of defendants on a fixed yearly budget. One public defender is assigned to each courtroom on a semi-permanent basis, and he represents all defendants determined to be indigent by the trial judge. Betaville does not have a public defender's office. Instead, it has a system whereby private attorneys are paid a fixed hourly rate to represent indigents. The ordinance provides twenty-five dollars per hour for research (up to a reasonable limit) and thirty-five dollars per hour for trial work. It also has provisions to cover expert witnesses and other reasonable defense-related expenses. While judges have some discretion as to which attorneys are appointed, the ordinance provides that at least half of the assignments must go to the local legal aid society.

Table 3-1 summarizes the significant differences in the setting and environment in which the two court systems process cases. These differences have important implications for sentencing decisions in each city. Before these decisions are discussed in light of the mode of analysis suggested earlier, the role of trial courts within the felony disposition process must be set forth.

Trial Courts Within the Court Organization

If the "felony court organization" is considered to be that entity responsible for processing serious criminal offenses in a community, the court organization in Alphabille and Betaville really contains two separate divisions—a preliminary hearing division and a trial division. Each performs a different task and each is composed of several work groups (courtrooms) charged with the day-to-day processing of criminal cases. Because police work under a different incentive system than judges and prosecutors, many cases are put into the system that, from an internal organizational perspective, are undesirable. Weak or nonserious, "junk" cases need to be eliminated at an early point, before a substantial amount of scarce resources is invested in their processing. Because preliminary hearing court work groups are the first point in the judicial process, the task of screening falls to them.

The preliminary hearing court work groups do a good job of

Table 3-1. Differences Between Hypothetical Criminal Court Systems

	Setting		Environment	
City	Indigent Defense System	Case Assignment	Media Coverage	Political Situation
Alphaville	public defender's office	stable, known assignments	general	machine dominated
Betaville	assignment to private attorneys; hourly fees	uncertain, largely unknown assignments	highly specific, extensive	highly competitive

screening in both Alphaville and Betaville. They eliminate over half the cases that they process, and most cases they do send to the trial court are quite strong. Given this, the role of the trial court groups within both court organizations is to procure convictions—an important task because many external evaluations of the court organization hinge upon how well it is performed. If this conviction procurement function were not executed adequately, many would question whether the court organization was properly performing its role within the societal division of labor.

The conviction procurement function can be performed in a number of different ways. This situation is, of course, analogous to the car company example. While the securing of car doors is an important task, there are many ways to do it. Also as in the car example, not all alternative methods are equally desirable. Full-blown, adversary jury trials are one way to secure convictions, but the enormous investment of resources and the degree of uncertainty involved in such a mode of disposition make it undesirable from the perspective of the courtroom elite's interests. Highly informal and arbitrary proceedings in which the defendant has no opportunity to cross-examine state witnesses, make legal motions, or present evidence would be an alternative way of securing convictions. However, this mode would also be unacceptable: although it would meet internal needs, it would not conform to external expectations as to how criminal courts should operate. One example of a satisficing mode of disposition—meeting both internal and external considerations—is the guilty plea. It is informal, expeditious, and not contrary to contemporary notions of due process.

The trial courts of Alphaville and Betaville perform their conviction procurement function quite well, although they do it in different ways. Alphaville trial courts have a conviction rate of 70 percent, and 85 percent of their convictions are the result of guilty pleas. Betaville trial courts have a conviction rate of 80 percent, but 65 percent of their convictions come after a trial. The differences in conviction procedures do not mean that the interests of the courtroom elite were reflected in this aspect of Alphaville's operations, but frustrated in Betaville. Rather, because of differences in the two systems, the interests of the courtroom elite are manifested in different ways. While 85 percent of Betaville's convictions were obtained after a trial, the vast majority of those trials were, in reality, "slow pleas." In Betaville, slow pleas are informal, nonadversary, highly truncated bench trials. As they are used in Betaville, slow pleas are functionally equivalent to guilty pleas.

These two types of dispositions are functional equivalents because they are both manifestations of a successful co-alignment of internal and external considerations in two different settings. However, there are some significant differences between them. First, slow plea dispositions are a shade closer to the adversary ideal, and, perhaps even more significant, on paper indistinguishable from full-length trials. Second, slow pleas are not as controversial as guilty pleas. Guilty pleas, decried by reformers since the 1920s, conjure up thoughts of "bargain justice," shady dealings, giveaway pleas, coercion, and so forth. Third, while the successful use of the slow plea requires a loose but generally acknowledged set of understandings, no *specific* a priori understandings or commitments need to be made.

Several factors related to the setting and environment of the trial courts in Betaville make the slow plea—with its distinctive characteristics—a more desirable mode of disposition than traditional guilty pleas. The unstable and uncertain nature of case assignment procedures makes it difficult to obtain the specific kinds of commitments and understandings essential to a guilty plea system. If a deal were to be reached by a prosecutor and defense counsel that was acceptable to the judge to which the case was initially assigned, a last-minute reassignment to a different, disapproving judge could undercut all the previous negotiations. The slow plea system, which requires only very broad understandings, is much better suited to such a situation. Also, the fact that many defense counsel can actually make money by going to trial, because of the structure of the indigent defense system, often makes it in their financial interest to go to trial even if the "trial" is really a slow plea. Finally, environmental factors have contributed to the development of Betaville's slow plea system. The trial courts there operate within an environment dominated by highly conscientious media and a highly competitive political situation. Slow pleas are advantageous in such a situation because they insulate the participants from many types of criticism that might result from a more traditional guilty plea system.

Implications for Sentencing

From what has been said, it is clear that, from an organizational perspective, guilty pleas and slow pleas are satisficing modes of performing the conviction procurement function in the trial courts of Alphaville and Betaville. But while this is true, for external reasons, a formal adversary jury or bench trial is always a viable option for the defense. In fact, such trials occur with some frequency in both court systems; this fact has important implications for the sentencing decision. Because of the differences in the two court organizations, these implications are somewhat different in each.

Internal Factors and Sentencing. The existence of satisficing and nonsatisficing conviction modes has one very basic implication for sentencing decisions in Alphaville: there are really two different sets of sentencing decision rules, one for guilty plea cases and another for trial cases. Because the former represents situations where the interests of the courtroom elite are realized and the latter represents situations where those interests are frustrated, different criteria are embodied in the two sets of rules and similar criteria are weighted differently. A graphic representation will illustrate this.

External considerations dictate that the most important criterion in both sets of sentencing decision rules be the seriousness of the crime. The gravity of an offense and the circumstances surrounding it cannot be ignored consistently in sentencing decisions, any more than consumer demands can be ignored in important decisions by a commercial entity. In both cases, ignoring external considerations would have undesirable long-term repercussions. Figure 3-1 represents the relationship between seriousness of the crime and sentences in hypothetical guilty plea and trial cases in Alphaville.

Two interesting relationships are evident from the figure. First, while case seriousness is a strong predictor of sentence after both satisficing and nonsatisficing types of dispositions, the relationship is significantly different in each. Similar offenses get more severe sen-

Figure 3-1. Relationship Between Seriousness of Crime and Sentences in Alphaville

The Study of Criminal Courts, Part III: The Organizational Approach 87

tences in trial cases than in guilty plea cases. This sentencing differential reflects an important difference in the two sets of decision rules that is due to internal considerations. The sentencing differential embodied in the two sets of decision rules is maintained because, if costs were not imposed upon defendants who invoked their right to trial, it would be very difficult for the court organization to obtain convictions in a satisficing manner.

A second point evident from Figure 3-1 is that case seriousness does not entirely explain sentencing in either situation. A substantial amount of unexplained variation exists in both situations. What the figure does not reveal, however, is that different factors account for the unexplained variance in each situation. This again reflects differences in the structure of the two sets of decision rules. Because a guilty plea is a satisficing conviction mode that requires some negotiating to attain, a good deal of the unexplained variance depicted in Figure 3-1a can be explained by differences in negotiating positions. Defendants with no arrest records and some financial backing who hire defense counsel with no ties to other members of the court organization (nonregulars) will get shorter sentences than other defendants pleading guilty to a similar crime.

These types of criteria are embodied in sentencing decision rules for guilty plea cases because they relate to certain realities that must be dealt with in negotiations in order to attain a plea. These types of criteria are not relevant to sentencing after a trial, when nothing remains to be negotiated. Factors important in explaining the unexplained variance depicted in Figure 3-1b relate to the type of trial that was conducted. The more a trial deviates from informal expectations and desires, the longer the sentence. Defendants convicted after hotly contested jury trials in which many witnesses were called and many legal motions were argued are apt to get much longer sentences than defendants convicted after bench trials consuming only one afternoon. Such criteria are embodied in sentencing decision rules in trial cases because they relate to the extent to which the courtroom elite's desires were frustrated.

In Betaville, the sentencing decision is structured somewhat differently. Instead of two different sets of sentencing decision rules, there are three: one for guilty pleas, one for slow pleas, and one for trials. The structure of the guilty plea and trial decision rules in Betaville is similar to those in Alphaville. Seriousness of the crime plays a major role in both sets of decision rules in Betaville, as do the other types of factors mentioned above. The structure of sentencing decision rules for slow pleas can best be explained and related to the other two types of cases by reference to Figure 3-2, which depicts

Figure 3-2. Relationship Between Seriousness of Crime and Sentence in Betaville

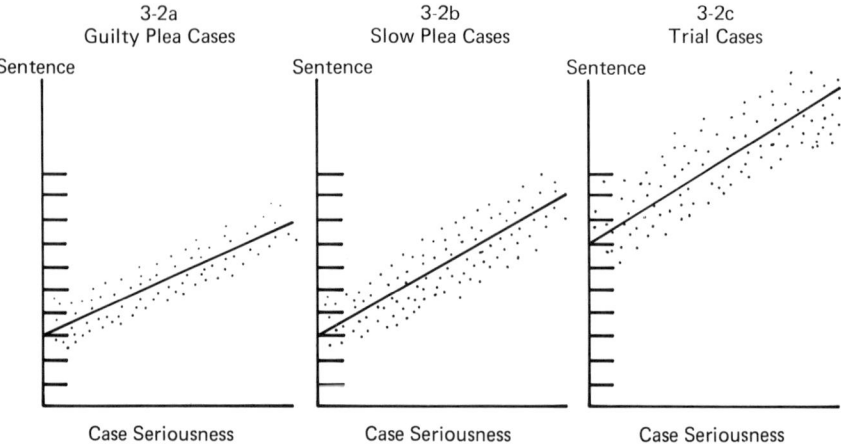

the relationship between case seriousness and sentence in the three situations.

As would be expected, cases convicted after a slow plea receive sentences similar to those given after a guilty plea but lower than those given after a full-length trial. This is, of course, because slow pleas are functionally equivalent to guilty pleas; both are satisficing modes of conviction. While the slope and intercept of the seriousness regression lines in guilty pleas and slow pleas are similar in Figures 3-2a and 3-2b, the types of factors explaining the deviations from those lines are different. Unlike some other slow plea jurisdictions, in Betaville explicit bargaining concerning sentence in slow plea cases does not take place. Thus factors related to bargaining position do not affect sentence in such cases. Instead, factors related to the defendant's background and the judge's attitudes and role perceptions become more important. The latter set of factors is more significant in slow plea cases than guilty plea cases because the negotiation process suppresses much of the impact that differences in judicial orientations can have upon sentence.

External Differences and Sentencing. The examples discussed so far have primarily illustrated how certain internal considerations, presumably constant across systems, are differentially manifested in sentencing decision rules. These internal factors affect the structure of decision rules differently in each court system because of certain differences in the setting within which cases are processed (i.e., dif-

Figure 3-3. Relationship Between Seriousness of Crime and Sentence After a Guilty Plea in Alphaville and Betaville

ferent contexts often require different strategies to pursue a given goal). What the examples have not directly addressed, however, is the relationship between external factors and decision rules. A graphic representation will again be useful in illustrating a possible impact that differences in external factors can have upon the structure of sentencing decisions across jurisdictions. Figure 3-3 represents the regression lines for case seriousness and sentence in *guilty plea cases* only, for each city.

What is obvious from this figure that was not evident before is that similar crimes receive significantly more severe sentences in Betaville than in Alphaville—even though both sets of cases reflect satisficing conviction modes. This difference in sentencing levels can be explained by differences in the environments within which the two court systems operate. Crime is much more of a political issue in Betaville than in Alphaville. Moreover, as noted earlier, the residents of Betaville are generally more conservative than those in Alphaville; they tend to place more faith in the deterrent power of the criminal sanction. These differences in community orientations and preferences are embodied in the prevailing sentencing decision rules in the two court organizations, and manifested in the form of different sentencing levels for similar crimes. This suggests that while internal considerations lead to sentencing differentials between satisficing and nonsatisficing modes of conviction, baseline sentencing levels are dictated by external considerations.

Another way to analyze the differential impact of external factors

Figure 3-4. Relationship Between Seriousness of Crime and Sentence in Alphaville and Betaville at Two Points in Time (Guilty Plea Cases Only)

upon the structure of sentencing decisions is to examine sentences longitudinally. Consider the following situation. In January 1973 a public opinion poll conducted by local newspapers in Alphaville and Betaville revealed parallel and significant increases in the public's concern over crime. Sixty-five percent of the respondents in each city also expressed dissatisfaction with the handling of cases by the criminal court system. An overwhelming majority in both cities thought defendants were treated too leniently. These polls were followed up by a series of editorials advocating stiffer sentences in each city's papers.

Figure 3-4 represents regression lines depicting the relationship between case seriousness and sentence for guilty plea cases handled during the last six months of 1972 (dotted line) and the first six months of 1973 (continuous line) in each city. As the figure reveals, Betaville judges responded rather swiftly to changes in public sentiment by increasing baseline sentencing levels. Alphaville judges, politically much more insulated than Betaville judges, did not.

In the months that followed the initial poll, Betaville papers contained many stories of severe penalties given to various defendants and many interviews of prosecutors and defense counsel commenting upon the difficulty of securing probation in felony cases. The newspapers in Alphaville did very little follow-up on the impact of the poll upon courtroom operations. In May 1973, however, they ran a series of front-page articles on a group of bungled cases and sensational crimes. This led to highly publicized community meetings in several wards. Various neighborhood groups decried the crime problem and sharply criticized local criminal justice officials. Leaders from business, civic, and labor groups met with the mayor, police chief, and chief judge. A bill was introduced in the state legislature to limit the discretion in judges' sentencing power severely by imposing fixed sentences for many types of crimes. In June, when a follow-up poll was conducted, concern for crime was still high in each city. However, the percentage of respondents expressing dissatisfaction with local criminal justice officials in Betaville dropped forty points, while the percentage increased fifteen points in Alphaville.

An analysis of sentencing decisions made in the period from July 1973 through December 1973 showed no change in Betaville. In Alphaville, however, a marked increase in the severity of sentences (an upward shift of the regression line) was observed. Thus, while both systems ultimately reflected the shift in community sentiment, the politically insulated judges in Alphaville responded less quickly. Moreover, the *types* of political pressure that had to be exerted to effectuate change differed in the two cities. Betaville judges responded to media pressure. Alphaville judges did not begin to respond until party officials—at both the top and the bottom of the party hierarchy—began to feel pressure from their traditional sources of support.

A BROADER VIEW

Having laid out in very broad terms what the mode of analysis suggested here entails, as well as some of its potential contributions, several tangential but important issues arise as to its role in the study of criminal courts. Two such issues are of particular significance. First, does the perspective here exhaust the potential contributions that the organizational literature can make to the study of criminal courts? This is easily resolved. The approach suggested here does not attempt to draw upon all facets of the organizational literature, and no claim is made that it does. Rather, this approach is concerned with the role of three types of considerations—internal, external, and contextual—in criminal court decision making. The overall decision-making emphasis was selected because, as Lawrence Mohr correctly asserts: "If the essence of behavior in all organization is not captured by models of decision making, as Simon proposed, it may well be at least for courts, especially trial courts. Trial courts are instruments for rendering decisions. Their organizational product is a certain kind of decision."[25] The decision was made to focus primarily upon the effects of internal, contextual, and external factors upon decision making because such a model provides a general, flexible approach and, at the same time, substantive guidance. This was considered crucial during the developmental stages of the organizational paradigm. The relevance of other facets of the organizational literature may become clearer as this perspective becomes more developed and refined.

A second important issue concerns the relationship between the organizational mode of analysis suggested here and other contemporary approaches to criminal court decision making, such as those advocated by Levin[26] and Gibson.[27] While primarily examining the effect of backgrounds, attitudes, and role perceptions on decision making, Levin and Gibson have discussed some of the same issues (environmental linkages) and used some of the same variables (case seriousness) that would arise from the application of the perspective advocated here. This, of course, leads one to ask whether the mode of analysis suggested here is necessary to uncover some of the insights discussed earlier. Also, as acknowledged earlier, the mode of analysis suggested here is not expected to lead to a complete understanding of criminal court decision making. This raises the question of whether theories such as those advocated by Levin and Gibson are consistent with the approach advocated here and whether they can be integrated with it to enhance our understanding of criminal courts.

With regard to the first point, it should be noted that the value of the organizational perspective outlined here asn an analytical mechanism is not compromised simply because other modes of analysis lead to similar focuses or stress the importance of similar factors. What is unique about this mode of analysis, whether compared to earlier approaches or contemporary ones such as Gibson's or Levin's, is that it explicitly acknowledges the role that mutual self-interests play within the dispositional process.[28] It also attempts to blend these internal considerations with other factors. Thus, what is unique about this organizational mode of analysis is not that it stresses environmental linkages but that it leads one to think about the impact that external factors may have in view of internal considerations, and in different settings. In addition, an organizational perspective on sentencing does not merely stress the importance of case seriousness as an explanatory variable. Rather, it leads one to consider the role of case seriousness as well as other factors after satisficing and nonsatisficing dispositions.

While approaches such as those of Gibson and Levin cannot supplant the perspective outlined here, they can be quite useful in supplementing it. One of the strengths of the mode of analysis proposed here is that it is not inconsistent with approaches that focus upon the role of backgrounds, attitudes, and role perceptions. Just as the attitudes, biases, and backgrounds of participants affect what goes on in corporate boardrooms, assembly lines, and sales offices, they are expected to affect criminal court operations. This having been said, however, it should be stressed that while differences among individuals are expected to be reflected in their behavior within organizations, *the impact of these factors is structured and mitigated by organizational mechanisms.* Expectations emanating from the requirements of performing a designated task in accordance with certain ends impose certain constraints upon the performance of that task, regardless of who is performing it. Coordinated efforts aimed at achieving common ends require that members of an organization be able to rely upon others to perform their designated tasks in accordance with commonly acknowledged or prescribed standards. If common expectations are not fulfilled routinely, coordinated efforts are not possible.

This is particularly noteworthy in the courtroom setting because it is through coordinated efforts that individual interests can most easily be pursued. Thus the court organization, like other organizations, utilizes such mechanisms as socialization techniques, control of information flows, division of labor, and inducements in an attempt to control individual deviations from expectations. To the extent that an organizational perspective on criminal court decision making leads one to recognize the various types of constraints upon criminal justice officials it can enhance our understanding of the role these other factors play. In addition, an integration of these factors into the organizational mode of analysis can lead to an enhanced understanding of how criminal courts operate. An example will illustrate.

Levin's Political Culture Approach

To illustrate how an organizational mode of analysis can be meshed with other approaches, the sentencing decision in Betaville will be reexamined in light of a somewhat modified view of Martin Levin's ideas on sentencing.[29] Levin's basic contention is that different political cultures result in different judicial recruitment procedures, which in turn result in the selection of judges with different types of backgrounds. Judges with different backgrounds use different criteria in sentencing decisions; thus political culture indirectly affects sentencing policies. To illustrate his ideas, Levin contrasts Minneapolis (a reformed city) with Pittsburgh (a traditional city). In Minneapolis, bar politics largely determines a judicial selection; in Pittsburgh, the selection process is dominated by the local Demo-

94 Approaches to the Study of Criminal Courts

cratic party. These differences result in the selection of very different types of judges. Minneapolis judges tend to come from a Protestant, middle-class background, and their pre-judicial careers tend to be concentrated in private, business-oriented law firms. Because of their backgrounds, Levin argues, Minneapolis judges tend to be primarily oriented toward the needs of society. Moreover, they employ legalistic, universalistic decision-making processes, eschewing personal and policy considerations. Pittsburgh judges, in contrast, tend to have ethnic, lower-class backgrounds, and the pre-judicial careers of most are largely in local government. Most have close, long-standing ties with the local Democratic party. Pittsburgh judges tend to be primarily defendant oriented. Their backgrounds and pre-judicial careers have made them sensitive to the types of problems and concerns that trouble defendants. Their decision making tends to be nonlegalistic and particularistic.

These differences in judicial orientation have several implications for sentencing decisions. Judges who are oriented toward society's needs would be expected to sentence more severely than those oriented toward the defendant's needs. This is seen in Figure 3-5, which displays case seriousness regression lines with different inter-

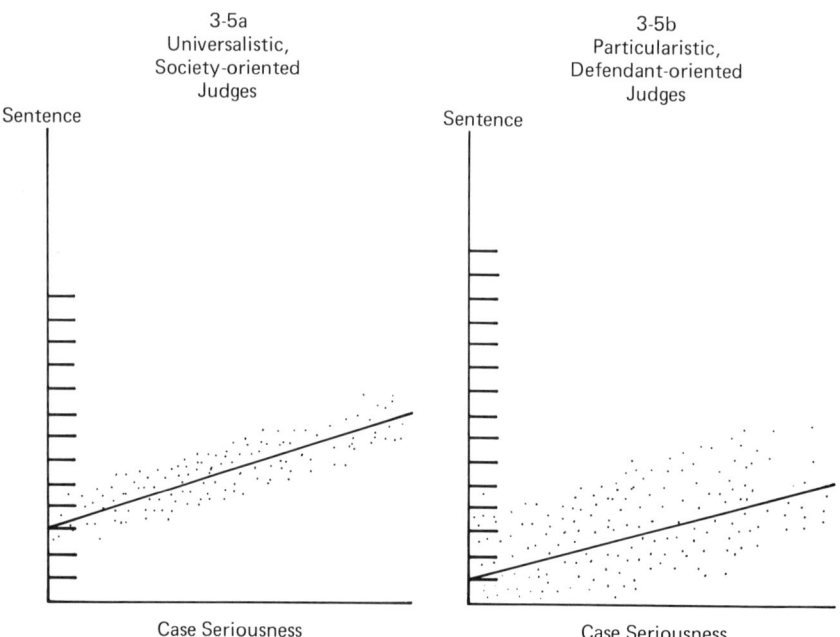

Figure 3-5. Sentencing Decision Disaggregated by Type of Judge

cepts. The figure also shows a second important difference in sentencing patterns: There is much more variation around the case seriousness regression line for particularistic judges than for universalistic judges, since the former define as relevant more extraneous factors than do the latter.

If Figure 3-5 is examined in light of Figure 3-2, a more refined approach to analyzing the impact of judicial orientations upon sentencing is evident. It was argued earlier that differences in the three prevalent types of conviction modes in Betaville led to the development and use of different sets of decision rules. If this were empirically the case (Chapter 8 provides some evidence that it is), it would make little sense to analyze the impact of judicial orientations without regard to conviction mode. Not only would the type of considerations discussed with regard to Figure 3-2 confound an understanding of the effects of judicial orientations, but their effect may differ across the various conviction modes. Hence, a more meaningful analysis of judicial orientations would require a disaggregation of sentencing by type of judge *and* mode of conviction. Figure 3-6 is a hypothetical illustration of what a series of disaggregated scattergrams of Betaville cases might reveal.

The two hypothetical plea bargaining scattergrams (Figures 3-6a and 3-6b) reveal slightly different intercepts and standard errors about the case seriousness regression line. The differences are not, however, as great as those in the two slow plea scattergrams (Figures 3-6c and 3-6d). While both sets of differences are in the predicted direction, the differences in their magnitudes are important to note. Magnitudes are greater between Figures 3-6c and 3-6d than between Figures 3-6a and 3-6b because there are fewer internal con-

Figure 3-6. Betaville Sentences Disaggregated by Judge and Conviction Mode

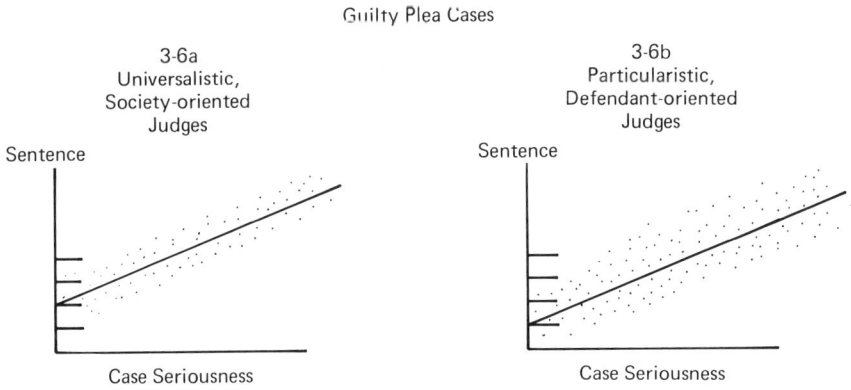

Figure 3-6. (continued)

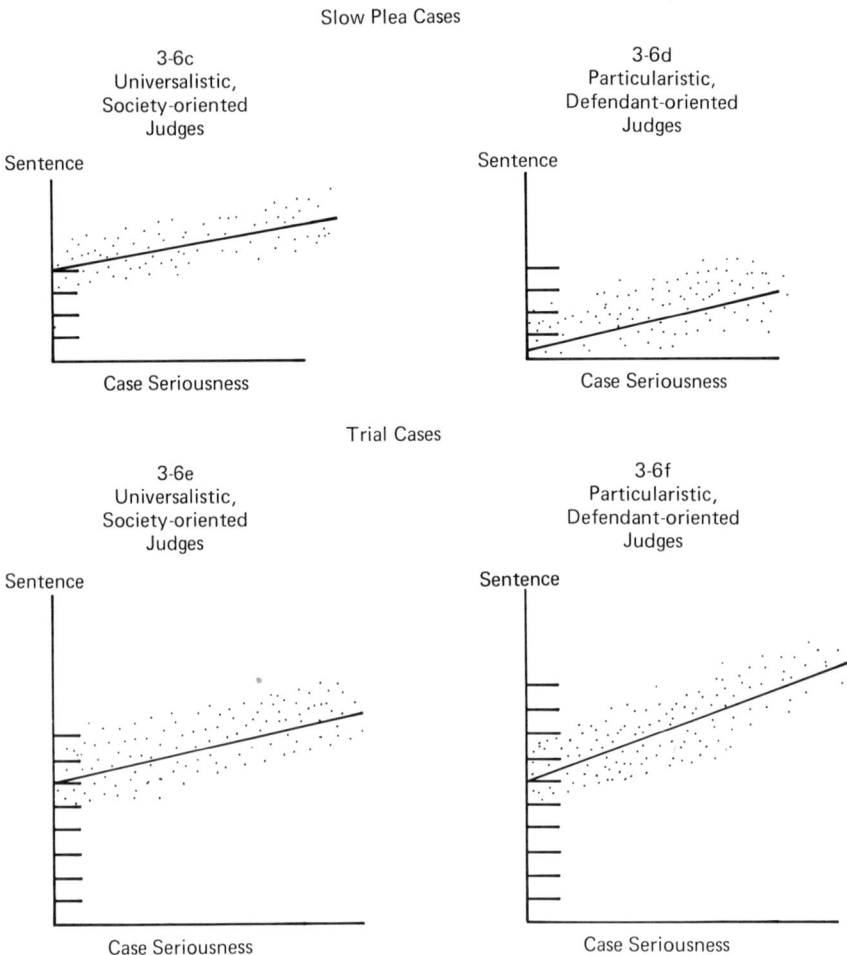

straints upon judges in slow plea cases than in guilty plea cases. The most significant internal constraint upon judges in slow plea cases is the expectation that sentences will generally be lower than those given after a full-length trial. While repeated violations of this expectation would undermine the ability of the system to process cases expeditiously and would bring to bear certain informal pressures upon the judge, few other constraints are present on his sentencing power in slow plea cases. He would be free to act upon many of the considerations he deemed relevant. This accounts for the large differences between intercepts and standard errors in Figures 3-6c and 3-6d.

The magnitude of these differences is smaller between Figures 3-6a and 3-6b because in guilty plea cases a judge's ability to act upon his own inclinations is not only constrained by the "going rate" for various types of offenses but also by the structure of the bargaining process. Often, but not always, the defense counsel and the prosecutor come to the judge with a "package" already in mind. The defense counsel, for example, may want two to four years, while the prosecutor may insist upon four to six years. These intervals reflect, among other things, the "going rate," the relative bargaining positions of the parties, and individual considerations that the defense counsel and prosecutor deem relevant. Moreover, they structure the bargaining process and mitigate the impact of the judge's predilections. Under these circumstances, the judge may impose a sentence of three to five years, but it would be very unusual for him to sentence between one and two or six to eight years.[30]

Given what has been said about the role of constraints, one might expect Figures 3-6e and 3-6f to look very different. After a full-length trial, the sentencing power of a judge is affected by only one internal constraint: In general, the sentence must be longer than it would have been after a slow plea or guilty plea. Given this, one might expect differences in intercepts and standard errors on a par with those observed in Figures 3-6c and 3-6d. Instead, there are no systematic differences at all. While this might be an extreme representation, what is seeks to emphasize is that Figures 3-6e and 3-6f represent sentencing after a nonsatisficing conviction mode. And, as magnanimous as Levin's defendant-oriented judges may be, their recognition of a defendant's needs may be contingent upon the defendant recognizing the needs of the judge and his associates. After all, Levin bases his characterization of defendant-oriented, particularistic judges on a model of old-time machine politicians. Although they distributed favors generously, special considerations were always contingent upon other factors (votes, ward heeling, kickbacks). Hence, the impact of differences in judges' orientations may not only be constrained by certain factors in the dispositional process, but it may also be contingent upon the defendant's deference to the informal rules which govern the process.

SUMMARY

This chapter has tried to outline and illustrate, in a systematic way, the essentials of one way of viewing the operations of criminal courts. It incorporates certain considerations that were lacking in earlier approaches. While it is not viewed as a comprehensive theory, it is believed that this mode of analysis will remedy many of the shortcomings noted in earlier research and will lend valuable insights into new approaches to criminal court reform. At this point, however, such propositions are little more than articles of faith. It is one thing to structure a diagram to illustrate a point, it is quite another to examine real data in light of certain a priori expectations. The remainder of this book is an attempt to extend and apply some of the fundamental ideas presented in this chapter to the felony court system in Chicago, as it existed in 1972-73. The following chapters outline one way of operationalizing this approach and shed some light upon its potential contribution to the study of criminal courts.

NOTES

1. These works include Abraham Blumberg, *Criminal Justice* (Chicago: Quadrangle, 1967); Jerome Skolnick, "Social Control in the Adversary Process," *Journal of Conflict Resolution* 11 (1967):52-70; Maureen Mileski, "Courtroom Encounters," *Law and Society Review* 5 (1971); Malcolm Feeley, "Two Models of the Criminal Justice System," *Law and Society Review* 7 (1972):407-26; George Cole, The Decision to Prosecute," *Law and Society Review* 4 (1970):313-43; James Eisenstein and Herbert Jacob, *Felony Justice: An Organizational Analysis of Criminal Courts* (Boston: Little, Brown, 1976); and Lawrence Mohr. "Organizations, Decisions, and Courts," *Law and Society Review* 10 (1976):621-42.

2. Recognition of the importance and existence of these common interests can be found in Blumberg, *Criminal Justice*, p. 61; Skolnick, "Social Control," p. 53; Feeley, "Two Models," pp. 416-17; Eisenstein and Jacob, *Felony Justice*, p. 9; and Mohr, "Organizations, Decisions, and Courts," p. 637.

3. Most of the organizational analyses of courts cited above are somewhat ambiguous as to the actual nature of these shared interests. The definition of these interests as the shared desire to process cases expeditiously seems, however, to be an accurate, generalized statement of their theses. For some support on this see Feeley's discussion ("Two Models," pp. 418-19), and Blumberg's emphasis on efficiency (*Criminal Justice*, p. 61 and elsewhere). It should also be noted that while the definition offered above might reflect some kind of consensus, no consensus exists on the consequences of the pursuit of these shared goals for the quality of criminal justice. Compare, for example, Blumberg's work with that of Skolnick. The empirical work reported in later chapters will shed some light on this debate.

4. Amitai Etzioni, *Organizations* (Englewood Cliffs, N.J.: Prentice Hall, 1964), p. 3.

5. Herbert Simon, "Comments on the Theory of Organizations," *American Political Science Review* 46 (1963):1130.

6. Phillip Selznick, "Foundations of the Theory of Organizations," *American Sociological Review* 8 (1948):25.

7. Peter Blau and W. Richard Scott, *Formal Organizations* (San Francisco: Chandler's, 1962), p. 5.

8. The phrase "organizational mode of analysis" is consistently used throughout this section because it is meaningless to talk about "organization theory." There is no such thing as organization *theory*. Rather, there is a plethora of *theories* relevant to organizations. Some are partial theories, others are more general, and many are not even relevant to courtroom operations (for reasons cited in Mohr, "Organizations, Decisions, and Courts"). Moreover, many of the relevant theories are expressed in such parochial and nongeneral terms that an extension to the study of courts would require considerable abstraction and modification. What I have attempted to do here is abstract three very fundamental and general considerations explicit or implicit in much of the theoretical literature on organizations and blend them into a mode of analysis that I consider to be helpful in studying the operations of criminal courts. Some of the most influential works considered in this endeavor were: James D. Thompson, *Organizations in Action* (New York: McGraw-Hill, 1967); Herbert Simon, *Administrative Behavior* (New York: The Free Press, 1957); Phillip Selznick, "Foundations of the Theory of Organizations," *American Sociological Review* 8 (1948):25; Peter Blau and W. Richard Scott, *Formal Organizations* (San Francisco: Chandler's, 1962); James D. Thompson and William J. McEwen, "Organizational Goals and Environment," *American Sociological Review* 23 (1958):23; Talcott Parsons, "Suggestions for a Sociological Approach to the Study of Organizations," Parts I and II, *Administrative Science Quarterly* 1 (1956):63-85 and 225-39; and James March and Herbert Simon, *Organizations* (New York: Wiley, 1958). Some may quibble with the types of considerations employed, others may wish to refine the mode of analysis, and still others may insist on a wholly different emphasis. These inevitabilities notwithstanding, I believe the mode of analysis to be proposed will provide a sound base for the development of an organizational perspective on the operations of criminal courts that will remedy many of the shortcomings noted in Chapters 1 and 2.

9. See Eisenstein and Jacob, *Felony Justice*, p. 9; Skolnick, "Social Control," p. 28; and Mohr, "Organizations, Decisions, and Courts," p. 63.

10. The classic statement of the role which the magnitude of work loads plays in this regard can be found in Blumberg, *Criminal Justice*, p. xi. He states:

> Intolerably large caseloads, which must be handled with limited resources and personnel, potentially subject the participants in the court community to harsh scrutiny from appellate courts and other public and private sources of condemnation. Thus there is an almost irreconcilable conflict: intense pressures to process large numbers of cases, on the one hand, and the stringent ideological and legal requirements of "due process of law," on the other. The dilemma is frequently resolved through bureaucratically ordained short cuts, deviations, and outright rule violations by members of the court, from judges to stenographers, in order to meet production norms.

While this position has been adhered to by many criminal justice scholars it has recently come under attack in several works. See Milton Heumann, A Note on

Plea Bargaining and Case Pressure," *Law and Society Review* 9 (1975):515-28; Malcolm Feeley, "The Effects of Heavy Caseloads," paper presented at the 1975 Annual Meeting of the American Political Science Association, September 2-5, 1975; and Peter F. Nardulli with Kathleen Proch, "The Caseload Controversy and the Study of Criminal Courts" (unpublished mimeograph). Data presented in Chapter 1, which show high dismissal and guilty plea rates as far back as 1920 in both urban and rural courts, also cast doubt upon the heavy case load thesis. What is important to note for the present analysis, however, is that this case load thesis is not a necessary tenet of the organizational approach advocated here. Indeed, the arguments about to be made provide a much broader base for an organizational mode of analysis, one that will allow its extension to all types of criminal courts.

11. Feeley, "Effects of Heavy Caseloads," p. 35.

12. Herbert L. Packer, "Two Models of the Criminal Process," *Pennsylvania Law Review* 113 (1964):12.

13. Blumberg, *Criminal Justice*, p. 6.

14. Packer, "Two Models," p. 12.

15. Edward L. Barrett, "The Adversary Proceeding and the Judicial Process—1984," Lectures to the National College of the State Trial Judges (1967), p. 29, as quoted in Lynn M. Mather, "Some Determinants of the Method of Case Disposition: Decision-Making by Public Defenders in Los Angeles," *Law and Society Review* 8 (1973):187-88.

16. A classic quotation on this point can be found in Wesley G. Skogan, "The Politics of Judicial Reform: Cook County, Illinois," *Justice System Journal* 1 (September 1975):11-23. One judge who was queried concerning the reasons he sought a judgeship responded: "I ran at the urging of my wife. I took a real interest in a judgeship because she wanted me to take a position of semi-retirement. And that's basically what a judge's position is—one of semi-retirement."

17. This is especially true with regard to the prosecutor and judge, but somewhat less true for the public defender, who occasionally may be able to complete his cases before his cohorts do. As a general rule, however, many courts first dispose of private attorney cases.

18. James Thompson, *Organizations in Action* (New York: McGraw-Hill), p. 126 (emphasis added).

19. Although only one aspect of these complex structures is stressed, the mode of analysis to be developed here is not inconsistent with the existence of other factors such as role perceptions, attitudes, and backgrounds. Indeed, theories stipulating the effect of such extraneous factors and the organizational mode of analysis can be mutually supportive. More will be said of this shortly.

20. Thompson, *Organizations in Action*, p. 147.

21. See Thompson, *Organizations in Action*, pp. 161-62.

22. Thompson would probably consider the car production process as an example of a long-linked technology and the dispositional process as an example of an intensive technology. See Thompson, *Organizations in Action*, Chapter II, for a treatment of these different processes.

23. It should be stressed that this does not imply that these individuals *never* modify the techniques they use in performing their tasks. On the contrary,

Implicit in this whole approach is that these techniques are flexible. However, they are not in constant flux. Once necessary adaptations are made the procedures (techniques, criteria) can be considered relatively constant and the basis for their derivation is not reexamined with every application.

24. One way to conceptualize sentencing decision rules would be to view them in multiple regression terms. The criteria embodied in the decision rules would correspond to variables in the equation, with the B coefficient corresponding to the weights applied to each criteria. For some purposes differences in the intercept (A coefficient) will also be important.

25. Mohr, "Organizations, Decisions, and Courts," p. 627.

26. Martin Levin, *Urban Politics and the Criminal Courts* (Chicago: University of Chicago Press, 1977).

27. James L. Gibson, "Judges as Representatives: Constituency Influence on Trial Courts," paper presented at the 1976 Annual Meeting of the American Political Science Association, Chicago, Illinois, September 2-5, 1976; and "Judges' Role Orientations, Attitudes, and Decisions: An Interactive Model," *American Political Science Review* (forthcoming, September 1978).

28. It should be noted that while Levin, early in his book, acknowledges the significance of these mutual interests, he fails to integrate them into his quantitative analyses—even though they have direct implications for what he does. See below in this chapter for discussion on this point.

29. This elaboration of Levin's ideas differs from his own in two ways. First, it is developed in multiple regression terminology. This is to make it consistent with earlier examples and to allow for a more sophisticated treatment of some of the ideas emobidied in his approach. Second, while Levin's analysis deals mainly with differences in sentencing levels for given offenses in two different cities, this example focuses upon differences in sentencing by type of judge within a given jurisdiction. This will simplify the analysis of the impact of differences in judges somewhat by controlling for the types of environmental differences noted above, something that Levin does not do.

30. It should be emphasized that this view does not ignore the fact that the defense counsel's and prosecutor's recommendations may reflect, in part, what they *anticipate* the judge's feelings to be. The only argument here is that while the judge's views may be reflected in these recommendations, and thus in the sentence, the impact of these views is more constrained than in a slow plea case.

✻ *Part II*

Preliminaries to the Empirical Analysis

The remaining chapters in this work are based upon a study of the felony court system in Chicago conducted in the 1972-73 academic year. During this time period extensive field work was done in these courts. The access enjoyed during this observational phase was quite good. Proceedings in the preliminary hearing courts were often observed by sitting on the bench next to the judge; trial proceedings were viewed from the jury box or a special chair located near the bench. Plea bargaining sessions and coffee klatches in judges' chambers were attended, and many informal discussions were held with various participants. Some questionnaire and interview data were also collected. In addition, observational and file data were collected on several samples of cases processed during this period.

These data were used to conduct the empirical analyses reported in Part III (Chapters 6, 7, and 8). These analyses are structured in light of the ideas developed in Chapter 3. Because this is a study of one court system during a relatively brief period of time, however, the focus of the empirical analyses is somewhat different from that outlined in Chapter 3 (i.e., environmental considerations and the setting are relatively fixed). Chapter 4 addresses this issue and the problems it raises; it also suggests some factors that are important to consider in attempting to understand micro-level courtroom phenomena from an organizational perspective. Chapter 5 describes in greater detail the types of data available for the empirical analysis as well as the sampling techniques employed. It also discusses the approaches used to operationalize some of the basic concepts introduced in Chapter 4.

 *Chapter 4*

The Organizational Perspective: An Extension

As discussed in Chapter 3, a basic tenet of the organizational perspective advocated here is that the interests of the governing coalition in the court organization (the courtroom elite) are relatively constant across systems. Within this mode of analysis, what accounts for most of the variations in criminal court operations and outputs are differences in the environment and setting within which the courts operate. However, because this study is limited to one court system at one point in time, the focus in the empirical aspects of this work cannot be on the impact of such factors. Rather, it must be on the implications of the interests of the courtroom elite for processing criminal cases within a particular system at one point in time (i.e., within a given environment and setting, what does it mean for the structure of operations and decisions that it is in the interests of the dominant coalition within the court organization to process cases expeditiously?). Thus, the concern of this chapter will be with developing the implications of the theoretical perspective outlined in Chapter 3 for a study of the felony court system in Chicago as it existed in 1972-73. First, the setting of these courts will be analyzed, then various environmental considerations will be discussed.

THE SETTING OF THE FELONY COURTS OF CHICAGO, 1972-73

The setting of a court system is important to analyze, even in a case study: To understand why a given organization mobilizes its resources in a given way to pursue given ends, it is essential to know something about the structure and nature of its inputs, its physical plant, the characteristics and capabilities of the available work force, the state of technological development, and other relevant aspects of its immediate setting. In order to understand how the interests of the courtroom elite are manifested in the structure of the felony disposition process in Chicago, one must be familiar with the formal structure of the courts, the nature of the inputs these courts process, some of the characteristics of the personnel that man them, and the types of procedures available to these individuals to process inputs.[1]

Formal Structure[2]

The felony court system in Chicago is composed of several levels of organization, as depicted in Figure 4-1.[3] Most of the work, however, is done in two sets of work groups—preliminary hearing court work groups and trial court work groups—and these entities constitute the primary focus of the empirical aspects of this work.

After arrest, many felony suspects in Chicago have their first encounter with the felony court system in bond court before an associate judge. Normally, the suspect appears in this court after the police complete initial processing. In bond court, the defendant is apprised of his rights, bond is set, and he is given a date for his first appearance in a preliminary hearing court. If he does not post bond immediately, usually he has his first appearance in the preliminary hearing court the following morning; those who do post bail are assigned dates several weeks later.[4] If a defendant is not processed before bond court recesses (usually 2:00 A.M.), bail is set in the preliminary hearing court that morning.[5]

As Figure 4-1 reveals, in Chicago during 1972-73 there were five preliminary hearing courts (two general courts, two drug courts, and one murder court) that handled adult felony cases. The formal role of these courts—as their title implies—is to conduct preliminary hearings aimed at determining whether there is probable cause to believe a given crime was committed and a given defendant was involved in its commission. Many other important functions, however, were performed by these courts. Bonds were set, bond rehearings conducted, and public defenders appointed; hearings on motions were conducted; cases were dismissed; and guilty pleas were accepted. Although it generally took about four months to dispose of a case in these courts (four to five appearances), some cases were disposed of within ten days; others took over a year. To perform these various activities, a set of public officials was semi-permanently assigned to each of the five courtrooms; assignments ranged from several months to over a year. One associate judge, two assistant

Figure 4-1. Formal Structure of the Felony Disposition Process in Chicago, 1972-73

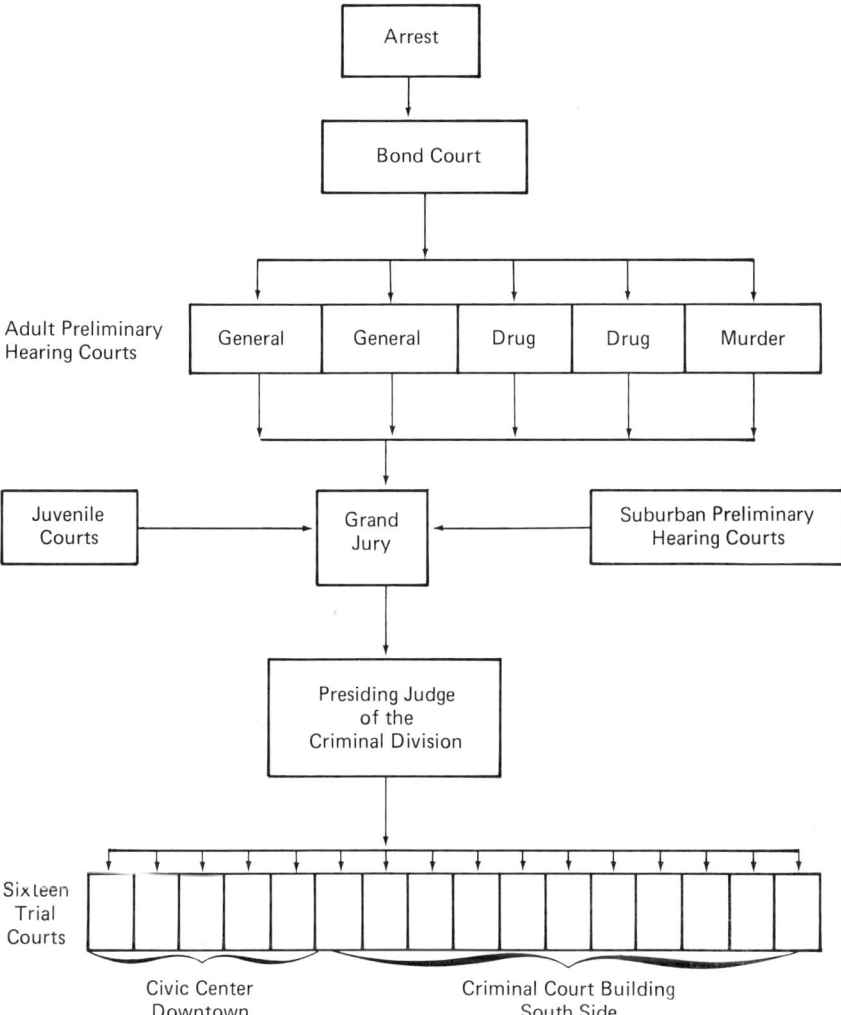

state's attorneys, and two public defenders manned each courtroom. Many of the private attorneys who represented defendants in these courts were only infrequent participants in criminal proceedings. Others were full-time criminal practitioners who spent most of their time in trial courts. Still others attached themselves informally to the various preliminary hearing courtrooms. Among the latter, some practiced primarily in either the drug or general courts, while others worked in all five.

The fairly specialized nature of the preliminary hearing courts is important to note for reasons other than that the system led to a somewhat specialized private defense bar. This specialization resulted in markedly different climates in the different courts. Murder court, for example, handled only very serious cases, and its docket was very light (two to three cases per session). Proceedings were very somber, formal, and deliberate. Only the most respected assistant state's attorneys, public defenders, and private attorneys appeared in this court. The two drug courts, on the other hand, resembled circuses more than courts. They handled extremely high caseloads—usually close to one hundred cases per day, and not infrequently more than that. Most of their cases, however, were not considered serious. Almost half of them were simple possession of marijuana cases. In the drug courts, there were no victims, very few civilian witnesses, and usually the only issue in question was the legality of the search used to obtain the evidence. Defendants in the drug courts also appeared to be socially more heterogeneous and younger than those in the other courts.

The two general felony courts fell somewhere in between these two extremes. Their clientele appeared to be largely lower class black males. While the cases they handled were generally less serious than those in murder court and more serious than those in drug court, there was also a tremendous range of variation in seriousness. Dockets included armed robberies, rapes, and aggravated batteries, as well as thefts and posssession of firearms cases. Moreover, while their dockets were not as strained as the drug courts (a normal range was from forty-five to seventy cases per day), personnel usually had victims as well as a large number of civilian witnesses with which to deal. This caused considerable management problems because many cases involved intense personal disputes among irate participants. Others were less personal but involved considerable sums of money.

If a finding of probable cause is entered in any case handled by one of these courts—or a suburban or juvenile court—it goes to a grand jury. The only exception to this is if a guilty plea is entered in one of the lower courts. The function of the grand jury is to determine whether an indictment should be returned in cases that come before it. An indictment, much like the complaint at the preliminary hearing, lists the crimes with which the defendant is charged. The returning of an indictment is almost a perfunctory proceeding. The state is the only party that presents evidence to the grand jury, which usually accepts the recommendation of the state. True bills are returned in over 99 percent of the cases that come before the grand jury.

After an indictment is returned, the case comes before the presiding judge of the criminal division, usually about two months after a finding of probable cause in the preliminary hearing court. The presiding judge reads the charges in the indictment to the accused and assigns the case to a trial court judge. If the defendant is on bond, he is often assigned to one of five courtrooms at the Civic Center in downtown Chicago. If he is confined, he is assigned to one of the eleven judges in the Criminal Court Building adjacent to the jail. The actual assignment to a specific courtroom was neither totally random nor totally biased. Normally, the presiding judge would assign all cases on a given afternoon or morning to a particular judge. Particularly sensitive, highly publicized, or extremely serious cases, however, would receive special assignments to judges in whom the chief judge had confidence. Although most unrepresented defendants would receive random assignments, a knowledgeable private defense counsel could usually request and receive an assignment to a particular judge. One last point should be noted about this assignment. As in the preliminary hearing courts, once a case was assigned to a given trial court judge the chances were great that he would ultimately dispose of it. No efforts were made to reassign cases that were ripe for trial from busy courtrooms to idle ones.[6]

The formal role of trial courts is to determine the guilt or innocence of indicted defendants and sentence convicted defendants. In addition, trial court judges perform many attendant tasks such as conducting bail rehearings, ruling on legal motions, and appointing public defenders. While in 1972 it generally took about six months from the day a defendant was arraigned by the presiding judge for the trial court to dispose of a case, some cases were disposed of in a month. Others took well over a year.

As in the preliminary hearing courts, public officials in the trial courts were semi-permanently assigned to each courtroom. One judge, two assistant state's attorneys, and one public defender were assigned to a courtroom for periods often extending well over a year. Assignments were longer in trial courts because, at least in the case of public defenders and assistant state's attorneys, there were no higher line positions to which they could go. Many of the private defense attorneys practicing in the trial courts were regular full-time criminal practitioners, but there were also many nonregulars. Moreover, while many of the regulars could get preferential courtroom assignments, they did not focus their practice in given courtrooms to the extent that many regulars in the preliminary hearing courts did.

Nature of Inputs

Several important points should be made about the inputs processed by the Chicago felony court system. As always, the important dimensions of these inputs vary with the type of questions asked. From one perspective, the fact that the inputs processed by criminal courts involve people is important to note. Defendants are reactive agents who can anticipate and respond to organizational attempts to process them. Inanimate objects, unlike people, are nonreactive agents that are much more susceptible to manipulation by an organization if the appropriate technology is applied. This is not to suggest, of course, that organizations processing inanimate objects do not encounter problems in manipulating them to produce an output. They do. What is important to note is that they encounter different problems from organizations processing reactive agents.

From a quite different perspective, another important facet of the inputs processed by the court under examination is that they all allegedly involve felony offenses. For the individuals involved, the stakes are much higher in felony cases than they are in traffic or misdemeanor cases. Also, the felony courts handle the kinds of cases of most concern to the community. Even though the nature of felony court outputs are as abstract as those of other entities administering "justice," the greater saliency of the cases these courts handle sets them apart. Individuals and groups concerned with "law and order" as well as civil liberties are apt to be more sensitive to the operations of felony courts than misdemeanor or traffic courts.

In one sense, neither of the two aspects of the court's inputs just discussed is relevant for the purposes of this study. If the operations of the court organization were being compared with those of a manufacturing concern, then the distinction between reactive and nonreactive inputs would be of considerable significance. If the operations of Chicago felony courts were being contrasted with the operations of the city traffic court, then the distinction between the felony and quasi-criminal nature of the cases would be important. However, even though this is not a comparative study, the characteristics mentioned above are important because they lead us to focus upon certain facets of the court's inputs that are important for the microlevel analyses to be performed. That is, while all inputs involve defendants who, by definition, are reactive agents, defendants differ in their capabilities and inclination to react. They vary in their *susceptibility* to organizational pressures. Moreover, while all inputs are felony cases, they differ in terms of their saliency to the community. They vary in terms of their *dispositional value*. An extended discussion of these terms will clarify their meaning as well as their role within this analysis.

Dispositional Value. Dispositional value is a concept that relates to the importance of acquiring a conviction in any given case; it is primarily important because of external considerations. For the purposes of organizational maintenance, it is more important that certain types of cases result in a conviction than others. The court organization seeks to satisfy the societal expectations outlined in Chapter 3 with a minimal expenditure of resources. In order to allocate its resources rationally to satisfy even the most minimal societal expectations, the organization must be able to rank cases in terms of their relative importance.

A concrete example will clarify this proposition. The societal role of the court organization is to protect the community from criminal transgressors by determining the guilt or innocence of defendants arrested by the police and charged with felony offenses. The court's role is also to sentence those defendants found guilty. While the organization is not expected to let guilty defendants go free, the community would feel much more threatened if armed robbery charges were dismissed in a case involving a convicted murderer-rapist than if theft charges against a housewife were dismissed. This may be true even if the evidence against the murderer-rapist was marginal while the evidence against the housewife was conclusive. Thus the former case can be said to have a higher dispositional value than the latter; in the former, it would be more important for the court organization to obtain a conviction.

There are two dimensions to the concept of dispositional value. The first involves case seriousness. The greater the seriousness of a case, the greater its dispositional value. Various factors affect case seriousness, for example, the offense(s) involved, the circumstances surrounding the offense, and the characteristics of the victim. For instance, an armed robbery by a drunk male against a female may be considered more serious than an armed robbery by a male against another male. Both, however, may be more serious than a murder case in which a wife kills her husband in the heat of a marital dispute.

The second dimension of dispositional value is evidentiary: the greater the weight of the evidence in a case, the greater its dispositional value. The reason that the weight of the evidence is a component of dispositional value is quite simple. The court organization is expected to attain some minimal conviction rate. It is usually easier to obtain convictions in cases where there is a good deal of evidence than where there is little evidence. And, given a limited amount of resources, the importance of obtaining a conviction increases with the ease of obtaining one. Another reason the weight of the evidence is an important component of dispositional value is that, if the evidence in a case is not adequate, the dispositional value of the case cannot be high. A defendant may be charged with a highly publicized, brutal crime, but if substantial evidence is not available to link him to the crime, the court system would not be under a great deal of pressure to obtain a conviction. A dismissal or an acquittal would be defensible because the organization would have legitimate reasons to support its actions.

The evidentiary dimension of dispositonal value has two components, one relating to the *strength* of the available evidence and the other to the *admissibility* of this evidence. With regard to the strength of the evidence, it is important to consider both the availability of evidence and the value of the available evidence. If all things are considered equal, when there is a good deal of evidence available to prove all of the elements of an offense, it is considered to be a stronger case than when only some evidence is available to prove only some of the elements of the offense. Unfortunately, all things are usually not equal. In this instance, the value of the available evidence often varies from case to case. For example, an intelligent, reliable, respectable witness is considered to be a better witness than one who is slow, unreliable, and a social aberration. Also, a gun recovered from the defendant at the scene of the crime is a better piece of physical evidence than one recovered in a vacant lot two days after the incident. Hence, the value as well as the availability of evidence must be considered in evaluating the strength of the evidence of a case.

The weight of the evidence in a case cannot be considered great if the evidence that is available is potentially inadmissible. If evidence was collected as a result of an arguably illegal search or arrest, it may well be held inadmissible at some point in the criminal process. That holding could come at the appellate level as well as the preliminary hearing or trial level. Hence, if all other things are considered equal, the weight of the evidence in a case is considered greater when the available evidence is not susceptible to a meritorious charge that it was illegally collected.

Defendant's Susceptibility. Another important facet of the court's inputs, for the purposes of this analysis, is the defendant's organizational susceptibility. This concept concerns the extent to which a defendant is amenable to organizational pressures and sanctions administered by various members of the courtroom elite. It is an important concept primarily because of internal considerations. With the dispositional value of a case held constant, differences in susceptibility have important implications for processing cases at various stages of the dispositional process. Cases must be handled expeditiously in order to meet internal and external considerations simultaneously—and this often requires the cooperation of the defendant. Because cooperation is more apt to be forthcoming in some cases than others, due to differences in defendants' susceptibility, this consideration is central to many important decisions.

More will be said of the implications of this concept with regard to specific decisions when the empirical analyses are presented in Chapters 6, 7, and 8. What is important to note here is that organizational susceptibility is really a multidimensional concept, three of the most important elements of which are situational, psychological, and economic. Situational susceptibility relates directly to the nature of the defendant's predicament in the court system. One indicator of situational susceptibility is the seriousness of his criminal record. A defendant with a long criminal record must take the prosecutor's threats of a long sentence after a trial much more seriously than a defendant with no criminal record. The latter can rely upon the leniency of a parole board, but the former cannot. The only way a defendant with a long criminal record can be *assured* of a "reasonable" sentence is to play by the rules of the game. His need for the cooperation of the judge and the prosecutor makes him more susceptible to organizational pressures.

Psychological susceptibility relates to differences in the psychological makeup of defendants. The dispositional process is fraught with ambiguities and uncertainties, and some individuals are better equipped psychologically than others to deal with these matters. Defendants with a lower tolerance for ambiguities, and who are less willing to gamble, are more amenable than other defendants to threats and pressures.

The economic aspect of susceptibility relates to the defendant's financial status. A defendant who can afford an adequate defense is in a better position to meaningfully and forcefully assert his rights and formal prerogatives than is one who must deal with monetary pressures in addition to those emanating from the courtroom elite.

Personnel

In Chapter 3 it was noted that the formal arrangement of personnel has important consequences for criminal court operations. Earlier in this chapter, it was also noted that Chicago has a public defender system to represent indigents, that public officials are semi-permanently assigned to each courtroom work group, and that a well-established private criminal bar exists. These are important facets of the court's setting to consider if one is viewing criminal court operations from a comparative perspective: Structural aspects of personnel assignment have direct implications for the predominant types of dispositional modes used to process cases. Although these structural aspects are important to note in a case study because they help to put its findings in perspective, they are also constants whose impact cannot be examined. What becomes important in a case study such as this are variations in certain personal attributes of the individuals who man the sytem.

As acknowledged in Chapter 3, various aspects of a judge's, defense attorney's, or assistant state's attorney's background or psyche may affect his behavior within the courtroom setting. However, only such factors essential to an elaboration of the organizational perspective outlined here are set forth in this work.[7] One individual-level attribute that is essential to elaborating upon the perspective espoused here is the notion of organizational responsiveness.

Organizational responsiveness is a concept relating to a judge's, defense counsel's, or prosecutor's commitment to the welfare of the court organization. Stated differently, it concerns their inclination to accept and adhere to informal operating procedures necessary to process cases in an organizationally satisficing manner. For various reasons (such as background factors, future aspirations, present status, and psychological predispositions), not all courtroom participants are equally concerned with the maintenance of the prevailing set of interrelationships. The notion of responsiveness has significant implications for the processing of criminal cases. Moreover, the implications of responsiveness vary by participant and at different stages in the process. Elaboration of these implications will be discussed in the empirical analyses; the purpose of this section is a further elucidation of the concept.

Like the other concepts introduced in this chapter, organizational responsiveness is a complex, multidimensional notion. No definitive statement encompassing all of its complexities can be provided at this early, developmental stage. Rather, the most that can be hoped for is a delineation of some of the most obvious dimensions. With this in mind, it can be said that there appear to be at least two general dimensions to the notion of responsiveness. The first relates to the participants' orientation to their role within the dispositional process; the second could be labeled an independence dimension.

The orientation dimension can perhaps be best conceptualized in terms of a pragmatism-formalism continuum. Individuals—regardless of their status as judge, defense attorney, or prosecutor—approach their various tasks in different ways, and this affects their responsiveness significantly. Some define and approach their tasks in highly pragmatic ways. They are most concerned with what can be done in a given situation and tend to be more responsive. Others approach their task more formalistically and are not as concerned with what can be done as how it should be done. They tend to be less responsive. As an aside, it might be noted that probably the most variation in this dimension of responsiveness occurs among new, unsocialized recruits and private defense attorneys. The rather routine nature of most criminal cases and the social structure in criminal courts, described in Chapter 3, probably influence most regular criminal justice practitioners toward the pragmatic end of the scale.

The independence dimension of responsiveness must be discussed separately for each individual because, while factors affecting an individual's independence concern the nature of his ties to the system, they vary by role.[8] Judges, for example, are usually (but not always) at the apex of their careers; most have attained a judgeship only after years of public and private service in the community. Moreover, because of the nature of their prior service or record some judges can afford to be more independent than others. This greater independence may lead them to be less responsive to the internal needs and demands of others in the system. Such considerations are important in a city like Chicago, where judgeships are often given as a reward for long and loyal party service. Judges who have paid their dues can afford to be more independent than others because they have a claim to a judgeship independent of their performance on the bench. They need not worry about being reslated. Also, powerful allies in the party will ensure that they will not be sanctioned for their recalcitrance by such devices as undesirable or inconvenient assignments.[9]

Unlike judges, most assistant state's attorneys and public defenders are in the formative stages of their legal careers. Often their positions in their respective offices are their first legal jobs. Hence, the factors most important to gauging their independence from the system are those related to their career aspirations, not their past endeavors. Some assistants aspire to a private, largely civil legal career. They desire only a brief stint in the state's attorney's office, which is merely a stepping-stone for the advancement of their personal careers at the state's expense. They want courtroom experience with a steady, if not enriching, salary. These attorneys tend to be somewhat more oriented to their own needs rather than those of the organization, and hence tend to be more independent and less responsive.

Other assistants aspire to a legal career in the public sector and are more concerned with "getting by" than with "getting experience." They envisage a career leading to an administrative post in their present office or some other legal post in local government. Some may even aspire to a judgeship. These assistants tend to be more oriented toward learning and working within the system. So also are assistants who desire a private, largely criminal practice. They recognize that the benefits from a cooperative posture during their apprenticeship in the system can be invaluable to them as budding private practitioners. Both sets of practitioners sacrifice an element of independence in exchange for possible future benefits.

With regard to private defense counsel, the most important factors affecting their independence within the system concern the extent to which their economic interests are dependent upon the cooperation of other members of the court organization. In turn, this dependency is primarily related to the extent of a lawyer's participation in the criminal court system and his legal ability. The more a private attorney participates in the criminal court system, the greater his dependence is expected to be. The economic interests of a defense counsel who only occasionally practices in the criminal courts are not significantly affected by the nature of his relationship to other participants. He does not normally care to become familiar with all of the informalities and will rely upon them only when he deems it advantageous to do so. The economic interests of full-time criminal practitioners, on the other hand, are affected significantly by the nature of their relationship with other participants. To maintain a lucrative practice, they must be able to turn over large numbers of cases expeditiously; to accomplish this, they need the cooperation of others.

Legal ability is important with regard to defense counsel responsiveness because it can gain private attorneys—especially full-time criminal practitioners—a measure of independence not enjoyed by others. Skilled attorneys know how to try cases in a combative, adversary manner, posing a threat to the other participants. Moreover, private attorneys who have developed a solid reputation as trial attorneys are not dependent upon the court organization for referrals and can attract wealthier clients. Thus, skilled private attorneys can afford to be less responsive than unskilled ones.[10]

Tools

Each year the preliminary hearing courts in Chicago receive approximately 20,000 new complaints, and the trial courts, between 2,000 and 2,000 new indictments. Each work group must do *something* with each case it receives, but there are a number of different things it can do, and often there are a number of different ways it can do each. Preliminary hearing work groups, for example, can make final disposition of a case or send it to the grand jury for final disposition in a trial court. If the case is finally disposed of at the preliminary hearing level, it can be dismissed,[11] resolved through a guilty plea to a felony or a misdemeanor, or tried on misdemeanor charges. Once a case reaches a trial court, it can be disposed of by a dismissal, a guilty plea, a bench trial, or a jury trial.

Two important points should be noted about these various dispositional tools. First, they vary significantly in terms of the resources required to attain them. Dismissals at the preliminary hearing level are the most expeditious type of disposition available (i.e., they consume the least amount of resources). Dismissals and guilty pleas are the most expeditious modes of disposition at the trial level, while jury trials and some bench trials consume considerable amounts of resources.

A second point to note is that there are very few formalized internal constraints either upon the use of these various dispositional modes or upon the ability of the participants to use other, supplementary devices to attain them. At the preliminary hearing level during the time of this study, there was an office policy to the effect that prosecutors had to get the consent of the victim, if one existed, to any plea offer. At the trial level, there was a fairly well-enforced policy against reducing armed robberies to simple robberies to obtain a guilty plea. At the same time, however, there was no requirement that *trial* prosecutors check with victims in plea bargaining cases. Nor was there a requirement that prosecutors state in writing their reasons for dismissing a case or reducing charges. In addition, judges were not bound by policies of the prosecutor's office. They had the power to dismiss cases as well as to accept plea bargains which the prosecutor rejected.

The judge's ability to encourage such dispositional modes as the guilty plea was constrained somewhat by the penal code. Offenses like murder and armed robbery have statutorily imposed minimum sentences. This does not, however, prevent the judge from accepting a plea to a reduced charge. Moreover, the penal code stipulates that a judge always has the option of granting probation. One last constraint, which both judges and prosecutors labored under, was a temporal constraint. At the time of this study, the prosecutor's office had to begin a defendant's trial, or otherwise finally dispose of the case, within a specified time—120 days for confined defendants, 160 days for released defendants. The only exception to this "term requirement" was when the defendant requested a continuance. When he did, the term period began anew.

In light of what has been said about the interests of the courtroom elite and the lack of formal constraints in the Chicago felony court

Table 4-1. Cases by Mode of Disposition in Chicago Felony Court System, 1972-73

	Preliminary Hearing Courts		Trial Courts	
Dismissals	(669)	60.8%	(111)	16.5%
Finding of no probable cause	(84)	7.5%	—	—
Guilty plea to misdemeanor	(68)	6.0%	—	—
Guilty plea to felony	(55)	5.0%	(378)	56.1%
Bench trial	(97)	8.7%*	(129)	19.1%
Jury trial	—	—	(56)	8.3%
Sent to the grand jury	(132)	12.0%	—	—

*All of these cases were misdemeanor trials.

system, it should come as no surprise that the vast proportion of all cases handled by these felony courts were disposed of using the more expeditious modes of disposition. Table 4-1 summarizes cases by mode of disposition during the period of this study.[12]

As the figures in Table 4-1 make clear, the vast proportion of cases handled in the preliminary courts during 1972-73 were dismissed. Of those not dismissed, almost as many resulted in lower court convictions as were sent to trial courts, where a greater expenditure of resources would be needed to pursue a conviction. Even when only the trial court figures are examined, the preponderance of expeditious dispositions is clear. While the guilty plea was the primary mode of disposition, guilty pleas and dismissals account for over 70 percent of all dispositions. Jury trials accounted for only 8.3 percent of trial court dispositions and only about 1 percent of all dispositions.

While most 1972-73 dispositions resulted from expeditious dispositional modes there was also a considerable amount of variance in type of disposition. The questions to be addressed in the empirical section of this book are: What accounts for these differences? and What are the consequences for those who resist informal, expeditious processing? It is believed that some light can be shed on these questions by viewing the operations of the Chicago felony court system in light of the general perspective outlined here. Cases are not and cannot be dismissed indiscriminately at the preliminary hearing court level. Guilty pleas do not just "happen" at the trial court level. The interactions of people making these decisions are influenced by the types of internal and external considerations discussed earlier. These considerations have direct implications for how cases, which vary in terms of dispositional value and involve defendants who vary with regard to organizational susceptibility, are processed by participants who vary in their responsiveness to the court organization.

The empirical chapters in this work report how these various considerations are integrated into an overall dispositional strategy. But, before these empirical analyses can be properly interpreted, a few comments are necessary with regard to the environment within which the court organization in Chicago operated in 1972-73.

ENVIRONMENTAL CONSIDERATIONS

At the time of this study the court system in Chicago, like most other public agencies in that city, enjoyed a highly insulated position vis-à-vis its environment.[13] The Daley machine dominated most facets of local political life. Slating by the Democratic party was tantamount to election to most local posts, including judgeships. Indeed, because after their initial election Illinois judges merely have to receive a 60 percent affirmative vote in noncompetitive referenda, initial election was almost equivalent to life tenure on the bench. Wesley Skogan, in a study of judicial recruitment in Cook County, concluded that "the impact of this political environment upon the distribution of judicial posts is apparent. They go to political veterans with long records of public service who grew up in service of the organization and who serve as the ethnic representatives of their constituents on the bench. Judgeships in Cook County are terminal positions to which warriors retire."[14]

While Skogan may overstate the case a bit—not every judge has had extensive party service, and some do go on to other posts—his observations do underscore the fact that in Chicago political realities dictate that judges be more sensitive to the needs and concerns of the local party than to the public. These realities extend beyond circuit court judges. Associate judges—those manning the lower courts—are selected by the circuit court judges; they also tend to have close ties to the party. In fact, political considerations help explain, in large part, why certain associate judges who are routinely ruled unqualified to serve by local bar associations are consistently reelected by the circuit judges. The chief judge of the circuit court (also elected by the circuit judges) and the presiding judge of the criminal division of the circuit court (appointed by the chief judge) are also very active and prominent party members; both were close allies of Mayor Daley. During the time of this study, 1972-73, political considerations also played a role in selecting other criminal court personnel. Bailiffs and clerks were essentially patronage workers. When the Democrats held the state's attorney's office, a letter from a ward committeeman facilitated a young lawyer's appointment as an assistant state's attorney.

The implications of the highly insulated position enjoyed by Chicago's felony court organization are not altogether clear. It is doubtful, however, that this insulation means that the conceptual framework developed here is not applicable outside Chicago. In system terms what is being argued here is that the Chicago system is not wholly open to many types of environmental influences (the public, civic reform groups). But, implicit in much of the discussion of environmental considerations in Chapter 3 is the notion that court systems, vis-à-vis other types of organizations, are relatively closed systems. That is, if organizations were evaluated on a scale measuring "openness to environmental influences" that ranged from 0 to 100 (0 being totally closed), court systems may vary only from 30 to 60. Commercial entities may vary from 50 to 90. Thus, the court organization in Chicago is not a unique system. Rather it is merely more "closed" than many of its counterparts in other jurisdictions.

What this means is that the concepts introduced thus far, as well as their interrelationships (to be explicated in the empirical chapters), have utility outside the confines of the present study. It may also mean, however, that the magnitude of the expected relationships may vary in systems that differ in terms of openness. An example will illustrate.

Consider the relationship between a defense counsel's responsiveness and his client's sentence in guilty plea cases. It will be argued later that, because less responsive defense attorneys are in better bargaining positions than more responsive attorneys, they are able to negotiate better plea packages from judges and prosecutors. Thus, in guilty plea cases, a positive relationship is expected between defense counsel responsiveness and sentence. The magnitude of this relationship may, however, vary in systems that differ in terms of openness. Because the constraints upon the ability of the participants to manipulate internal processes are greater in more open systems, the magnitude of the abovementioned relationship would be expected to vary inversely with system openness.

Figure 4-2 illustrates this point. It represents hypothetical regression lines in three jurisdicitions. These three systems have identical settings. Moreover, environmental expectations as to qualitative and quantitative aspects of court operations are similar in each. They vary only in terms of their openness to external influences. As Figure 4-2 makes clear, the relationship between defense counsel responsiveness and sentence is much stronger in the relatively closed

The Organizational Perspective: An Extension 121

Figure 4-2. Defense Counsel Responsiveness and Sentence Across Systems (Guilty Plea Cases Only)

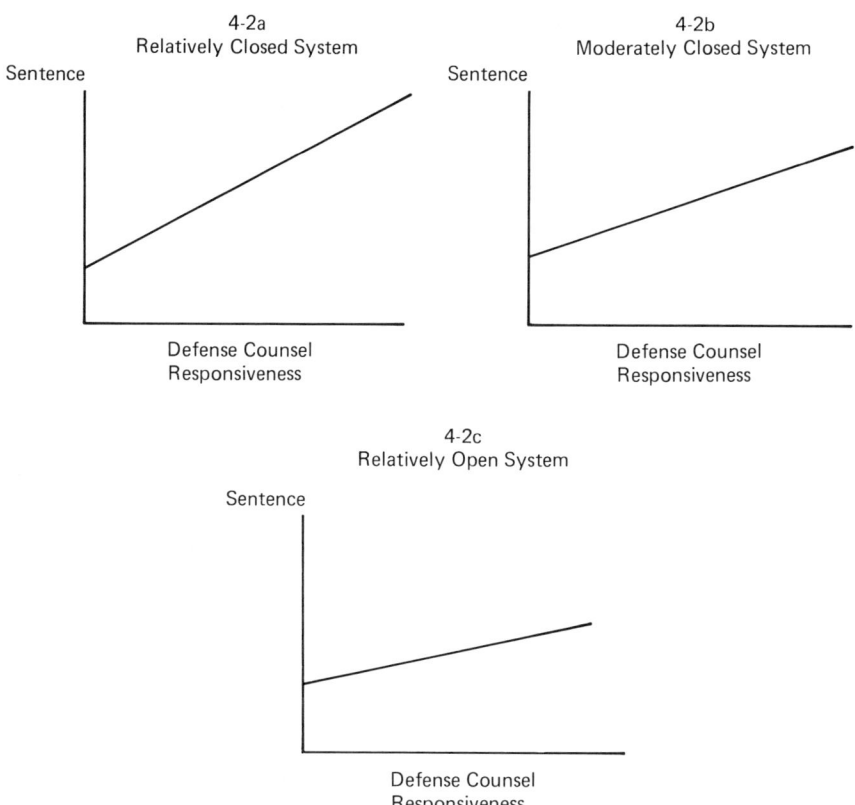

system than in the relatively open system. Other relationships are also expected to vary with system openness, but not always inversely. Consider, for example, the relationship between case seriousness and sentence in guilty plea cases discussed in Chapter 3. The magnitude of that relationship would be expected to vary directly with system openness as it is largely reflective of external considerations.[15]

Hopefully this discussion has somewhat clarified questions concerning the generalizability of the results to be reported in the empirical chapters of this work. With this proviso in mind it is now possible to present the approaches used to measure some of the rather abstract concepts introduced earlier and, finally, the empirical analyses.

NOTES

1. These four facets of the setting are merely those deemed to be most important for the purposes of the present study. It may well be that other dimensions of the setting would be more important for other purposes (e.g., a comparative analysis such as was outlined in Chapter 3).

2. It should be emphasized that various aspects of the criminal court system in Chicago have changed in the years since the observational phase of this study. Some of the descriptive aspects of this section are no longer accurate. A more detailed and current description of the formal structure can be found in the Chicago Bar Association's *Program for Action* (Chicago: Chicago Bar Association, 1975).

3. The term "felony court system in Chicago" is technically inaccurate because the courts actually included in this study are formally part of the circuit court of Cook County. References are usually prefaced by "Chicago" instead of "Cook County" because the sampling design of this study included only Chicago cases. No suburban preliminary hearings, which take place outside the city, were observed, and suburban trial cases, which are handled by trial courts located within the city, were excluded. This procedure was adopted because this study was part of a larger, comparative research project. For a report on the comparative results from a somewhat different theoretical perspective, see James Eisenstein and Herbert Jacob, *Felony Justice: An Organizational Analysis of Criminal Courts* (Boston: Little, Brown, 1976).

4. It should be noted that in Illinois a defendant merely has to post 10 percent of his bond to be released. If, for example, bond is set at $2,000, he has to post $200 at the clerk's office to be released. Moreover, he is entitled to receive 90 percent of that amount ($180) at the termination of his case, regardless of outcome. Thus, bondsmen play an insignificant role in the felony disposition process in Chicago. One important consequence, however, is that the clerk's office often acts as an escrow agent for private defense attorneys. The bond money is very often assigned directly to the attorney as partial payment of his fee. To the attorney the bond deposit is like "money in the bank."

5. It should be emphasized that the bond decision is not merely important because the amount at which bail is set determines, in large part, whether someone will be released or confined for the duration of the criminal proceedings. It is also important because the amount of bond set determines *where* confined defendants will be housed. Confined defendants with bonds set below $3,500 were kept in the House of Corrections; others were housed in the Cook County jail. While neither is an especially desirable place to spend idle time, the clientele and facilities (sleeping, eating, working, recreation) in the House of Corrections are vastly superior to those in the jail.

6. It should be noted that, while there was almost no chance for reassignment in the five preliminary hearing courts, a defendant could as a matter of right receive a reassignment from a trial judge whom he might claim to be prejudiced against him. This was rather infrequent, however, and was usually done at an early stage of the trial court proceedings. Moreover, it did not upset the gen-

erally stable nature of the case-assignment procedures in Chicago, since the probability that the new judge would dispose of the case was great.

7. In certain instances background data on some of the participants were collected and used when essential to an analysis. More will be said of this in subsequent chapters.

8. Although these two dimensions of responsiveness are considered distinct, they are probably not unrelated empirically. Moreover, the relationship between the orientation and independence dimensions probably varies with each set of individuals (judges, prosecutors, etc.).

9. This notion of independence, of course, is not confined to machine-dominated political systems like that of Chicago. It is just as applicable in other, more conventional systems. For example, a highly visible and successful former state's attorney with a large following in the community may be more independent, and hence less responsive, than a younger, inexperienced judge with no large following. The latter type may be less apt to "buck the system." This notion of independence has parallels in private organizations: Consider, for example, the boss's son coming into an entry-level position in a business. He needs to be much less concerned with informal conventions and niceties than a new recruit just out of school. Also, Walter Murphy notes parallel influences in his classic study of the Supreme Court. See Walter Murphy, *Elements of Judicial Strategy* (Chicago: University of Chicago Press, 1964), p. 63.

10. While the notion of defense counsel responsiveness is really a continuous variable, the observational phase of this study uncovered three rather distinct types of private attorneys—nonregulars, clubhouse regulars, and adversary regulars. Nonregular criminal attorneys are those who seldom practice in the criminal courts and whose total practice is only marginally affected by their relationship with the organization. They are the least responsive type of private attorney. "Clubhouse regulars" are full-time criminal attorneys who tend to congregate in the chambers of various criminal court judges for frequent coffee sessions. The purpose of these sessions is to cement relationships within the organization as well as to dispose of cases informally. They maintain large caseloads and depend upon the organization for referrals as well as cooperation. The last type of defense counsel, the adversary regular, is a regular criminal practitioner, but also a skilled trial attorney. He only represents clients who can afford his fees. Because he receives relatively high fees he does not need to maintain an overly large caseload.

11. There are several different ways a case can be dismissed at the preliminary hearing court level. It can be stricken off the docket with leave to reinstate (SOL); it can be "DWP'd" (dismissed for want of prosecution), or a nolle prosequi can be issued. Also, for some purposes, a finding of no probable cause can be considered a dismissal.

12. These data are based on a sample of cases drawn from the preliminary hearing and trial courts. The sampling procedures will be described in Chapter 5.

13. Much has been written on the rather unique political system in Chicago and it will not be reiterated here. Some of the best sources include: Edward C. Banfield, *Political Influence* (New York: The Free Press, 1961); sections of

Edward C. Banfield and James Q. Wilson, *City Politics* (Cambridge, Mass.: Harvard University Press, 1967); and Milton Rakove, *Don't Make No Waves, Don't Back No Losers* (Bloomington: Indiana University Press, 1976).

14. Wesley G. Skogan, "The Politics of Judicial Reform: Cook County, Illinois," *The Justice System Journal* 1 (1975):20.

15. With regard to the notion of case seriousness, the impact of differences in system openness should not be confused with the impact of differences in environmental expectations as to appropriate sentencing structures. As noted in Chapter 3, differences in environmental expectations in Alphaville and Betaville led to different intercepts in the case seriousness regression lines in guilty plea cases. If the two systems had differed *only* in terms of system openness, similar intercepts would be expected. What would be different would be the standard errors—the variance around the regression line. Larger standard errors would be expected in more closed systems.

Chapter 5

The Measurement of Organizational Phenomena

To empirically examine some of the ideas discussed earlier, Chicago felony cases processed during the observational phase of this study (1972-73) will be analyzed. The screening process at the preliminary hearing level, the plea bargaining process at the trial level, the decision to pursue a case once negotiations have failed (at the trial level), and the sentencing decision will all be examined. The empirical analysis of these varied stages of the dispositional process, from an organizational perspective, requires the use of several different data bases and rather involved derivations of several indices of organizational phenomena. There are, for example, three entirely different data bases—one with the defendant as the unit of analysis, one with the judge, and one with private defense counsel—used at different points of the empirical analysis. Data from each of these sources were used to construct measures of such phenomena as seriousness of the case, strength of the state's evidence, the responsiveness of the participants, and the susceptibility of the defendant. Because of the complexity and centrality of these methodological concerns, the description of the data bases to be used in various aspects of this study and of the derivation of the measures of courtroom phenomena to be employed in the data analysis are the focus of this chapter. This will greatly facilitate the presentation of the data analysis in Chapters 6, 7, and 8.

DATA BASES
Defendant-oriented Data Bases

In the four samples of cases used in this study, the defendant was the unit of analysis.[1] The most basic of these samples is the preliminary hearing sample. It is the only one of the four samples that has as its universe all adult felony cases processed by the Chicago felony court system. This sample was observational and systematically selected. Each of the five adult preliminary hearing courts (two general felony courts, two drug felony courts, and one murder court) was observed, but for varying amounts of time. In the general felony courts and the murder court, every other case was selected. In the two drug abuse courts, where the caseloads are larger and proceedings move more swiftly, every third case was observed. This sample contributed 514 cases to the entire data base of 1,476. Because a different number of days was spent in each courtroom and different sampling procedures were used, the contribution from each court had to be weighted in order to treat the various subsamples as a single sample.[2]

The second group of cases selected was a sample of cases in which the defendant pleaded guilty to an information at the preliminary hearing level. It consists of 144 cases randomly selected from a master list of all informations processed during the first nine months of 1972. These cases were selected because, while they were of particular interest, the general preliminary hearing sample yielded too few to permit any type of meaningful analysis.

The last two groups of cases, both trial court samples, were selected for the same reason the information sample was selected. One of the trial court samples was a systematically selected, observational sample of cases processed in the trial courts during the observational phase of this study. To obtain it, each of the fifteen trial courts was observed for one week. All cases that were the subject of significant proceedings (i.e., not merely continued) during that week became part of the sample. This procedure contributed 220 cases to the data base. The other trial sample was a random sample of all Chicago cases processed by the trial courts during the first nine months of 1972. Like the information sample, it was selected from a master list of all cases sent to a trial court. It contains 596 cases. For the purposes of this study, the two trial court samples were merged into one general trial sample consisting of 816 cases.

Two basic categories of data were collected on the various samples described above—observational data and archival data. Because of the greater reliability of the archival data and because it was available across all of the four samples (not merely in the two observational samples), the quantitative analysis relied almost exclusively upon these data. The basic source of the archival data was the clerk's file. This file contains the arrest report, attorney appearance slips, copies of motions filed, the bail record, and half sheets (a record of court appearances and transactions). These documents contain information on characteristics of the defendant (age, race, sex, occupation, etc.), type of offense, circumstances surrounding the offense and arrest, witnesses to the crime, evidence collected, bail amount and whether it was ever posted, type of disposition, and sentence (if applicable). These documents also generally contain the name of the participants who handled the case (judge, defense counsel, and prosecutor).[3] In addition to the clerk's file, information from the prosecutor's file was available for many—but not all—cases in the information and trial court samples. The prosecutor's file was also employed to discern archival data. In addition to much of the same information found in the clerk's file, the prosecutor's file contains information on the defendant's request for a plea bargaining session and the initial plea offer made by the prosecutor (if applicable). This file also contains extensive information on witnesses and other evidentiary matters.

Table 5-1 summarizes the information on the defendant-oriented samples employed in this study.

Judge-oriented Data Bases

Two files of data on trial court judges were used to construct various indicators of judicial behavior that, in turn, were used in several analyses reported below. Unfortunately, similar data were not available for preliminary hearing court judges. The first trial judge data base consisted of aggregate indicators of outputs for each judge, by month, over a two-year period (1972-73). Among these indicators were the number of jury trials a certain judge conducted in a given month, the number of cases on his call for a given month, the number of indictments a judge disposed of, the number of convictions he

Table 5-1. Defendant-based Samples

	Preliminary Hearing Sample	Information Sample	Trial Court Observational Sample	Trial Court Random Sample
N	514	144	220	596
Type	systematic	random	systematic	random
Weighting procedure used	Yes	No	No	No
Observational data	Yes	No	Yes	No
Clerk's file data	Yes	Yes	Yes	Yes
State's attorney's file data	No	Yes	Yes	Yes

obtained, and the number of defendants he sent to the penitentiary. The unit of analysis for this file was a judge-month, and there were approximately twenty-four months of data on twenty judges. Hence, there were approximately 480 observations in the file (24 × 20 = 480).

The second file of trial judge data consisted of information obtained from interviews with the twenty judges permanently assigned to a trial court during the observational phase of this study. Included in this file was such information as party affiliation, extent of a judge's participation in party politics, law school attended, type of prior legal practice, and length of time on the bench.[4] Some summary information from the file of monthly output data was added to the background data. For each important output indicator (conviction rate, number of jury trials, number of cases disposed of, etc.) in the file on monthly output data, the mean, standard deviation, and coefficient of variation $\left(\frac{\text{standard deviation}}{\text{mean}}\right)$ were computed. These measures were added to the file of judge background data. This combined file was then used to construct the various indices of judicial behavior to be described later in this chapter.

Private Defense Counsel Data Base

A file of data with private defense counsel as the unit of analysis ($n = 326$) was used to examine the characteristics of *private* defense counsel practicing in Chicago's criminal courts. This file was also used to construct an indicator of these attorneys' responsiveness to the concerns of the court organization. Two types of information were included in the sample. The first came from responses to a questionnaire sent to each of the 326 private defense counsel who were represented in one of the four defendant-based samples. Unfortunately, only 94 of these questionnaires were completed and returned. The second type of data in this file contained information on each private defense counsel's participation in the Chicago felony court system. More specifically, the participation data related to the number of times each defense counsel appeared in each of the defendant-based samples. Since this information was available for each of the private defense counsel, it was the primary data employed in constructing the private defense counsel responsiveness scale.

OPERATIONALIZATION OF KEY CONCEPTS

This section will outline the manner in which some of the key concepts introduced earlier were operationalized by means of the data bases described above. First, the procedures used to derive three case-related indices—case seriousness, strength of the state's evidence, and dispositional value of a case—will be described. Second, three measures of the defendant's susceptibility to organizational pressures will be discussed. Finally, the derivation of the responsiveness measures for the judge, defense counsel, and prosecutor will be outlined. While from time to time other indices of courtroom phenomena will be employed, the measures to be described here are the indicators of the central theoretical concepts in the organizational perspective espoused here, and they will constitute the basis for most of the empirical analysis.

Seriousness of the Case

Although the model espoused here gives little guidance as to the types of factors affecting the seriousness of a case, courtroom observations indicated that two types of factors do affect it: seriousness of the offense and situational factors surrounding the offense (such as defendant's sex, victim's sex, and the presence of threatening behavior). The following procedure was used to gauge seriousness of the *offense*. Using the merged trial court sample, a subset of *guilty plea cases* was identified in which only one offense (or one offense and a lesser included offense) was involved. Then a series of dummy offense variables (scored 1 if a case involved the offense, 0 if it did not) was constructed for every major offense in the sample. These variables were then entered into a multiple regression analysis on the subset of guilty plea cases described above, with sentence as the dependent variable.[5] The resulting regression equation was used to compute *offense* seriousness scores. These scores ranged from 123.6 for murder, to 85 for rape, to 56.5 for armed robbery, to 35 for the sale of heroin, and to 0 for the possession of marijuana. A offense seriousness score was given to each offense alleged in the preliminary hearing complaint. Hence, there were several offense seriousness variables—seriousness of the first offense, seriousness of the second offense, and so forth. If a defendant had only one or two offenses alleged in the complaint, all other offense seriousness variables were scored 0.[6]

The offense seriousness variables and a series of situational variables were then used in a multiple regression analysis on *all* guilty plea cases, with sentence as the dependent variable. In addition to seriousness of the first offense charged, the following variables were all significant beyond the .01 level: seriousness of the third offense charged, defendant's sobriety at the time of the offense, defendant's sex, and victim's sex. Moreover, the last three terms interacted with the seriousness of the first offense charged. Equation 5.1 explained 45 percent of the variance in sentence ($R^2 = .448$) in 360 guilty plea cases:

$$Y = 7.5 + .007\ X_1 + .42\ X_2 - 4.75\ X_3 + .7\ X_3 X_1 - .78\ X_4 + .26\ X_4 X_1 - 2.75\ X_5 + .46\ X_5 X_1, \tag{5.1}$$

where

Y = Sentence (in months)
X_1 = Seriousness of first offense
X_2 = Seriousness of third offense
X_3 = Defendant's sex
X_4 = Victim's sex
X_5 = Defendant's sobriety at the time of the occurrence.

This equation was used to compute the case seriousness scale.[7] The proper interpretation of a case seriousness scale score is the best estimate (considering only case-related characteristics), in a least square sense, of the sentence in a case after a guilty plea. If, for instance, a case had a case seriousness score of 48, the best guess as to that defendant's sentence after a guilty plea would be forty-eight months. This procedure produced considerable variance within categories of offenses. In the trial sample, the seriousness of murder cases ranged from 8.5 to 227.6; of rape, from 56 to 138; and of armed robbery, from 8 to 111.

Weight of the Evidence

One facet of the dispositional process seldom addressed by criminal justice researchers is the weight of the evidence in criminal cases. While there is undoubtedly a good deal of variance in the weight of the evidence across criminal cases, no attempt has ever been made to incorporate the weight of the evidence in a statistical analysis of outcomes in criminal cases.[8] Indeed, no one has ever even attempted to outline how such an index might be constructed.

Unfortunately, as was true for case seriousness, the organizational framework developed here deals only with the predicted impact of the weight of the evidence; it lends little insight into the composition of such a scale. Courtroom observations indicated, however, that at a minimum a refined, sensitive measure of the weight of the evidence in a criminal case would have to do several things. First, it would have to weight, or at least rank order, various types of evidence (e.g., eyewitnesses, physical evidence, and confessions) by specific types of offenses. This is important because, while an eyewitness may be very important to a case involving a personal offense (e.g., murder, rape, and assault), it may be less important in a case involving a drug charge (such as the sale of heroin). A sensitive weight of the evidence measure would also have to reflect variations in the value of different types of evidence within broad categories of evidence (such as physical evidence and eyewitnesses). For example, in certain types of cases, a policeman may make a better eyewitness than a prostitute. Likewise, in certain types of cases a weapon may be a better piece of physical evidence than a piece of clothing or a set of fingerprints. Finally, an evidence measure would have to incorporate the impact of legal deficiencies in the available evidence. For instance, a confession may not be very valuable if it was illegally obtained.

While the data necessary to the construction of a refined, sensitive measure of the weight of the evidence were not available, data on several plausibly relevant evidence variables were available. The evidence-related variables contained information on the number of eyewitnesses, the number of other witnesses, items of physical evidence, time of arrest, existence of an oral or written statement, and so forth. Also available was information on whether or not motions were made to suppress various pieces of evidence. Although no information was available to evaluate the relative significance of various types of evidence within the different categories, it was possible to weight the different evidence variables by type of offense and to incorporate the impact of possibly tainted evidence. Given the types of data used, however, the resulting composite index is more accurately characterized as the "strength of the state's evidence" than the "weight of the evidence." No data on defendants' evidence (such as witnesses, alibis, or legal defenses) were available.

Two indices of the strength of the state's evidence were constructed by linearly combining the various evidence-related variables described above. One index was for the preliminary hearing courts; the other, for the trial courts. Two evidence measures had to be constructed because decisions made by preliminary hearing court personnel are fundamentally different from those made by trial court personnel and because the former are made at a different point in the "life" of a case. In essence, preliminary hearing court personnel decide whether a case should be pursued or dismissed. Trial court personnel, on the other hand, are concerned with the procurement of convictions. Moreover, they are examining cases that have already undergone rigorous screening, at a time quite far removed from the date of the alleged occurrance.

A few examples will clarify the implications of these differences for the construction of an evidence index. Because lower court personnel handle all cases in which felony charges are alleged, they are apt to see much more variance with regard to certain pieces of evidence than trial court personnel, and this might influence their perceptions concerning the relative significance of these pieces of evidence. It might be, for example, that a weapon in an armed robbery case is recovered in only 40 percent of preliminary hearing court cases, while a weapon might be recovered in 85 percent of all armed robbery cases filtering through to the trial courts. Thus trial court personnel might not perceive recovered weapons to be as valuable as might lower court personnel. In addition, for similar types of cases, the evidentiary value of different types of evidence may vary in the two types of courts because they handle cases at temporally different stages of the dispositional process. An irate witness who testified vigorously at the preliminary hearing may well have disappeared by the time a date is set down for a trial. If this happened frequently enough, trial court personnel may tend to discount the value of witness-derived information. On the other hand, trial court personnel might place a higher value on physical evidence than lower court personnel. Unlike a witness's memory, the proceeds from a robbery will not fade. Nor can these proceeds be subjected to a cunning cross-examination a year after an incident occurred. For these reasons, separate analyses were conducted to derive separate evidence scales for preliminary hearing courts and trial courts. The two scales are similar only in the sense that both were derived using the same basic types of evidence-related data.

To derive the two evidence scales, multiple regression analysis was employed in a manner similar to the way it was used to derive the case seriousness scale. In the preliminary hearing court sample a dummy "pursued" variable was constructed (1 = pursued, 0 = dismissed). The sample was broken down into three groups: personal offense cases, property offense cases, and drug offense cases. Each of the evidence-related variables (number of witnesses, number of eyewitnesses, number of pieces of physical evidence, existence of a motion to suppress a confession, existence of a motion to suppress the evidence, etc.) was then entered into a regression analysis on each of the three subsets of cases.[9] The three resulting regression equations were then used to compute the strength of the state's evidence variable. The values predicted by a regression equation using a dummy dependent variable are interpretable as probabilities. Hence, the proper interpretation of strength of the state's evidence scores in the preliminary hearing court is the probability that a case will not be dismissed (considering evidentiary factors only). An identical procedure was used in the derivation of the trial court evidence scale, except that the dummy dependent variable was a convicted/not convicted variable. As expected, this procedure resulted in very different equations for each of the six regression analyses conducted.[10]

Dispositional Value of the Case

As described in the theoretical framework, dispositional value is a two-dimensional concept with both an evidendiary dimension and a seriousness dimension. But while the theory specifies the nature of these dimensions it says very little about their interrelationships. There are several ways in which the seriousness and evidence measures just described could be combined into a composite dispositional value index. Since it is far too early in the development of this perspective to specify an a priori combination of these measures, this will be treated as an empirical matter. That is, whenever the notion of dispositional value is relevant to an analysis, the evidence and seriousness measures will be employed separately and in conjunction with one another (as an interaction term) to determine their impact upon the dependent variable. This approach was thought to be preferable to an a priori, theoretically groundless combination of the seriousness and evidence measures because it permits empirically based insights into the interrelationships between these two measures in different contexts. The a priori approach would tend to inhibit the uncovering of such insights.

Defendent's Susceptibility

In the theoretical analysis it was mentioned that there were at least three important facets of the defendant's susceptibility—situational, psychological, and financial. The psychological dimension relates to a defendant's ability to deal with uncertainty and ambiguity. Data necessary to construct such a scale would have required psychological examinations of individual defendants; such data were not available for this study. Data did exist, however, to allow the construction of indicators of the situational and financial dimensions of susceptibility.

The notion of situational susceptibility concerns the nature of the defendant's predicament in the court system. For various reasons some defendants, due to their immediate situation, are more susceptible to organizational pressures than are other defendants. Two indicators of situational susceptibility were employed here. The first concerned the number of other indictments or complaints (in the preliminary hearing courts) pending against the defendant. Defendants who are arrested, released, and then rearrested on a separate set of charges are expected to be more susceptible than other defendants. If convicted on each set of indictments or complaints, such a defendant faces the possibility of consecutive sentences. This weakens his bargaining position considerably and makes him highly susceptible to organizational pressures. Two versions of this variable were employed in different analyses. One variable reflected the number of other indictments or complaints pending against a defendant (it ranged from 0 to 4); the other was a dummy variable reflecting the existence of one or more additional indictments or complaints (0 = no other, 1 = one or more).[11]

The second indicator of situational susceptibility was a surrogate measure of the seriousness of the defendant's criminal background—his arrest record. The defendant's criminal record is a meaningful indicator of situational susceptibility because, if convicted, a defendant with a long criminal record has more to lose than other defendants. He is more apt to get a longer sentence and less apt to receive leniency from a parole board. This weakens his position vis-à-vis the judge and prosecutor and provides his defense counsel with leverage in persuading him to plead guilty. In the trial court sample the arrest record variable was a continuous variable which ranged from 0 to 52; in the preliminary hearing court sample the arrest record variable was merely a dummy variable indicating whether the defendant had been previously arrested *in Chicago*. An ideal measure of the seriousness of the defendant's criminal record would incorporate much more information (the number of convictions on felony and misdemeanor charges, the seriousness of the cases in which the defendant was convicted, the amount of time the defendant had been incarcerated, etc.). Unfortunately, however, extensive information on these other factors was not available.[12] Thus the arrest variables available here must be used as a rough indicator of this complex concept.

No data were available on the financial status of defendants (current income, savings, availability of funds from other sources). Information was available, however, on defendants' occupations. In conjunction with a U.S. Department of Commerce scale ranking broad occupational categories in terms of socioeconomic status, this information was used to derive a rough indicator of the defendant's economic susceptibility.[13] There were, however, several problems with this procedure. One major problem was the fact that almost one-third of all defendants reported themselves unemployed and occupationless. These defendants were arbitrarily accorded the lowest score on the scale, but this procedure resulted in a highly skewed distribution. In the trial sample, for instance, about two-thirds of all cases were in the lowest two categories, while the remaining third were in the other six categories. This was resolved by creating a trichotomous scale. Occupationless and unemployed were scored 1, laborers 2, and all other occupations 3.

Responsiveness of the Participants

Judge Responsiveness. The concept of judge responsiveness relates to a judge's commitment to the welfare of the court organization or, stated differently, his inclination to adhere to the informal operating procedures necessary to process cases in a organizationally satisficing manner. More responsive judges would be expected to more readily use the sanctions under their control to induce the expeditious handling of cases than would less responsive judges. While the data were not available to construct a sensitive, refined measure of judge responsiveness, there were several plausible indicators of this concept in the judge data.

Some of the background variables relating to prior party and public service were thought to be relevant here: years in a public role other than judge; whether a judge had held an elected office prior to becoming a judge; whether the judge had held a formal party role (ward committeeman, for example) before becoming a judge; and so forth. These were thought to be important because they indicated that the judge had "paid his dues" and that he probably had some "clout" within the local political party responsible for slating judges. This is particularly important in Chicago because slating by the Democratic party is tantamount to election to the Cook County Circuit Court. These factors have important implications for judge responsiveness because, independent of their performance on the bench, judges who have paid their dues or have clout within the party have a claim to a judgeship (a traditional party reward for faithful service). These judges need not be as concerned with internal needs and demands of the court organization as judges who are less secure in their tenure. Judges with powerful party allies are more insulated than other judges from hierarchial pressures by the presiding or chief judge. This could well lead them to be more independent (i.e., less responsive).

Beyond these background variables there were also three summary measures of judge outputs which could be construed as responsiveness indicators. Each related to the extent of a judge's concern for expeditious dispositional procedures. These measures were the mean proportion of jury trials (the jury trial variable), the mean proportion of all nonconvicted cases that were dismissed before trial $\left(\frac{\text{dismissals}}{\text{acquittals} + \text{dismissals}}\right.$, the dismissal variable $\Big)$, and the mean absolute number of cases disposed of each month (the dispositions variable).

Attempts to combine the background and output indicators into an index of judge responsiveness by means of factor analysis proved to be fruitless. After a good deal of analysis it was decided that the best indicator of judge responsiveness was the dispositions variable. Several criteria were used in the selection of this variable. First, it was very meaningful conceptually. Consistently high absolute dispositional figures are indicative of a judge's concern with keeping the docket current and moving cases through the system. Judges concerned with such matters are thought to be highly committed to the maintenance of informal procedures aimed at facilitating dispositions and hence to be highly responsive.

Second, the correlations between this variable and other plausible indicators of responsiveness indicated that it was the best indicator of judicial responsiveness. For example, the dispositions variable had a strong positive correlation with the dismissal variable ($r = .55$) and a moderate negative correlation with the jury trial variable ($r = -.36$), while these two variables (dismissal and jury trial) were not highly intercorrelated ($r = .01$).[14] Moreover, further analyses indicated that the dispositions variable had moderate negative correlations with the coefficients of variation $\left(\frac{\text{standard deviation}}{\text{mean}}\right)$ of the dismissal variable ($r = -.43$) and the jury trial variable ($r = -.27$). In other words, over the two-year period observed, judges who consistently disposed of a large number of cases varied little from their individual means on the dismissal and jury trial variables. Conceptually, this indicates that these judges were responding more to internalized organizational norms (the need to dispose of cases expeditiously) that were farily constant over time, not to stimuli that varied from month to month (individual cases).

The pattern of correlation between the dispositions variable and several background variables, which indicated that a judge had a claim to a judgeship quite independent of his performance on the bench, were also important in selecting the dispositions variable as the judge responsiveness indicator. For instance, the dispositions variable had a strong negative correlation ($r = -.57$) with a variable reflecting the number of years a judge had spent in a government position other than judge or public attorney (assistant state's attorney, corporation counsel, etc.). This variable also had a strong negative correlation ($r = -.47$) with a dummy variable indicating whether the judge had ever held an elective office other than judge (scored 1 if he had; 0 if he had not). There were weaker negative correlations between the dispositions variable and a dummy variable indicating whether a judge ever held a formal party office (scored 1 if he had; 0 if he had not; $r = -.17$), as well as between the dispositions variable and a dummy variable indicating whether the judge's entire career since being admitted to the bar had been in the public sector (scored 1 if virtually all jobs were government related; 0 if not; $r = -.23$). These relationships were significant in the decision to select the dispositions variable as the indicator of judge responsiveness: while these background variables were consistently related to the dispositions variables, they had no consistent pattern of correlations with the other potential indicators of judge responsiveness (the dismissal variable and the jury trial variable). Hence, when viewed in light of the patterns of correlation among plausibly meaningful indicators of judge responsiveness, the dispositions variable emerged as the central variable.[15]

Defense Counsel Responsiveness. The operationalization of the defense counsel's responsiveness presented several difficult problems. As was noted earlier, efforts to systematically collect background questionnaire data on private defense counsel and public defenders were frustrated. Almost no questionnaires were returned by public defenders, and less than one-third of the questionnaires were returned by private defense counsel. This situation led to the use of a measure of the extent to which a defense counsel participated in the preliminary hearing courts of Chicago as an indicator of responsiveness for private defense counsel. For reasons to be discussed later, these participation rates were not meaningful indicators of responsiveness for public defenders, and they will be treated separately. These rates were meaningful for private defense counsel, however, because private attorneys who participate in the system regularly depend upon the availability of expeditious operating procedures for their economic livelihood. Fees in criminal cases tend to be relatively small; to maintain a lucrative practice, criminal lawyers must be able to quickly turn over large numbers of cases with a minimal amount of preparation. Hence, they are as dependent upon expeditious procedures as are judges and prosecutors.

To derive the participation scale for private defense counsel, the preliminary hearing court and merged trial court samples were used to estimate the extent to which each private attorney practiced in the preliminary hearing courts of Chicago.[16] To obtain a meaningful set of participation scores, each of these samples had to be broken down by courtroom (cases in the preliminary hearing sample from Branch 24 constituted one subsample, cases in the trial court sample from Branch 24 constituted a second subsample, cases in the preliminary hearing sample from Branch 57 constituted a third subsample, etc.). There was a total of eight subsamples—one for each of the four preliminary hearing courts in each of the two basic samples. In each of these subsamples a score was given to each attorney that corresponded to the percentage of the total cases in the subsample in which that attorney represented a defendant. For example, if there were 250 cases in a subsample and Attorney A represented defendants in 5 of those cases, his score for that subsample would be .02. Each attorney in the sample of 326 was given a score in this manner for each of the eight subsamples.[17]

These participation scores were then used to derive both continuous and discrete versions of the private defense counsel participation scale. For the continuous version of this scale, a z-score transformation was performed on each of the eight sets of scores. This was necessary because different sample sizes and different means in each subsample made the scores incomparable. The eight scores were then averaged. This average score was then put in standard form and translated so that the lowest scale score was 1. Scale scores ranged from 1 to 4.5. The discrete version of this scale was constructed by assigning defense counsel clustering around 1 on the continuous scale a 1 on the discrete scale, while assigning defense counsel scoring above 2 on the continuous scale a 3 on the discrete scale (the reason for these particular cutoff points will become clear in a moment). All other defense counsel were assigned a 2 on the discrete scale.

As was noted earlier, too few private defense counsel (94 of 326) returned questionnaires for the questionnaire data to be used in constructing the defense counsel responsiveness scale. However, the questionnaire information can be used in a rather limited way to outline some of the differences in the legal practices of defense counsel who vary in terms of the participation scale just developed. Some of the more interesting differences observed are reported in Table 5-2. As these figures indicate, defense counsel scoring very low on the participation scale tend to belong to large law firms and tend to spend much more time on noncriminal legal work than do other defense counsel. These data are important because they indicate that the economic livelihood of these attorneys is not as dependent upon their criminal practice as is that of the other attorneys. The data in Table 5-2 also show that attorneys scoring low on the participation scale do not have as litigation-oriented a legal practice as the other

Table 5-2. Questionnaire Data on Nature of Law Practice for Different Types of Criminal Practitioners

Score on Discrete Version of Private Attorney Participation Scale	Average Number of Members in Law Firm	Average Number of Hours Devoted to Non-criminal Legal Work*	Average Number of Defendants Represented in a Preliminary Hearing Court*	Average Number of Defendants Represented in a Misdemeanor Court*	Average Number of Defendants Represented in a Criminal Trial Court*	Average Number of Criminal Defendants Represented in Federal District Court*
1	5.9 (n = 63)	42.4 (n = 50)	1.7 (n = 64)	3.3 (n = 64)	3.3 (n = 64)	.5 (n = 64)
2	2.1 (n = 22)	16.1 (n = 20)	7.6 (n = 20)	3.8 (n = 20)	9.0 (n = 20)	1.4 (n = 20)
3	2.0 (n = 8)	3.7 (n = 8)	16.6 (n = 8)	7.2 (n = 8)	6.0 (n = 8)	.5 (n = 8)

*These figures are for the two-week period prior to the date when the defense counsel received the questionnaire.

types of attorneys. These attorneys score lowest on all of the questions concerning the number of defendants represented in the different types of courtrooms. The data on client representation also reveal an interesting, but expected, difference in the nature of the practices of the two types of *regular* criminal attorneys. Those scoring high on the participation scale tend to have large clienteles in the preliminary hearing and misdemeanor courts but relatively fewer cases in the more prestigious trial courts and federal courts. Attorneys accorded a 2 on the discrete participation scale, on the other hand, represent more clients in the trial and federal courts. Hence, while both of these two types of attorneys have criminal, litigation-oriented practices, their focus is quite different.

The defendant-oriented data bases also can be used to shed some light on the differences in the nature of these defense counsel's practices. For example, there are significant differences in the nature of these defense counsel's clients and the types of cases in which they became involved. An examination of some of these data (using cases from the trial sample) reveals a pattern of correlation that indicates that defense counsel scoring high on the participation scale tend to represent clients in cases where the likelihood of a guilty plea is quite high. Significant positive correlations exist between the continuous version of the participation scale and two of the measures of the defendant's susceptibility: the indictments variable ($r = .21$ significant beyond .001) and the arrest record variable ($r = .16$, significant beyond .001). There are also significant correlations between the participation scale and the strength of the state's evidence variable ($r = .20$, significant at the .001 level).[18] Each of these variables, in turn, is significantly related to the attainment of a guilty plea at the trial level. Thus, these relationships at least imply that different types of criminal practitioners structure their practices in different ways. Some tend to attract cases where the likelihood of a expeditious, nontrial disposition is great; others tend to attract cases where a genuine controversy exists and where the chances for a negotiated settlement are lower.

Public Defenders. While the participation rate of a private defense counsel constitutes a rough surrogate for his responsiveness, it was not a meaningful measure for public defenders. In regard to responsiveness, the participation rate of a public defender would not have differentiated him adequately from private attorneys or from other public defenders. Undoubtedly *most* public defenders are more responsive than are *most* private attorneys. Unlike most private attorneys, public defenders are part of the permanent courtroom team. They share working quarters, coffee breaks, and similar work loads with the judge and prosecutor. This constant interaction leads to a sense of common destiny and shared perceptions of roles. It is this unity of perspective that makes most public defenders more highly responsive members of the courtroom work group than most private attorneys. While this state of mind varies within the ranks of public defenders, the variations are due to differences in value structures, professional orientations, and career ambitions, not to differences in participation rates.

Because no personal information was available on individual public defenders, the problem of assigning them scores on the defense counsel responsiveness scale was reduced to ranking them vis-à-vis private defense counsel (i.e., the variation in responsiveness among public defenders could not be tapped). One approach to this problem was to assign public defenders the highest score on the private defense counsel participation scale. This approach was acceptable for preliminary hearing court public defenders but not for trial court public defenders. Lower court public defenders are generally young, inexperienced, recent graduates of local law schools. Many joined the public defender's office to gain trial experience, which they believed would be valuable to them in later stages of their legal careers (often in private trial practice). Such an attorney's stay in a lower court is similar to an apprenticeship, one that must be successfully completed in order for him to be promoted to a trial court where he can obtain the experience he desires. During this apprenticeship these public defenders are saddled with extremely heavy case loads. To manage them successfully, they are very dependent upon the cooperation of other members of the permanent courtroom team; hence they must be very mindful of informal norms and practices. For these reasons, in the preliminary hearing court analyses, public defenders were assigned a 4.5, the highest score on the continuous version of the defense counsel participation; on the discrete version of the scale, they were assigned a 4.

This same approach could not be adopted for trial court public defenders. These attorneys are in a significantly different stage of their careers in the legal profession and within the court organization than are lower court public defenders. After their apprenticeship and a brief interval in a trial court, these public defenders have done more trial work than most lawyers do in a career. Many have earned reputations as competent trial attorneys. Moreover, the substantially reduced case loads at the trial level make these public defenders somewhat less vulnerable than their lower court counterparts. Indeed, trial court observations indicated that many private defense counsel were significantly more dependent than public defenders upon the cooperation of the other courtroom participants and upon expeditious, informal operating procedures. Unlike public defenders, the economic livelihood of the less competent, regular criminal practitioners was dependent upon their ability to rapidly turn over cases with a minimal expenditure of effort.

These considerations led to an attempt to empirically rank trial court public defenders vis-à-vis private attorneys on the participation scale using the following procedure: Initially public defenders were accorded a 0 on the continuous version of the participation scale, while private attorneys were ranked between 1 and 4.5. Then a dummy attorney status variable was constructed (public defender = 1, private attorney = 0). Both of these variables were then entered into a regression analysis using guilty plea cases in the trial sample with sentence as the dependent variable. Controlling for all other statistically significant factors, both attorney variables were highly significant (beyond the .001 level). Moreover, an examination of the B coefficients revealed that public defenders had an impact upon sentencing equivalent to a private attorney with a participation score of 2.0. This, of course, indicated that assigning trial court public defenders a score of 2.0 on the continuous version of the defense counsel participation scale would be a reasonable solution to this aspect of the public defender ranking problem.[19]

An analysis of guilty plea rates lent additional support to this conclusion. Using the merged trial court sample, private attorneys with a score of 1 on the discrete version of the participation scale had a guilty plea rate of .43 ($n = 163$), while those with a score of 2.0 had a guilty plea rate of .56 ($n = 147$), and those who were scored 3.0 had a rate of .86 ($n = 42$). Trial court public defenders had a guilty plea rate of .61 ($n = 303$). This, of course, ranks them above private attorneys with a score lower than 2 on the continuous version of the above 2.0. Given these two separate pieces of evidence, trial court public defenders were assigned a 2.0 on the continuous version of the participation scale. This ranked them above 90 percent of all private attorneys and below those attorneys whom the questionnaire data revealed to be lower court specialists. Public defenders were assigned a score of 3.0 on the discrete version of the participation scale; private attorneys who were accorded a 3.0 on the discrete scale were assigned a 4.0.

Prosecutor Responsiveness. As in the case of the public defender, extensive personal information on assistant state's attorneys was unavailable. A rough indicator of prosecutor responsiveness for trial court prosecutors was constructed, however, using data on initial plea bargain offers made by these prosecutors. In an effort to induce expeditious dispositions (guilty pleas), it would be expected that more responsive prosecutors would be more apt to offer more reasonable (i.e., lower) bargains than less responsive prosecutors and would also be more inclined to utilize the tools within their control to secure the defendant's consent. To differentiate among prosecutors in terms of their inclination to offer more reasonable plea packages, a "reasonableness of the offer" variable was constructed by subtracting the case seriousness score (measured in months) from the initial offer made by the prosecutor (also measured in months). The case seriousness scale score for a given case represents the best estimate (in a least squares sense) of the sentence (in months) given to all cases with similar characteristics (similar offense, same sex, etc.) after a guilty plea. If a case had a case seriousness score of 36, for example, the best guess as to that defendant's sentence after a guilty plea would be 36 months. The initial offer made by the prosecutor was also scaled in months. Hence, if the initial offer was 48 months and the case seriousness score was 36 months, the "reasonableness of the offer" variable (initial offer minus case seriousness) would be equal to 12. Substantively, this would indicate that the initial offer was about a year above the "going rate" for a similar type of crime.

The plea offer variable (initial offer minus case seriousness) was broken down by prosecutor, and the average score obtained was the raw prosecutor's responsiveness score. The average n on which these average scores were based was about 15. Only three of twenty-two subsamples had fewer than nine cases and these three prosecutors accounted for only a small percentage of the cases. As constructed here the prosecutor's responsiveness scale is a reflection of his inclination to make reasonable offers. A score of 0 would have indicated that, on the average, a prosecutor's initial offers corresponded closely to the "going rates" for a given offense. The raw scores ranged from −2 to 130, with a mean of 40. These scores were then inverted, standardized, and translated so that (1) prosecutors with low average offers were given high responsiveness scores and (2) the lowest scale score was 1. The final scale scores ranged from 1.0 to 5.22

With the available data and measures in mind, it is now possible to proceed to the empirical analyses.

NOTES

1. These samples were part of a larger comparative data base containing cases from Baltimore, Chicago, and Detroit. The comparative study was made possible by a grant from the National Science Foundation (#GS 33965). The co-

principal investigators were Herbert Jacob of Northwestern University and James Eisenstein of Pennsylvania State University. Their analysis of these data can be found in James Eisenstein and Herbert Jacob, *Felony Justice: An Organizational Analysis of Criminal Courts* (Boston: Little, Brown, 1976).

2. The weighting scheme adopted was devised by Jacob and Eisenstein, and I thank them for making it available. In the scheme the relative contribution of each court to the total caseload for one year is estimated. Then weights are assigned to the cases actually observed in each court to make its weighted contribution to the sample equivalent to its estimated annual contribution.

3. It should be noted that defense counsel appearance slips were not filed for all cases in the preliminary hearing courts. This caused some serious problems, which will be discussed later, with regard to attorney identification in the preliminary hearing court sample.

4. These data were collected by myself and Wesley G. Skogan, and our efforts were partially supported by Northwestern University's Program in Law and Society.

5. In Illinois, sentences must be given in ranges (two to four years, three to nine years, etc.). Thus, the dependent variable was measured by taking the average of the maximum and minimum. Probation cases were scored 0, since they involve no time in jail.

6. The import of this procedure is as follows: The offense seriousness score given to each offense is the mean sentence given to all defendants charged with the same offense (or the same offense and a lesser included offense) in the subset of guilty plea cases used. Given the available information, this procedure provides the best estimate of participants' perceptions of the seriousness of various offenses—a much more direct measure than statutory maximums or minimums. This technique also provides a way to handle the effects of multiple-count indictments upon case outcomes.

7. Initially an attempt was made to construct this scale separately for personal offenses, property offenses, and drug offenses. The presumption was, of course, that the types of situational factors affecting seriousness vary by type of offense. While early analyses indicated that this was correct, the relatively small number of cases in each subset led to an abandonment of this more refined approach. The regression equation predicting sentence was much more stable when all cases were analyzed together than when they were analyzed by type of offense. Larger samples may make it possible to use the more refined approach in future research projects.

8. A possible exception to this might be Eisenstein and Jacob's *Felony Justice*, which employs evidence-related variables (number of witnesses, pieces of physical evidence, etc.). However, Eisenstein and Jacob do not attempt to construct a weight of the evidence index using the variables.

9. Multiple regression could be performed on these subsamples for the evidence variables because the subsamples were much larger than those in the case seriousness analysis, which dealt with only guilty plea cases.

10. It should be noted that no variable was included in the computation of the evidence scales unless it had a statistically significant impact (beyond the .05 level) upon the dependent variable. The three sets of scores produced by the three regression analyses in each of the two basic samples were easily combined

into a general evidence scale because the predicted scores were all similarly scaled (each was a probability score ranging from 0 to 1). The actual equations derived from the regression analysis were:

Preliminary Hearing Court Evidence Scale Equations

Personal Offense Scores = .05 + .74* Existence of defendant statement + .21* Number of eye witnesses

$$(R^2 = .20, n = 188)$$

Property Offense Scores = .09 + .43* Existence of a defendant statement + .29* Existence of more than one piece of physical evidence + .22* Type of arrest (proactive = 1, reactive = 0) + .09* Existence of an eye witness

$$(R^2 = .10, n = 232)$$

Drug Offense Scores = −.19 + .25* Existence of more than one piece of physical evidence + .18* Existence of a witness − .23* Existence of a motion to suppress the evidence

$$(R^2 = .13, n = 547)$$

Trial Court Evidence Scale

Personal Offense Scores = .41 + .13* Number of pieces of physical evidence + .16* Existence of an eye witness

$$(R^2 = .05, n = 376)$$

Property Offense Scores = .83 + .17* Existence of more than one piece of physical evidence −.28* Existence of a motion to suppress an identification −.28* Existence of a motion to suppress a confession

$$(R^2 = .06, n = 178)$$

Drug Offense Scores = .97 − .29* Time of arrest

$$(R^2 = .11, n = 96)$$

11. The existence of indictments or complaints other than those in the case sampled was uncovered through references in the case file and through references on the daily call sheets (if the case was from an observational sample).

12. Some of these variables were available, but only on a small number of cases in the trial sample. Even the arrest record variable was missing on a significant number of trial cases. The missing data problem on the arrest record variable led to an estimation procedure using the average number of arrests in cases with defendants of similar age, race, and sex, charged with a similar type of offense, to fill in missing data. In no instance did these estimated data constitute more than 13 percent of the cases used in an analysis.

13. For more information on the scale, see U.S. Department of Commerce, Bureau of the Census, *Methodology and Scores of Socioeconomic Status*, Work Paper no. 15 (Washington, D.C.: U.S. Government Printing Office, 1963).

14. All of the correlations discussed in this section are based on a small number of cases ($n = 20$). Moreover, the correlation between the dispositions variable and the jury trial variable is based on only eighteen cases because examinations of the scattergram indicated that two extreme cases were obscuring the relationship between the jury trial and the dispositions variables.

15. It should be noted that the judge responsive scale scores ranged from 1 to 4.8. However, these scores are not interpretable as the average number of cases each judge disposed of each month over the two-year period. The scale scores are standardized scores that were translated so that the lowest scale score was 1. This was done to facilitate the interpretation of B coefficients and the analysis of interaction. This same procedure was used on the defense counsel and prosecutor responsiveness scales.

16. It should be mentioned here that the data used from the trial court sample related to the name of the defense counsel who represented the defendant at the *preliminary hearing level*. What was desired in the participation scale was a ranking of private defense counsel in terms of their appearances in lower courts, not in trial courts. Defense counsel scoring high on a scale measuring trial court participation might well be skilled trial specialists. Those ranking high on a lower court participation scale, on the other hand, are more likely to be journeymen attorneys who rely more upon their contacts within the system than upon their legal abilities to earn a living.

Ideally, a scale of lower court participation rates of defense attorneys would be constructed using only a sample of cases from the lower courts (the preliminary hearing sample, in this instance), and, indeed, this approach could have been adopted here. The approach used here—combining a trial court sample estimate of lower court participation rates with the lower court sample estimate—was adopted because the rather limited size of the preliminary hearing sample (514 cases) produced a rather fragile estimate of participation rates. Only 204 cases involving identifiable private attorneys were contained in this sample. (There were 80 cases in which a private attorney was known to have represented a defendant but could not be identified.) The use of the merged trial sample more than doubled the amount of available information—at a minimal cost. While combining these trial court sample estimates with those from the preliminary hearing court sample may introduce a slight bias (overestimating participation rates of defense counsel who are more apt to have their cases sent to a trial court), it was thought that this procedure would enhance the reliability of the participation estimates.

17. At first glance, the derivation of eight different participation scores would seem to be an overly cumbersome method of computation. For several rather technical reasons, however, the attorney participation rates had to be estimated separately for each of the eight subsamples. First, the preliminary hearing court sample could not be treated as a single sample for the purposes of this analysis. Here—unlike other analyses to be conducted using the preliminary hearing court sample—the defense counsel, not the defendant, was the unit of analysis. The weighting scheme used to combine the four preliminary hearing court samples made meaningless a general participation score based on the combined sample. A defense counsel's score would have been based almost solely upon the court in

which he practiced. A nonregular criminal practitioner appearing once in a courtroom assigned a low weight in the weighting scheme would, for example, receive a much lower score than a nonregular attorney appearing once in a courtroom receiving a high weight. For this reason attorney participation rates had to be computed separately for each of the four preliminary hearing court samples.

There are different reasons why the trial court sample was broken down by preliminary hearing courtroom to derive participation rates. The trial court sample is a sample of cases sent to trial from the preliminary hearing courts. But all preliminary hearing court judges do not send the same proportion of their cases to trial. Some are more inclined to dispose of their cases at the preliminary hearing level. This creates a problem when one wants to use the trial sample to estimate preliminary hearing participation rates. If an attorney practices predominantly is a preliminary hearing court where the judge is more inclined to dispose of cases at this level, his chances of appearing in the indictment sample are not as great as those of an attorney who predominantly practices in the courtroom of a judge who is less inclined to dispose of cases at the preliminary hearing level. If courtrooms are analyzed separately, however, and scores are determined on the basis of deviations from courtroom means, the problem is largely mitigated.

18. This last correlation was obtained using the discrete version of the defense counsel scale; the other two were computed using the continuous version. The correlation between evidence and the continuous version of the scale is .13 (significant beyond .01).

19. This is a modified version of a technique advocated by Jacob Cohen and others for handling missing data. Public defender cases were considered as very special types of missing cases on the defense counsel responsiveness scale. See Jacob Cohen and Patricia Cohen, *Applied Multiple Regression/Correlation Analysis for the Behavioral Sciences* (New York: Lawrence Erlbaum, 1975), Chapter 7.

�֍ *Part III*

The Empirical Analysis

Chapters 1 and 2 discussed earlier traditions in the study of criminal courts and noted various shortcomings in their analysis due to their failures to take into account certain institutional characteristics of criminal courts. Chapter 3 outlined an organizational mode of analysis that incorporates some of the important considerations earlier researchers neglected. Chapter 4 extended this framework somewhat, and Chapter 5 dealt with some of the methodological problems involved in implementing it. This section uses the data and measures described in Chapter 5, as well as some additional measures of courtroom phenomena, to examine the operations of the felony court system in Chicago from the perspective outlined earlier.

The focus of the chapters in this section is on the types of tasks performed by the different work groups, how they are performed, and how they relate to one another in the context of the court organization's overall plan to process their workloads. Chapter 6 discusses the various instrumental tasks performed by the the preliminary hearing courts as well as these courts' primary task—screening. Preliminary hearing court screening is analyzed in light of its importance for the trial courts' performance of the conviction procurement function. After describing the atmosphere surrounding trial court operations, Chapter 7 examines conviction procurement in trial courts. Because conviction procurement in Chicago is highly guilty plea oriented, Chapter 7 first examines the factors affecting the attainment of a guilty plea. Then it analyzes the considerations involved in the decision to pursue a case to trial if plea negotiations fail. Finally, Chapter 8 examines trial court sentencing in light of its role within the court organization's dispositional strategy. It is argued that sentencing is the courtroom's most potent tool in its efforts to procure convictions expeditiously. The implications of this for the sentencing decision are outlined and tested empirically.

 *Chapter 6*

The Operations of Preliminary Hearing Courts

The preliminary hearing courts are the workhorses of the felony court organization in Chicago. Members of these work groups begin their day well before those in trial court work groups and often do not complete their work until their trial court brethren have been gone for several hours. While there were only five preliminary hearing courts in Chicago at the time of this study, they handled between 15,000 and 20,000 cases per year. In contrast, the sixteen trial courts normally handle between 2,000 and 3,000 cases. Thus, what the preliminary hearing courts do and how they do it is very important. Most defendants and victims will never have their case heard in any other forum. Defendants who will eventually have their cases heard in a trial court are affected by many preliminary hearing court decisions, such as bail and rulings on legal motions. The operations of these lower courts are also important for the community at large. Because of the scope of cases they handle, their policies probably have a greater impact upon serious street crime than do those of any other judicial body in the city. Finally, the operations of the preliminary hearing court work groups are important for another constituency, the court organization itself. The preliminary hearing courts act as channeling mechanisms to other parts of the court organization, "feeding" cases as well as court personnel. It is important to note this channeling role because it sensitizes one to the fact that the preliminary hearing courts affect the system in ways that other organizational components do not or cannot.

This chapter will outline some of the important ways in which preliminary hearing courts act as channeling mechanisms and perform channeling functions. It will also be concerned with other activities of these courts that have repercussions at other levels of the organization. The most straightforward and important channeling activity—and the one that will receive the most attention here—is the screening function, the decision to dismiss a case or to pursue a conviction. As indicated in Chapter 4, most cases involving felony charges in Chicago never reach the trial level. Thus, the decision to dismiss a case at the preliminary hearing level is an important one. The dismissal of important cases, or merely of too many cases, could activate environmental control devices. The pursuit of "junk" cases wastes trial court resources and impedes participants' ability to process cases expeditiously in an externally acceptable manner. Some of the considerations discussed in Chapter 3 and 4 have implications for the decision to dismiss at the preliminary hearing level; they will be explored here.

While the screening function is perhaps the most important task performed by preliminary hearing work groups, they also perform other important functions, often affecting what happens elsewhere in the organization. Some of these are directly related to their role as channeling mechanisms; others are not. These other, instrumental functions include the performance of degradation ceremonies, informal sanctioning of defendants, socialization and training of organizational recruits, placement of responsive defense attorneys, and neutralization of time constraints. After a brief discussion of each, a more lengthy treatment of the screening function will be presented.

INSTRUMENTAL ACTIVITIES

Degradation Ceremonies

One of the tasks performed, or at least begun, in the preliminary hearing courts is conveying to the defendant that his status as a human being has changed. He is now a criminal in the eyes of those charged with processing him if not in the eyes of the law. This process is important: once a defendant begins to view himself in light of his new status he becomes more amenable to manipulation and processing by members of the court organization. While such a redefinition of one's self is not unimportant in cases that are ultimately dismissed (arguably for deterrent purposes), it takes on an added significance in cases not dismissed. Blumberg, especially, stresses the importance of this process. Drawing on the work of Erving Goffman and extending it into the realm of criminal courts, he notes:

The accused is confronted by definitions of himself which reflect the various worlds of the agent-mediators—yet are consistent for the most part in their negative evaluation of him. The agent-mediators have seized upon a wholly unflattering aspect of his biography to reinterpret his entire personality and justify their present attitude and conduct toward him. Even an individual with considerable personal and economic resources has great difficulty resisting pressures to redefine himself under these circumstances. For the ordinary accused of modest personal, economic, and social resources, the group pressures and definitions of himself are simply too much to bear. He willingly complies with the demands of agent-mediators, who in turn will help "cool him out."[1]

How this process takes place at the preliminary hearing level is aptly described by Eisenstein and Jacob in their study of criminal courts in Baltimore, Chicago, and Detroit. After noting the formal role in the arraignment ceremonies performed by preliminary hearing judges, they state:

The ceremony conveys other meanings as well. It is the first of many occasions at which the defendant must stand in an open courtroom and be identified as a defendant. The courtroom treats him curtly if not roughly. He has to humble himself before the judge; the courtroom workgroup makes it clear that he would also do well to treat all official personnel (clerks, bailiffs, attorneys) with deference. The judge often reminds a bailed defendant that he is only a misstep away from jail; if he is in jail, he is brought to the courtroom under guard. The ceremony demeans; it strips the defendants of their self-respect and helps prepare them for entry into the lowest caste of American society, the prison convict's caste. Often not even addressed as "Mr." or "Miss," defendants experience the transition from citizen to subject.[2]

Informal Sanctioning

Although degradation ceremonies prepare defendants psychologically for later encounters within the court organization, the vast majority never get beyond the preliminary hearing stage. In fact, over 70 percent of the defendants in Chicago's preliminary hearing courts have their cases dismissed, are acquitted after a misdemeanor bench trial, or have a finding of no probable cause entered in their case, with the vast majority simply having their case dismissed. While this figure is staggering, it would be a mistake to presume that individuals leave the system totally unscathed. Most defendants who have the charges against them dropped at the preliminary hearing court level obtain their release only after an arduous ordeal. The psychological and economic costs involved in facing a prospective criminal prosecution are considerable and, in Chicago, are frequently drawn out over a fairly lengthy period of time. During the time of this study, on the average it took 142 days (median = 106 days) and between four and five appearances in court before a case was dismissed. Twenty-five percent of all dismissed cases took more than six months, while only 5 percent took less than a month. Thirty percent of all dismissed cases involved between six and eight appearances.

For released defendants these delays and appearances cause considerable problems—anxiety, time off from work, sitting around a courtroom for the greater part of the day. But for the confined defendants the costs are even greater. They suffer total deprivation of the most basic freedoms. While only 19 percent of all defendants who had their cases dismissed were confined for the entire dispositional period (average confinement for these defendants = 76 days, median = 57 days), only 18 percent escaped with no time in detention. Forty percent of all dismissal defendants spent only one day in jail, 11 percent spent between two and seven days in jail, and the remaining 16 percent spent between eight days and a year.

Even though most dismissed defendants were ultimately released, their release involved certain costs. The cost of a bond in Chicago is relatively cheap (1 percent of the total amount), but bonds were set fairly high and 10 percent of the face amount must be posted with the court until the case is completed. At the time of disposition 90 percent of the deposited money is returned by the clerk (see Table 6-1). This means that the defendant or his family loses the use of a considerable amount of money for a considerable amount of time. A defendant who can post a considerable amount of bail money will normally will not receive a public defender. If he hires a private attorney, the bond money held by the court is usually assigned directly to the attorney in partial or full payment of his fee. Hence, the defendant will probably never see that portion of the bond money

Table 6-1. Bail Information for Selected Offenses in the Preliminary Hearing Courts

	Mean Amount	Mean Deposit	Mean Cost
Rape	8,800	880	88
Armed robbery	7,020	702	70
Robbery	3,940	394	39
Burglary	3,190	319	32
Unlawful use of firearms	2,990	299	30
Theft	2,120	212	21
Possession of heroin	1,730	173	17
Possession of marijuana	840	84	8

that is theoretically returned to him. About 75 percent of dismissed defendants hired private attorneys, which in itself can be considered to be a cost of prospective criminal prosecution.

These costs can be viewed as an important part of the informal sanctioning process that is an integral part of the dispositional strategy used in the preliminary hearing courts to handle work loads. This sanctioning is an important part of this strategy because, while further processing of many dismissed cases would have undesirable consequences for the court organization (such as heavy trial court work loads and poor court statistics), dispositional procedures in the preliminary hearing courts that did not visibly impose hardships on dismissed defendants would have undesirable external consequences. An example will illustrate.

Consider a case, evidentially rather tenuous, which involves a relatively small amount of merchandise (say $150 worth) stolen from a local store. Although the court organization does not consider this case worth pursuing to a trial court, the defendant resists any suggestion of a guilty plea, even to a misdemeanor. Such a case is a prime candidate for dismissal. It is one thing, however, to dismiss the case at the first appearence in a preliminary hearing court and another to dismiss it at the fourth or fifth appearance. At the first appearance, likely to occur within a day of arrest, the complainant is still apt to be "hot" about the whole incident and rather insistent upon some form of retribution. By the fourth or fifth appearance, however, several things may have changed, mitigating the undesirable consequences of a dismissal. After several months and several appearances in court, the complainant may well lose interest in the case. In fact, of the 299 dismissals in the sample general felony court cases, 121, or 41 percent, were dismissed for want of prosecution. Many of these dismissals were the result of the complainant losing interest, but others were due to some form of restitution or reconciliation. Such informal resolutions are often fostered and monitored by the judge or prosecutor during the course of the proceedings; they placate complainants without requiring further proceedings.

Lengthy preliminary proceedings can mitigate undesirable consequences of the court organization's screening procedures even when they do not result in the complainant's diminished interest or in an informal resolution. By the fourth or fifth appearance the judge or prosecutor can make several arguments to the complainant that might satisfy his desire for retribution, arguments that were not possible to make in the early stages of the proceedings. For example, they can note that the defendant has been incarcerated for a period of time, even if not for the entire period. They can also argue that the defendant has already incurred substantial economic and psychological costs due to the pending prosecution, and that he has benefitted from his experience. As evidence they might cite the cost of bail and of hiring an attorney (when applicable). They might also note that the defendant has stayed out of trouble during the period of time since the arrest (if he has not, it is doubtful that the case would be considered for dismissal). While such arguments do not totally satisfy every complainant in every situation, they are effective in many instances.

Socialization and Training

One facet of preliminary hearing court operations that has been less well noted in the literature than the two just discussed is the court's socialization and training functions. Most, if not all organizations provide their members with some type of orientation. To perform in acceptable ways, recruits must learn the goals, norms, and structures of the organization. Because the court organization as conceptualized here is not a formal organization, formalized training and socialization programs do not exist. This notwithstanding, there is still a need for the functions performed by these mechanisms. In Chicago the preliminary hearing courts fulfill most of this need.

Performance of the socialization and training function falls mainly to the preliminary hearing court work groups because most new employees in Chicago's felony court system begin in these courtrooms. At the time of this study no assistant state's attorney or public defender practiced in a trial court without an internship in the preliminary hearing courts. Also, 50 percent of the trial court judges had previously served in a lower court.[3] Indeed, two of the preliminary hearing court judges observed in the field phase of this study were "promoted" to trial courts shortly after the field phase ended. Many regular private defense attorneys also began their criminal practices in a preliminary hearing court, often as prosecutors or public defenders. Thus, personnel as well as cases are channeled through the preliminary hearing courts to other parts of the system.

The orientation that participants receive at the preliminary hearing level is largely "on-the-job" training, although a good deal of it actually occurs in the hallways, in the judge's chambers, or between court sessions. Recruits learn much from their orientation period. They are taught the primacy of expediency as well as the importance and appropriate means of cooperation. Recruits develop an ability to isolate important facets of cases and evaluate them for various purposes (bail, dismissal, sentencing). They learn how and when to trade information as well as to whom and in exchange for what. They become familiar with the reputations of various important regulars. They develop valuable contacts, incur and accumulate debts. Finally, they learn to recognize when they are being sanctioned and for what as well as how and when to use their power to sanction others.[4] In short, their orientation period not only teaches recruits that the system is not run in accordance with law school notions of due process, but also how the system operates and how to operate within it. It is the effects of this orientation period that lead most regular criminal court practitioners to develop extremely pragmatic orientations to their roles, as noted in Chapter 4.

Defense Attorney Placement

In the short run, when a case is assigned to a given courtroom—preliminary hearing or trial—both the judge and the prosecutor are relatively fixed. The only participant who normally changes from case to case is the defense attorney. This is important because a defense attorney's orientation can have a significant impact on how a case is processed (legalistically or informally) as well as upon its ultimate disposition (dismissal, guilty plea, or jury trial). In general, more responsive defense attorneys, those who have been through some orientation period and who are closely tied to the court organization, will be much easier to work with than other attorneys. Thus, the court organization maximizes its ability to process cases expeditiously by increasing the probability that a highly responsive defense counsel will represent a defendant in any given case.

There are two ways in which highly responsive defense counsel are placed with defendants needing attorneys at the preliminary hearing level. The first is through the appointment of a public defender. Although technically public defenders are available only to indigent defendants, judges seldom inquired into a defendant's financial situation. When they did it was merely a cursory examination, such as "Can you afford a private attorney?" Negative responses were seldom followed up. Moreover, if a defendant was not represented on the day a hearing was scheduled, the judges often offered to appoint a public defender—and upon occasion appointed one over the defendant's objections. These practices, of course, enlarged the set of defendants represented by public defenders, who are normally highly responsive attorneys.

A second placement mechanism, which operates to maximize the probability that a highly responsive attorney will represent any given defendant who can afford a private attorney, is the bailiff's referral system. Before court, when the defendants are in the lock-up, the bailiffs solicit business for selected private attorneys. They emphasize the serious nature of the charges against the defendant and how "up-tight" the attorney is with the judge. Also, they promise that an attorney will secure a bond reduction, a "good deal," probation, a dismissal, and so forth. The bailiff, of course, gets a kickback from the attorney. Regular defense attorneys were observed in the preliminary hearing courts as early as 7:30 A.M. fraternizing with the bailiffs in an attempt to obtain referrals for that day's court session. It is advantageous for a defense counsel to be on the good side of the bailiffs and other members of the permanent work group because it is in the bailiff's best interests to be selective in their referrals. Recalcitrant attorneys who wage long hearings that keep the bailiffs in court until five or six at night are not apt to be prime recipients of referrals.

As an aside, it should be noted that access to the bailiff's referrals is not the only benefit accruing to cooperative private defense attorneys. They are tied to the system in a number of other ways that help them financially and assure their continued cooperation. For example, they are given scheduling preferences by clerks. While some attorneys sat for hours waiting for their case to be called, knowledgeable regulars often strolled into a preliminary hearing courtroom at 11:00 A.M. and promptly had all of their cases for the day heard in succession. Or, if that was not possible, they made arrangements with the clerk to return at a given hour when their cases could be called. Judges also regularly granted these attorneys continuances for "professional reasons" (i.e., the attorney was having difficulty collecting his fee and did not want the case concluded until it was in hand). Finally, judges and prosecutors often tolerated loud adversary "performances" by these attorneys. These performances are make-believe oral arguments made in open court, normally in front of a "full house." They may concern a bond reduction, a nonsubstantive issue, or a substantive issue that has already been resolved informally. These performances are valuable because, while they do not jeopardize private attorneys' relationships within the court, they help them attract clients. Several attorneys reported that after such performances unrepresented defendants in the courtroom would follow them into the hallway and make arrangements to retain them. Also, the defendant in the case would return to the lock-up feeling adequately represented and would refer coprisoners to his attorney.

Neutralization of Time Constraints

One problem that was of particular significance to courtroom regulars, especially prosecutors, was the time pressures resulting from Illinois' statutory term period for felony cases. As mentioned in

Chapter 4, depending upon whether a defendant has been released or confined, the prosecutor must have at least initiated the trial against him within 160 or 120 days, respectively. While the "term problem," as it was referred to, seldom accounted for a case's dismissal, it was constantly on the mind of courtroom regulars. In trying to arrange their schedules, judges and prosecutors were continually concerned with cases which were term problems. Some defense counsel would use concessions on term problem cases to ingratiate themselves with prosecutors and accumulate debts. Other defense counsel would use the term requirement in designing elaborate procedural defense strategies in multiple defendant cases (where some defendants had term problems and others did not). Another reason that the term problem was accorded so much significance was because when a term dismissal did occur it usually signaled serious trouble for the prosecutor. One such dismissal took place during the observational phase of this study. The prosecutor, a four-year veteran, was called "downstairs" for a two-hour session with the first assistant state's attorney. The atmosphere in the courtroom was quite grim while he was gone, and observers speculated that he would not be around for long.

The only usual instances in which pressures from the term requirement could be mitigated were when the defendant requested or consented to a continuance. Once a defendant's motion for a continuance was made and granted, the term period began anew. Not surprisingly, efforts were made at the preliminary hearing level to secure such motions. In some cases this was done simply by asking defendants whether they were ready to proceed with a hearing when their cases were called—the assistant state's attorney was never asked formally since the judge often knew the state's level of preparedness. If the defendant replied "no" to the judge's inquiry, a continuance on his motion was entered in the court record and the term stopped—regardless of the prosecutor's preparedness. This procedure was especially effective in the early stages of the preliminary hearing before the defendant obtained counsel and when he was often confused and unaware of the implications of his actions. In cases where the defendant was indigent and required a public defender, this procedure took on added significance. The public defender was not normally appointed until the day the assistant state's attorney was ready for a hearing (investigation completed and witnesses in court). After he was appointed, the public defender interviewed his client briefly and answered "ready for a hearing" the same day, thus enabling the state to dispose of the case as soon as it was ready to proceed. The assistant state's attorney did not need to worry about assembling his witnesses again. Moreover, because the defendant could not answer "ready" until he had an attorney, this mechanism allowed the state to use as little of its statutory term as possible at the preliminary hearing level.

SCREENING

While the performance of the activities described above consumed a considerable amount of the preliminary court's time and energy, the structure of the complaint initiation process in Chicago also required participants to devote a good deal of their resources to screening cases brought before them. At the time of this study, the Chicago police initiated almost all felony cases by merely filing a complaint in the preliminary hearing court. Because the incentive system for police officers differs markedly from that for members of the court organization, many cases initiated by the police were considered to be "junk" cases.[5] This term means either that the evidence supporting the allegations is insufficient or that the offense is trivial, though technically a felony. In the latter category were many personal disputes—involving families, lovers, or friends—as well as many nonserious felonies (relatively minor thefts by old people, for example).

Removing junk cases from the system required an extensive screening process. Because the preliminary hearing courts receive cases first, a rational division of labor within the court organization dictates that they perform the screening. This is perhaps the most important task they perform; both the level of screening (the proportion of the cases dismissed at the lower level) and the criteria used by the preliminary hearing courts to screen cases have important implications for the court organization's overall operations. Given the large number of cases these courts handle, slight shifts in screening levels could have significant internal and external ramifications. A lowering of standards (resulting in fewer dismissals) could lead to overcrowded dockets in the trial courts and much grumbling among trial court personnel. A raising of standards (resulting in more dismissals) could lead to external cries of inefficiency and laxness.

The criteria used in screening cases are also important because random screening could have undesirable external and internal ramifications. One consequence of random screening would be a significant portion of important cases dismissed at the lower level—resulting in disgruntled victims and police officers, editorial condemnations, and other undesirable external activity. Random screening could also lead to a significant portion of junk cases being sent to trial courts—resulting in wasted resources and less impressive trial court statistics. Evidentially weak cases are difficult to settle at trial.

Rather than ending in "good" bargains, they tend to result in "giveaway" pleas, trials, or dismissals, none of which is good for trial court statistics and some of which entail significant expenditures of resources. Junk cases involving personal disputes also cause problems. Even where there is a good deal of evidence, there may also be a good chance of informal settlements between the disputants, resulting in uncooperative witnesses and eventual dismissals.

The importance of the implications that the screening decision in the preliminary hearing courts has for trial courts statistics should not be underestimated. Trial court statistics are of the utmost significance in Chicago. They are employed as the court organization's measures of productivity and efficiency. During political campaigns, at public meetings, and in official publications, it is trial court statistics that are cited by the chief judge and the head of the state's attorney's office. Never, for example, do they give the conviction rate for all cases entering the system; only the rate for all trial court cases is given. These officials cannot control what comes into the system from the street, but they can control what flows into the trial courts. By carefully monitoring these case flows, they can protect their measures of productivity and efficiency.

Organizational Considerations and the Screening Decision

Although this study can say very little about the determinants of screening levels, it can shed some light on the criteria used in the screening decision. If this decision is viewed in light of the broad perspective outlined in Chapter 3 and some of the factors discussed in Chapter 4, several expectations emerge that can be tested using some of the measures developed in Chapter 5. First is the expected centrality of dispositional value. Dispositional value, it will be remembered, is a concept relating to the importance of acquiring a conviction in a given case. It has both evidentiary and seriousness dimensions. Not surprisingly, it is expected that, the greater a case's dispositional value, the smaller the probability that it will be dismissed by a preliminary hearing court. If implemented correctly, decision rules incorporating dispositional value would insure that important cases would not be dismissed, that cases sent to trial courts would be worth the expenditure of resources, and that most of these cases would be "convictable."

Given what has been said about the nature of the case input mechanism in the Chicago felony court system, another important criterion in the screening decision is expected to be the nature of the dispute involved in the case. Most cases involve clear-cut criminal violations—regardless of their seriousness or the strength of the evidence indicating culpability—but others do not. The police are often called upon to intervene in personal disputes merely to cool things down or as a means of retaliation or restitution. While such cases may, in fact, involve a criminal violation, no one really views them in that light. Although some of these cases find their way into the preliminary hearing courts (largely the two general felony courts), frequently they are resolved informally, with the complainant losing interest in the criminal proceeding. Also, such cases are frequently recognized by the courtroom participants. They often refuse to become a party to the dispute and merely dismiss it. Hence, it is expected that cases involving personal disputes are more likely to be dismissed than those involving nonpersonal disputes.

The organizational susceptibility of the defendant involved in the case is also expected to be an important criterion in the screening decision, mainly for internal reasons. It is expected that, independant of the types of considerations discussed above, the greater the defendant's susceptibility to organizational pressures, the less apt he is to have his case dismissed in the preliminary hearing court. Such a relationship is hypothesized because a screening strategy incorporating susceptibility increases the proportion of highly susceptible defendants appearing in trial courts. Cases involving these defendants are expected to be easier to handle, and thus such a strategy facilitates the attainment of organizational ends, as will be demonstrated in Chapter 7.

One last set of factors thought to be relevant in the screening decision is the responsiveness of the participants. It is expected that cases handled by highly responsive judges and prosecutors are less apt to be sent to trial than cases handled by less responsive judges and prosecutors. Because more responsive judges and prosecutors are more sensitive to internal considerations, doubt with regard to a case's dispositional value, the nature of the dispute, susceptibility, and other considerations are expected to be resolved in favor of resolving the case in lower courts. From time to time this may result in some external problems, but it enhances these individuals' reputation as people who are concerned with the smooth flow of cases through the court organization. Expectations with regard to the effects of defense counsel responsiveness are somewhat different. Here it is expected that the greater the responsiveness of the defense counsel, the less the probability of a dismissal. The reason for this expectation is similar to the argument relating to susceptibility. Because more responsive defense counsel are expected to be easier to work with at later stages of the process, the preliminary hearing courts are less inclined to dismiss cases involving them.

Analytical Problems

To examine the hypothesis just set forth, cases in the preliminary hearing court sample will be examined. Before these data can be presented and interpreted meaningfully, several problems encountered in the analysis must be discussed.

Comparability of Courts. The first and most easily resolved problem was that preliminary analyses indicated that the criteria used to screen cases in the two general felony courts were quite different from those used in the two drug courts.[6] This was not surprising in light of the differences in setting between the two types of courts (noted in Chapter 4), but it did raise problems in the data analysis. These problems were resolved by doing separate analyses for each type of court. While a single equation could have been used, separate analyses facilitated the straightforward presentation of results for each type of court as well as a comparison of the differences and similarities between them.

Dependent Variable. Another problem encountered concerned the operationalization of the dependant variable. A dummy dismissal variable (not dismissed = 0, dismissed = 1) was used, but the actual situation is somewhat more complex. As noted in Table 4-4, preliminary hearing courts do not merely dismiss cases or send them to the grand jury. They also accept guilty pleas to felonies or misdemeanors and upon rare occasions conduct misdemeanor trials. These complexities could have been handled by creating a dependent variable with three or four different categories for the various case outcomes and then applying a statistical technique such as multiple discriminant function analysis. Such an approach, however, would lead to some problems in interpretation. The expectations set forth above are quite straightforward with regard to a dummy variable, but their implications for a more complex dependent variable are considerably more problematic. More important, the small number of cases in some of the possible outcome categories made such an approach unfeasible. There were, for example, only four cases in the sample of general felony court cases in which a misdemeanor trial was held, only twenty-one cases in which a guilty plea to a felony was accepted, and only eighteen cases in which a guilty plea to a misdemeanor was accepted. For these reasons, the dummy dismissal variable approach was chosen.[7]

Independent Variables. A final problem encountered in the analysis of the dismissal decision was the unavailability of certain measures of relevant phenomena. As indicated in Chapter 5, no data at all were available on the responsiveness of the judge or prosecutor. This made it impossible to test the hypotheses concerning them. Also, no refined measure of the nature of the dispute was available. Such a measure could have been constructed if some data had been available on the nature of the prior relationship between the defendant and victim and on the origins of the situation giving rise to the alleged violation. However, since no such information was available, four rather crude, but still somewhat meaningful, dispute indicators were used. Each was a dummy variable relating to some aspect of the nature of the dispute involved in the case.[8]

The first dispute indicator is a resisting arrest variable, coded 1 if some assault was committed against the arresting officer and 0 if there was none. This was considered a dispute indicator because, regardless of the nature of the original dispute, once an assault is committed against the arresting officer, the dispute ceases to be personal. Thus it is expected that, all other things considered equal, dismissal rates will be higher in cases where there was no resistance than in cases where there was some. While this is truly a continuous variable (as there are various degrees of resistance), information was only available on the existence of some resistance, not its nature.[9]

A second dispute indicator was a type of offense variable. Offenses against a person (murder, rape, assault, battery, etc.) were coded 0; offenses against property (burglary, robbery, theft, etc.) and victimless offenses (usually unauthorized use of a weapon), 1. The rationale behind this variable is that criminological research has traditionally reported closer victim-offender relationships in crimes against the person than in other types of crimes. This does not mean, of course, that all crimes against the person involve close victim-offender relationships or that all such cases are perceived as purely personal disputes. It does mean, however, that the incidence of these types of cases is apt to be greater in offenses against the person than in other cases. This gives rise to the expectation that, other factors held constant, the proportion of personal offense cases dismissed should be higher than the proportion of other cases dismissed.[10]

A third type of dispute indicator is a dummy defense counsel variable (0 = no defense counsel appearing on behalf of the defendant, 1 = defense counsel appearing). This variable was considered to be meaningful because cases in which the defendant does not bother to retain an attorney or ask for a public defender *probably* do not involve real criminal disputes. This is a very crude dispute indicator, however, because the contrary does not hold true. There are probably many defendants not involved in truly criminal disputes who retain attorneys to protect their self-interests. Nonetheless, it is expected that the failure of a defense counsel to appear in behalf of a defendant will be negatively related to the dismissal variable (the proportion of cases dismissed will be greater when there is no defense counsel than when there is one).

The final dispute indicator is a dummy legal motions variable (0 = no legal motions, 1 = one or more legal motions). It is also expected to be negatively related to the dismissal variable. The reason for this expectation is that cases in which legal motions are argued are not apt to involve purely personal disputes. The issues involved in such disputes are not likely to be formulated in legal terms nor addressed as legal problems. Here again, however, the contrary is not true. There are many truly criminal cases in which legal motions are not raised at the preliminary hearing level. This may reflect a defense strategy, or the fact that no legal issues emerge, or other considerations. Thus this variable, like the other dispute indicators, is only a crude indicator of the nature of the dispute involved in a case.

The Decision to Dismiss in the General Felony Courts

Multiple regression analysis was used to examine the expected effects of the independant variables discussed earlier upon the dummy dismissal variable.[11] The following equation explained 30 percent of the variance ($R^2 = .297$) in 382 general felony court cases:

$$Y = 1.4 - .003X_1 - .59X_2 - .13X_3 - .27X_4 - .20X_5 - .47X_6 - .13X_7, \quad (6.1)$$

where

Y = Dismissal variable (0 = not dismissed, 1 = dismissed)
X_1 = Case seriousness
X_2 = Strength of the state's case
X_3 = Prior arrest record (0 = no prior record, 1 = prior arrests)
X_4 = Presence of a defense counsel (0 = none present, 1 = present)
X_5 = Legal motions (0 = no motions filed, 1 = motions filed)
X_6 = Resisted arrest (0 = no resistance, 1 = resistance)
X_7 = Type of offense (0 = offenses against person, 1 = all other).

Table 6-2. Essential Data on the Dismissal Regression Analysis for the General Felony Courts

Variable	Approximate Percentage of the Variance Accounted for	Beta Weight	F Value
X_1	7.0	−.16	11.0
X_2	9.0	−.28	33.9
X_3	2.0	−.13	8.3
X_4	6.5	−.25	32.0
X_5	1.0	−.11	6.6
X_6	2.5	−.18	16.1
X_7	1.5	−.12	7.2

As is evidenced by looking at Equation 6.1 and Table 6-2, while not all of the hypothesized relations held true, all factors that significantly affected the dismissal variable affected it in the hypothesized direction.[12] Although the proportion of the variance explained in this analysis is not high and no factor had a particularly strong impact, the results did give some insights into the types of factors embodied in the screening decision.[13] First, it is clear that a case's dispositional value (captured in the case seriousness and strength of the state's case variables) is reflected in the decision; together these two variables accounted for more than half of the variance that was explained. Their effect was linear and additive and, as expected, the greater a case's dispositional value, the lower the probability of a dismissal.

While the results with regard to dispositional value were as hypothesized, neither the defense counsel responsiveness measure nor two of the three susceptibility measures had significant effects upon the dismissal variable. With regard to the defense counsel variable, it should be mentioned that this was the only analysis conducted in this study in which the defense counsel responsiveness measure was hypothesized to have an impact but did not. This was clearly an unexpected result, but the drug court analysis will shed some light on possible reasons why the impact of the defense counsel's responsiveness may have been particularly constrained in the general felony courts.

Several factors should be noted in regard to the three susceptibility measures. First, while the arrest record variable did have a significant impact, this was rather negligible. The results may, however, understate the real significance of the underlying concept because of measurement problems. What was desired here was a measure of the seriousness of the defendant's criminal background, but what was available in the preliminary hearing court sample was only an indication of whether or not the defendant had ever been previously arrested. Thus, information on the number and nature of prior arrests, the number and nature of prior convictions, and the amount of time spent in confinement was unavailable. Similar arguments can be made for the SES variable. What was desired was a measure of financial status, but what was available was only a crude, trichotomous measure of occupational prestige. Such important information as current income, financial holdings, and access to money from relatives was unavailable. In regard to additional complaints variable, an indicator of situational susceptibility, different problems arose. The measurement error here was not considered to be great. Within the general felony courts, however, very few defendants are charged with additional complaints (about 4.5 percent). This is meaningful because it supresses the impact of the complaints variable.[14] Credence is added to this hypothesis by the fact that the complaints (or indictments) variable had a strong impact in every other analysis in this study where it was hypothesized to have one.

Finally, the data analysis shows that the addition of the four dispute indicators, crude as they are, makes a significant contribution to our understanding of the screening process in Chicago's preliminary hearing courts. Although far from being conclusive, the results suggest that criminal cases that are not perceived as truly criminal situations are "handled" in the lower courts. Unfortunately, little is known about how they are handled. Instances of informal restitutions were observed, but information on them was not collected systematically. Also observed were many situations involving various types of physical assaults where the parties made informal amends. Here again, however, no systematic data were recorded on the origins of the transgression, the prior relationships of the parties, or the role of the different members of the court organization in facilitating a settlement. Certainly this is an area that warrants further investigation. Much needs to be known about how these disputes are processed and how they fit into the overall dispositional strategy used by members of the court organization in handling their workloads.

The Decision to Dismiss in the Drug Courts

Here again multiple regression analysis was used to examine the effect of the same set of independent variables—except for the dispute indicators—upon the dismissal variable.[15] The following equation explained 25 percent of the variance ($R^2 = .252$) in 520 weighted drug court cases.[16]

168 The Empirical Analysis

Table 6-3. Essential Data on the Dismissal Regression Analysis for the Drug Courts

Variable	Approximate Percentage of the Variance Accounted for	Beta Weight	F* Value
X_1	2.0	−.12 (−.12)	3.8 (7.1)
X_2	1.0	.00 (−.10)	0 (5.3)
$X_1 X_2$	3.0	−.23	8.5
X_3	2.0	−.10	6.1
X_4	14.0	−.34	60.1
X_5	1.5	.04	0.34
$X_5 X_6$	1.5	−.23	11.5

*Figures in parentheses are the relevant data before the interaction term was entered.

$$Y = .94 + .01X_1 + .01X_2 - .06X_1 X_2 - .09X_3 - .49X_4 + .04X_5 - .06X_5 X_6, \tag{6.2}$$

where

Y = Dismissal variable (0 = not dismissed, 1 = dismissed)
X_1 = Case seriousness
X_2 = Strength of state's case
X_3 = Prior arrest record (0 = no prior arrests, 1 = prior arrests)
X_4 = Presence of other pending complaints (0 = no other complaints, 1 = other complaints)
X_5 = Presence of a defense counsel (0 = none present, 1 = present)
X_6 = Defense counsel responsiveness scale (continuous version).

Equation 6.2 is significantly different from Equation 6.1 in a number of ways.[17] First, while the proportion of variance explained is again not high (see Note 13), all hypothesized relationships except for those relating to the SES variable were confirmed at or beyond the .01 level. A case's dispositional value[18] and two measures of the defendant's susceptibility were negatively related to the probability of a defendant's receiving a dismissal. Moreover, when a defense attorney was present, the defense counsel's responsiveness was also negatively related to the dismissal variable (see Note 17).

A second important difference between Equation 6.1 and Equation 6.2 concerns the role played by a case's dispositional value (depicted in the seriousness and evidence variables). In terms of their relative significance, the seriousness and evidence measures are much more important in the general felony courts than in the drug courts. In the former case they explain 16 percent of the variance; in the latter, only about 6 percent. Another difference concerns the form of the relationship. The linear components of seriousness and evidence accounted for only 3 percent of the variance in the two drug courts; the nonadditive (interactive) component contributed the other 3 percent. Thus not only did dispositional value seem to play less of a role in the drug courts, but it appears that a case had to be relatively serious *as well as* evidentially strong before further resources were devoted to it. These differences may well be due to the different setting in the two types of courts (absence of physically present victims in drug courts and relatively less serious cases), but no empirical support can be given to this proposition.

Responsive Defense Attorneys, Flexibility, and Drug Court Operations

Additional insights into the impact of defense counsel responsiveness and the role of highly responsive defense counsel in the two drug courts can be gained by examining Table 6-4. This table is a cross-tabulation of dismissals, misdemeanor convictions (essentially guilty pleas), and cases sent to trial with the discrete version of the defense counsel responsiveness scale.[19] The data presented here document quite clearly the linear drop in dismissals across the categories of the responsiveness scale. They also demonstrate, however, a marked increase in the use of misdemeanor charges to dispose of cases in the lower courts. It should be noted that while no public defender cases were sent to trial courts, the proportion sent to trial increases across the three categories of responsiveness for private defense counsel.

Table 6-4. Cross-Tabulation of Disposition Mode by Discrete Version of Defense Counsel Responsiveness Scale (drug court cases only)

Mode of Disposition	Defense Counsel Responsiveness			
	1	2	3	4 (Public Defender)
Dismissal	94.0% (16)	84.1% (82)	74.5% (64)	58.9% (80)
Misdemeanor conviction	0% (0)	6.8% (7)	11.0% (10)	41.1% (56)
Sent to trial	6.0% (1)	9.1% (9)	14.4% (12)	0% (0)

170 The Empirical Analysis

These same results were not found in the two general felony courts, probably because of differences in the setting. More specifically, it was believed that the increased use of of misdemeanor convictions by cooperative defense counsel in the drug courts was due to the fact that the relatively trivial nature of many offenses and the absence of any aggravated complainants provided the members of the drug court work groups with added flexibility (i.e., they worked in a relatively more closed system). Moreover, at least in one instance, the effects of this flexibility can be examined empirically.

During courtroom observations it was noted that frequently a defendant who had been confined for a certain period of time was given an opportunity to plead guilty and be given probation or a sentence equal to the time he had already spent in jail. To examine how this affected the screening process, a confined variable (0 = released on bond, 1 = confined for the entire duration of the proceedings) and a variable denoting how many months a confined defendant had spent in jail awaiting disposition were created and added to the analysis reported in Equation 6.2.[20] The results are reported in Equation 6.3 and Table 6-5 ($R^2 = .30, n = 520$).

$$Y = .87 + .02X_1 + .03X_2 - .06X_1X_2 - .08X_3 - .47X_4 - \\ .004X_5 - .04X_5X_6 - .63X_7 + .17X_8, \tag{6.3}$$

where

Y = Dismissal variable (0 = not dismissed, 1 = dismissed)
X_1 = Case seriousness
X_2 = Strength of state's case
X_3 = Prior arrest record (0 = no prior arrests, 1 = prior arrests)
X_4 = Presence of other pending complaints (0 = no other complaints, 1 = other complaints)
X_5 = Presence of a defense counsel (0 = none present, 1 = present)
X_6 = Defense counsel responsiveness scale (continuous version)
X_7 = Confined (0 = released at time of disposition, 1 = confined at time of disposition)
X_8 = Months spent in confinement for confined defendants only.

The results of this analysis can best be demonstrated with a numerical example. Consider a sale of heroin case involving a public

Table 6-5. Essential Data on Revised Dismissal Regression Analysis for the Drug Courts

Variable	Approximate Percentage of the Variance Accounted for	Beta* Weight	F* Value
X_1	2.0	.21 (−.12)	12.1 (7.2)
X_2	1.0	.01 (−.10)	0 (5.3)
$X_1 X_2$	3.0	−.24	10.2
X_3	2.0	−.09	4.9
X_4	14.0	−.32	55.5
X_5	1.5	.00	0
$X_5 X_6$	1.5	−.14	4.0
X_7	1.5	−.44	33.0
X_8	3.0	.35	23.3

*Figures in parentheses are the relevant data before the interaction term was entered.

defender with values on variables X_1 through $X_5 X_6$ such that, considering just those variables, Equation 6.3 would predict a probability of dismissal of .49.[21] This would be the predicted probability of dismissal for released defendants. Table 6-6 shows the effect of the months of confinement variable upon the predicted probability rates. What is happening here is roughly as follows. Some confined defendants represented by public defenders agree to a misdemeanor guilty plea. In exchange they are given probation or a sentence equal to the time they have already served. An examination of the sentence given in this subset of cases revealed that only about 17 percent of defendants (seven of forty) who did plead guilty to a misdemeanor received a sentence in excess of time they already served. Moreover, these seven defendants received only one month in excess of time served (e.g., they served one month and were sentenced to two months). Confined defendants who resist pressures to plead guilty ultimately enhance their chances for a dismissal—as Table 6-6 and Equation 6.3 show. Although they may avoid formal sanctioning, they do not escape informal sanctioning. In the drug courts, sentences for misdemeanor convictions seldom exceed two months in a county detention center. But, as Table 6-6 shows, before a confined defendant's chances for a dismissal are significant he has already spent four to five months in jail. Thus, the results of this analysis suggest that, while it is possible to resist informal pressures, there are costs involved in such recalcitrance, at least for confined defendants in the drug courts. This is encountered again in the trial courts on a broader scale (Chapter 8).

Table 6-6. Predicted Dismissal Rates Across Different Confinement Periods

		Months of Confinement				
	0 (not confined)	1	2	3	4	5
Predicted probability of dismissal	.49	.02	.19	.37	.54	.71

One last point should be made with regard to the analysis contained in Equation 6.3. If the betas (standardized regression coefficients) and F values reported in Table 6-5 are compared with those in Table 6-3, it can be seen that while the addition of X_7 and X_8 slightly enhances the role of dispositional value in the equation, it causes a marginal reduction in the role of the two susceptibility measures and the defense counsel responsiveness variable. The reason for the reduction in the latter set of variables is that variables X_7 and X_8 represent a technique used by the courtroom elite to process cases expeditiously. All convictions among confined drug court defendants were misdemeanor convictions and the use of misdemeanor convictions was restricted almost exclusively to the most highly responsive categories of defense counsel (see Table 6-5). The reduction in importance of the two susceptibility measures also suggests that the technique described above to secure misdemeanor convictions and sanction recalcitrants works most effectively on more susceptible defendants.

These observations may also shed some light on the relatively poor showing of the susceptibility measures and especially the defense counsel responsiveness measure in Equation 6.1 (general court analysis). If differences in the setting of the drug courts and the general felony courts inhibit the use of such devices as misdemeanor convictions in the general courts, then they may also restrict other types of informal manipulations by work group regulars. This does not mean that such manipulations do not exist, but it suggests either that they are more complex than was initially thought or that they are too subtle for the crude indices used here to capture them.

NOTES

1. Abraham Blumberg, *Criminal Justice* (Chicago: Quadrangle, 1967), p. 69.
2. James Eisenstein and Herbert Jacob, *Felony Justice: An Organizational Analysis of Criminal Courts* (Boston: Little, Brown, 1976), p. 193.
3. While it is known that about 50 percent of these judges worked in a lower court within Cook County, it is not known whether they worked in one of the

five preliminary hearing courts being examined here. Some undoubtedly did serve in one of these courts, but others may have been in a misdemeanor or juvenile court, and still others may have spent time in each.

4. A multitude of different sanctioning tactics was observed during the observation phase of the study. Judges could, and frequently did, sternly lecture defense attorneys and prosecutors in open court. They could also refuse to schedule cases conveniently or could pressure the attorneys by marking a continuance "final." Marking a continuance final means that the hearing must be held on the next date or the case will be dismissed. Defense attorneys could retaliate against what they perceived to be unfair treatment by using delaying tactics, raising frivolous motions, not exchanging information freely, or not agreeing to a continuance desired by the prosecutor. If the defense attorney agreed to a continuance, the term period (160 or 120 days) would begin anew; if he did not then the amount of time available to proceed with the case would continue to dwindle, putting increased pressure on the prosecutor. Among possible prosecutor tactics are withholding informal disclosure, opposing reasonable bail reductions, and offering stiffer plea bargains.

5. It should be noted that this situation may be changing. In the latter phase of this study a pilot prosecutor-screening mechanism was set up in one police precinct. A prosecutor was to be in the station house twenty-four hours a day advising the police on charging and evidentiary matters. If instituted on a citywide basis, such a program could drastically affect inputs and alter the screening function performed by the preliminary hearing courts.

6. There were so few cases in murder court that they were not included in the quantitative analyses.

7. In constructing the dummy dismissal variable, findings of no probable cause and acquittals after a misdemeanor trial were treated as dismissals. This categorization was considered justifiable for several reasons. First, such outcomes are equivalent to dismissals in that the case is screened and nothing further happens to it. Second, such dispositions are often judge dismissals in the same sense that nolles are prosecutor dismissals and DWPs (dismissed for want of prosecution cases) are complainant dismissals. Probable cause hearings and misdemeanor trials are often very brief encounters that are handled quite informally. In many instances they were used where a regular dismissal was warranted but would have further irritated an insistent complainant. Guilty pleas to felonies (informations) and misdemeanors, misdemeanor convictions, and cases sent to the grand jury were categorized as cases that were not dismissed.

8. It should be noted that these variables will be used only in the general felony court analysis. The arguments relating to the expected impact of the nature of the dispute do not hold for drug court cases, which involve essentially victimless crimes.

9. It should be emphasized that while resistance to arrest can give rise to formal criminal charges, it seldom did in the sample of cases used in this study. An indication of resistance was gleaned from the arrest report. Hence, whatever differential handling of resistance cases occurs cannot be due to the existence of multiple charges, which in any case were controlled for in the case seriousness measure.

174 The Empirical Analysis

10. The "all other factors held constant" stipulation is particularly significant with regard to this hypothesis because, by and large, personal offenses are considered more serious than most property crimes. Thus, the bivariate correlation between type of offense and the dismissal variable is apt to be highly misleading.

11. It should be noted that the use of a dummy dependent variable formally violates certain basic assumptions underlying multiple regression analysis. It is assumed, for example, that the variance around every value of the dependent variable is constant. This *cannot* hold true for dummy variables except in the unusual case where the proportion of cases in one category equals the proportion of cases in the other category (i.e., 50 percent of the cases are coded 0 on the dependent variable and 50 percent of the cases are coded 1). While this is a formal assumption underlying multiple regression analysis, it is also known that except in extreme cases a violation of it is not very costly. D.R. Cox, a noted English mathematician-statistician, writes in his *Analysis of Binary Data* (London: Methuen, 1970), p. 16: "It is known that quite appreciable changes in var (Y_i) induce only a modest loss of efficiency. Further, at least in the range say, $0.2 \leq \theta_i \leq 0.8$, the function $\theta_i(1-\theta_i)$ changes relatively little. Therefore, within this range, there is unlikely to be a serious loss of efficiency arising from the changes in var (Y_i)." Empirical studies have shown that other more complicated techniques which are formally more appropriate for use with dummy dependent variables produce very similar results. See, for example, Morley Gunderson, "Retention of Trainees: A Study with Dichotomous Dependent Variables," *Journal of Econometrics* 2 (1974):79-93, in which Gunderson compares regression analysis with logit analysis, probit analysis, and other sophisticated forms of analysis designed for dichotomous dependent variables.

Given these findings, the problems associated with the use of other methods (some of which are noted in Gunderson), and the greater familiarity of multiple regression (on the part of the author as well as most readers), multiple regression analysis was chosen over other methods. There is a 70-30 split in the dependent variables used here (70 percent of all cases were dismissed, 30 percent were not), which falls within the 80-20 split discussed by Cox. The use of the multiple regression with a dummy dependent variable places this work well within conventional modes of statistical analysis in the social sciences. Other recent uses of this technique in well-respected journals include: Gerald C. Wright, Jr., "Contextual Models of Electoral Behavior: The Southern Wallace Vote," *American Political Science Review* 71 (1977):497-508; and Karen Mason et al., "Changes in U.S. Women's Sex Role Attitudes, 1964-74," *American Sociological Review* 41 (1976):573-96.

12. All variables reported in Equation 6.1 were significant beyond the .01 level; X_1, X_2, X_4, and X_6 were significant beyond the .001 level. Neither the indictments variable, the SES variable, nor either version of the defense counsel responsiveness variable had a statistically significant effect upon the dismissal variable. Moreover, it should be noted that, because there were some cases in which there was no defense counsel, a special technique had to be used to examine its effect. This will be discussed in the drug court analysis, where defense counsel responsiveness had a significant effect.

13. It should be noted that the proportion of variance explained in this analysis, as well as the other analyses employing dummy dependent variables, can be misleading indicators of the strength of the findings. The size of r is very dependent upon the distribution of the independent and dependent variables. It can reach a maximum of 1 only when the distribution of each is identical. As the distributions of the independent and dependent variables become increasingly disparate, the maximum value that r can take becomes increasingly lower. This is a very common problem when the variables being correlated are both dichotomies, as is the case in the analyses in this chapter and Chapter 7. The predictive power of the organizaitonal model being developed here increases markedly in Chapter 8, where the dependent variable (sentence) more closely approximates an interval-level scale. Hence, in this chapter and in Chapter 7 more attention should be paid to the nature of relationships reported than to the overall strength of the regression equation.

An excellent discussion of the impact of the distributions of the independent and dependant variables upon r can be found in Jacob Cohen and Patricia Cohen, *Applied Multiple Regression/Correlation Analysis for the Behavioral Sciences* (New York: Halstead, 1975), pp. 59-60.

14. Here again see Cohen and Cohen's discussion of factors suppressing the size of r cited in Note 13.

15. In this analysis the breakdown of the dependent variable is 72-28 (72 percent dismissed, 28 percent not dismissed). It is again within the 80-20 criterion D.R. Cox discusses (see Note 11). The dispute indicators were not used in this analysis because the notion of personal disputes, as developed earlier in the chapter, is not really applicable in drug court cases. There is no real victim and, hence, no chance of informal restitution or reconciliation before trial.

16. A significant missing value problem was encountered with regard to the identity of the defense counsel. While it was possible to determine whether or not a defense council represented a defendant, in 102 cases it was not possible to determine who the defense counsel was and thus assign a responsiveness score. Analyses were run with and without the 102 cases (using the mean defense counsel responsiveness score for missing cases). With the exception of variable X_4 (presence of additional complaints), the two analyses were virtually identical. Without the 102 cases, the B coefficient for X_4 jumped from .49 to .67; the F value, from 60 to 122. This resulted in an R^2 of .40. The only explanation that would have justified reporting this analysis as opposed to that reported in Equation 6.2 (using the mean responsiveness score for missing values) was that the information on additional complaints was poor for the same set of cases where the defense counsel's identity was unknown. Since this could not be documented, the more conservative approach was chosen.

17. A peculiarity about Equation 6.2 which requires some explanation concerns the procedures used to introduce the defense counsel responsiveness scale. About 21 percent of the defendants in the drug courts were not represented by an attorney and had no score on this scale. To examine the impact of the defense counsel's responsiveness without eliminating 21 percent of the cases, a dummy defense counsel variable (identical to the one used in the general felony

court analysis; 0 = no defense counsel present, 1= defense counsel present) and a multiplicative term involving it and the defense counsel responsiveness scale were used. In cases where there was no defense counsel, the defense counsel responsiveness scale was 0; in other cases it ranged from 1 to 4.5. This procedure allowed examination of the impact of a defense counsel's responsiveness where a defense counsel existed, while simultaneously controlling for situations where none existed.

An example will clarify how to interpret the two defense counsel variables. Consider a situation where, based upon a given set of values for variables X_1 through X_4, Equation 6.2 predicted a probability of dismissal of .72. The impact of X_5 (the defense counsel variable) and $X_5 X_6$ (the multiplicative term) could be determined as follows: If the defendant had no defense counsel the values for X_5 and $X_5 X_6$ would both be 0 and the predicted probability of dismissal would still be .72. If, however, there was a defense counsel ($X_5 = 1$) who was very unresponsive ($X_6 = 1$, $X_5 X_6 = 1$) then, using the B coefficients for X_5 and $X_5 X_6$ in Equation 6.2, the predicted probability of dismissal would be .70 (.72 + .04 − .06 = 70). If the defense counsel was a highly responsive private attorney ($X_6 = 3.0$), the predicted probability of dismissal would be .58 (.72 + .04 − .18 = .58). The predicted probability for a public defender would be .48 (.72 + .04 − .27 = .49).

What this analysis shows is that where a defense counsel is present, the greater his responsiveness, the lower the probability of the defendant's receiving a dismissal. Defendants not represented by an attorney fare about as well as those represented by a highly responsive attorney. This should not be interpreted to mean, however, that defendants in the drug courts do worse by retaining an attorney. The reasons for not retaining an attorney may well account for why this set of cases has a relatively high dismissal rate. Unfortunately, little can be said about the decision not to be represented by some type of attorney. In many cases defendants were offered an opportunity to attend drug abuse classes sponsored by the state's attorney's office. If a defendant accepted the opportunity and attended all of the classes, his case was automatically dismissed. In such cases the defendant would not ordinarily be expected to hire an attorney, nor would a public defender be appointed. This probably accounts for the relatively high dismissal rates among unrepresented defendants, but no empirical support can be offered. Thus, the most that can be said of this analysis is that where a defense counsel was involved, defendants with less responsive attorneys fared better than those with more responsive attorneys.

18. At first glance it may appear the X_1 and X_2, the seriousness and evidence measures, are positively related to the dismissal variable. It only appears that way because of the interaction term $X_1 X_2$. Often when an interaction term is entered the signs of the additive terms reverse themselves. However, the additive and net effect of the seriousness and evidence variables are negative.

19. There were no guilty pleas to a felony in this subset of cases.

20. The scores for released defendants on the "months spent in confinement" variable were all 0 even though these defendants may have spent some time in jail before being released. The concern here is with only defendants confined at the time of disposition.

21. See Note 17 for an explanation of how this value was obtained. The value for public defender cases was chosen because, as can be seen in table 6-4, most of the cases in which lower courts adjustments are made involve public defenders.

Chapter 7

Dispositions in the Trial Courts

In contrast to the preliminary hearing courts in Chicago, the trial courts observed during this study were "gentlemen's courts." In many courtrooms daily sessions were frequently preceded (as well as followed) by "coffee klatches" held in the judge's chambers.[1] The coffee klatches were usually attended by the judge, public defender, the two assistant state's attorneys, and a handful of regular private defense attorneys, who may or may not have had a case in that courtroom on the day in question. Conversations ranged from the fate of the Blackhawks or Bulls the night before, the potential impact of some changes in criminal law or procedure, the cases scheduled for that day, to what happened in the annual football game between the state's attorney's office and the public defender's office. "War stories" concerning unusual criminal cases in which the various participants had been involved were also related frequently, and occasionally some political gossip was exchanged. One judge even kept a television in his chambers—presumably to fill in when idle talk dropped off. Oftentimes these klatches evolved into plea bargaining sessions involving concerned participants, with opinions and comments of bystanders freely registered. In short, these sessions were not unlike those that might take place in any office or shop.

This relaxed atmosphere generally extended into the court session, which usually began between ten and eleven o'clock. Court was then recessed by two o'clock, after an hour's break for lunch.[2] These truncated working periods were possible because there were usually no more than (and frequently less than) ten cases per day on any given judge's call. Moreover, most of the cases on a call were merely given continuances, the majority of which took no more than a few minutes. Indeed, total dispositions (dismissals, guilty pleas, and trials) in 1972-73 averaged twenty-one per month or just about one per working day.[3] This is all the more impressive if it is realized, as noted in Chapter 4, that about 70 percent of these dispositions were guilty pleas or dismissals.

TRIAL COURT OPERATIONS: GENTLEMANLY PREROGATIVES

The genial atmosphere described above was manifested in many of the informal procedures characterizing trial court operations. Gentlemanly relations were perhaps most noticeable with regard to the scheduling privileges accorded many cooperative private defense attorneys. Scheduling was a problem for these individuals because a successful criminal practice entails a good deal of courtroom work, often requiring defense counsel to be in more than one place at a given time. Unlike other members of trial court work groups, their work is not confined to one physical setting.

Scheduling problems of cooperative private attorneys were mitigated in several ways. First, if a defense counsel had several different cases assigned to one judge, often the judge would arrange for all cases to be scheduled on a given day of the month. Most cases were continued for one month at a time. For example, Attorney Grollinger would have all of his cases before Judge Dooley set on the fifteenth of the month, which became known as "Attorney Grollinger Day." This allowed the attorney to complete all of his work in Judge Dooley's courtroom conveniently. Few dispositional problems arose from this practice because cases were seldom "ripe" for disposition on the same day. Even if they were, dispositions for the class of attorneys enjoying such privileges seldom entailed more than a guilty plea ceremony.

Another type of scheduling privilege enjoyed by cooperative private attorneys concerned the timing of court appearances. In the preliminary hearing court an attorney had to bribe a clerk to get his cases called at a convenient time during the session. In the trial courts private attorneys enjoyed such privileges without paying for them—especially when only a continuance was desired.[4] Motions for continuances were normally considered in the first hour of the session, but a private attorney could arrive at any *reasonable* point during the day (that is, not after two o'clock) without being sanctioned. Moreover, once an attorney seeking a continuance did arrive, his case would be called almost immediately and he could transact his business without undue delay.[5] On rare occasion when it would be extremely inconvenient for a defense counsel to appear in person, he could obtain a continuance over the phone. He merely called the judge's clerk, who made the necessary arrangements. Continuances for "professional reasons" were another type of scheduling privilege enjoyed by friendly private defense attorneys. These were granted when a case was ripe for disposition (for example, a bargain was struck or the state was ready for trial) but the defense counsel had not yet collected his entire fee, or as much of it as he thought he could collect. Such continuances were considered important because most private attorneys believed it was much more difficult to obtain their fee after final disposition than before.

One last type of scheduling privilege enjoyed by some private attorneys concerned the flexibility accorded them when, while they were engaged in some formal proceeding (a bench trial, for example), they needed to be somewhere else. This can best be explained by relating an incident observed in one of the trial courts. A regular defense counsel who had been around for a long time and was well liked and respected by his colleagues was engaged in a bench trial of a particularly vicious murder case. On the second day of the trial, however, he had a preliminary hearing scheduled in one of the general felony courts. After one of the prosecution witnesses completed his testimony the attorney asked for a conference in chambers. He explained to the judge that he had to "go downstairs and make some money." The judge promptly recessed the case—idling two assistant state's attorneys, several witnesses, and two policemen for several hours—while the defense counsel tended to his other business!

While cooperative private attorneys benefited from the scheduling privileges described above, it should be emphasized that they were not the only beneficiaries of the rather relaxed, gentlemanly atmosphere surrounding Chicago trial courts. Prosecutors and judges benefited also. For example, while various contrivances were used to secure the defendant's consent to a continuance in the preliminary hearing courts, in the trial courts defense counsel often agreed to continuances as a matter of course, thereby alleviating the term pressures on the state. This allowed all concerned to proceed with their business at a less harried pace. Thus, while Illinois law set time limits for dispositions of 120 days for confined defendants and 160 days for released defendants, it usually took twice as long to dispose of a case—on the average, 241 days to dispose of a case involving a confined defendant and 313 days for a released defendant.

Informal rescheduling of ripe cases was a second way in which judges and prosecutors benefited from the extremely cordial trial court atmosphere. This procedure entailed "moving up" the date of a case in which plea negotiations were completed. Normally it occurred near the end of a month (right before data on dispositions were forwarded to the presiding judge) during months in which a judge felt he was lagging in dispositions. The judge would make this known in daily coffee klatches or bring it up informally with the senior assistant state's attorney. A review would be made of candidates to be "moved up." When an agreement was reached the clerk would make the necessary arrangements. This was most apt to occur in public defender cases involving confined defendants scheduled for disposition the following month, since such cases posed the least troublesome logistical problems.

Ungentlemanly Behavior

Despite these examples of cordiality, not all was wine and roses in Chicago's trial courts. Indeed, the carrot (scheduling privileges) used to induce cooperation from defense counsel was often used as the stick to sanction them for violating informal norms or understandings. For example, a social-minded, nonregular patent attorney was assigned to the defendant in a rape case by the local bar association's Defense of Prisoners' Committee. The case involved a twenty-two-year-old black man who was accused of raping a sixty-eight-year-old white schoolteacher. In the view of the courtroom regulars the case was a "dead banger" (factually open and shut). This notwithstanding, the novice defense attorney had requested a jury trial and had prepared six pretrial motions requiring extensive preparation and oral argument by the assistant state's attorney. The case was scheduled for a Monday morning and the patent attorney was in court promptly at nine o'clock. Some informal discussions were held, but nothing more was done on the case that day. Nor, it should be pointed out, was the court preoccupied with any other pressing business. This pattern was repeated on Tuesday and Wednesday. Finally, on Thursday afternoon the judge began to hear some of the legal motions and quickly ruled in the state's favor in each. The defense attorney then requested a plea bargaining session, a deal was negotiated, and the defendant pleaded guilty on Friday. While the patent attorney lost a week of "billable hours," he learned a great deal about the realities of criminal justice in Chicago.

A similar incident occurred in a burglary case involving a professional burglar who was represented by a semiregular defense attorney with a sleazy reputation. While the defense attorney requested only a bench trial, innuendoes picked up in chamber talk revealed that he had bribed the two police officers involved in the case. The police officers had caught the defendant in the act of a daytime burglary (a neighbor notified the police of the break-in), but in trial testimony they garbled their story and contradicted much of what they had said at the preliminary hearing. The defendant was acquitted ultimately, but only after the relatively brief trial was spread out over several days, detaining the defense counsel in the courtroom for the entire court session each day. The judge took testimony in the case for an hour in the morning. He then recessed for a brief period, accepted a guilty plea in another case, or engaged in some other type of activity. He even began a second bench trial while the first was still in progress.

Defense attorneys had, of course, sanctioning power of their own. When the need arose they could, and often did, withhold their agreement to a continuance, thereby increasing term-related pressure and sometimes giving rise to scheduling problems. Moreover, in some instances defense attorneys concocted intricate defense strategies in term problem cases. An example of one such strategy that was observed occurred in a murder case. The case involved two defendants—one had a term problem (the statutory time period was nearly up) and the other did not. There were two defense counsel, and both requested a jury trial. The state had planned to try the defendants together, but on the day proceedings were to have begun the defense counsel in the case with no term problem surprised the state with a request for a mental examination for his client. Since the attorney alleged that his client was unfit to stand trial, the judge could not proceed until the exam was completed. The other attorney refused to agree to a continuance and entered a demand for trial. This posed problems for the state because proceedings had to begin in the term problem case by the middle of the following week. This was compounded by the fact that two other term problem cases were scheduled for that week. The only viable alternative was to try the defendants separately, roughly doubling the amount of resources required to achieve a disposition.

Cordiality and Convictions

While such incidents of ungentlemanly, even hostile, behavior were rare in the trial courts of Chicago, they were also functional: they tended to reinforce the virtues of cordiality in the minds of trial court participants. A cordial atmosphere reigned in the trial courts because its maintenance was in the interest of the courtroom elite. The benefits reaped by each member of the dominant coalition could be enhanced through the maintenance of cooperative relationships. Nowhere was this more evident than in the conviction procurement process within the trial courts. The desirability of cooperation in the procurement of convictions was enhanced by widely shared perceptions of the role of trial courts and the nature of trial court cases. These cases were, after all, a rare breed; only about 12 percent of all felony cases initiated in Chicago were carried through to a trial court. Given the extensive screening by preliminary hearing courts, very little pruning remained to be done at the trial level. Indeed, within the court organization's division of labor the preliminary hearing court's role was to screen cases, while the trial court procured convictions.

The impact of cordiality upon the conviction procurement process in the trial courts can be seen in the prevalence of guilty pleas. Fifty-six percent of all cases in the trial court sample were guilty pleas, accounting for about 80 percent of all convictions. Although cordiality is not a necessary condition for a guilty-plea-oriented conviction procurement process, it does facilitate plea bargaining. Plea discussions frequently evolved from coffee klatches and were often later reaffirmed in formal plea bargaining sessions. Regular informal contact bred common conceptions of the important facets of different crimes as well as appropriate sentences for various types of situations, and this facilitated the negotiation process. Finally, the informal set of privileges designed to meet the peculiar needs of the various participants tended to further cement close relationships. These privileges provided the parties with continuing tangible benefits that tied them together between dispositions and that reaffirmed mutual need and the importance of cooperation, thus contributing to a genial atmosphere conductive to plea bargaining.

Expeditious dispositions like guilty pleas were important because they enhanced the ability of the trial courts to procure convictions, and from an external perspective conviction procurement is one of the most important tasks performed by the court organization. Many external evaluations of the court's efficiency and productivity are based upon conviction-related statistics (such as conviction rates and aggregate conviction levels), and, as noted in Chapter 6, trial court statistics are virtually the only ones discussed publicly in Chicago. But as important as the external dimension to conviction procurement is, an internal dimension also exists. While external considerations revolve around conviction levels and rates, internal considerations relate to how these convictions are procured. At the "bottom line" of an annual report, convictions obtained after a jury trial do not look any different from those obtained after a guilty plea. The mode of disposition makes an immense difference, however, to the line personnel in the court organization.

Guilty pleas take very little formal preparation and once the bargain is struck very little work remains to be done. Moreover, there is little uncertainty with regard to the case's ultimate disposition—other than the chance that the defendant will make a mistake at the guilty plea ceremony. Just the opposite is true with a jury trial. Very little preparatory work is done in informal sessions with regulars, but rather in off-session hours with witnesses, policemen, lab technicians, and law books. Also, the preparatory work must be followed by a formal, straightforward, legally acceptable presentation to a second group of outsiders—the jury. Finally, once all of the formal work is completed there is a great deal of uncertainty as to the case's outcome, which is not determined by courtroom regulars.

The nature of this work is such that the court's performance of the conviction procurement function cannot be analyzed by examining conviction rates and aggregate conviction levels. What can be examined, however, are some of the factors affecting the attainment of expeditious convictions (guilty pleas), as well as what happens to cases in which expeditious processing is resisted (i.e., are they dismissed or pursued to trial?). The theoretical perspective outlined in earlier chapters has direct implications for both of these issues.

FACTORS AFFECTING THE ATTAINMENT OF GUILTY PLEAS

The conviction procurement process in Chicago trial courts can be characterized as guilty-plea oriented (80 percent of all convictions are the result of guilty pleas) and guilty pleas can be considered satisficing dispositional modes.[6] These two observations have implications for the trial courts analyses presented in this chapter as well as those in Chapter 8. For the immediate analysis, however, the most important consequence to note is that in a guilty plea system, as opposed to a slow plea system, before a satisficing disposition can be achieved the defendant's consent to the terms of any agreement or understanding must be obtained. A defendant has certain rights that must be waived before a guilty plea can be entered by the court.

The plea bargaining literature is replete with examples of the types of inducements and arguments made to defendants to secure their consent to a guilty plea. When this process is viewed in light of some of the considerations outlined in Chapter 4, however, it becomes clear that arguments and inducements are made by different participants with varying degrees of intensity and that their impact is different upon different types of defendants. Thus, the concepts of organizational susceptibility and responsiveness are expected to be important in understanding how guilty pleas are attained. With regard to susceptibility, it is expected that the greater the defendant's susceptibility to organizational manipulation, the greater the probability of a guilty plea. The rationale for this expectation is quite straightforward: pressures, threats, and innuendoes are thought to be most effective among more susceptible defendants. With regard to responsiveness, it is expected that the greater the responsiveness of the participants, the greater the probability of a plea. More responsive participants—whether they are judges, defense counsel, or prosecutors—are more likely than other participants to use more forcefully whatever tools are available to them to induce a guilty plea.

Despite these hypotheses, susceptibility and responsiveness are not expected to be the primary determinants of a guilty plea. Indeed, their real impact may not even be comprehensible without controlling for another important factor: the defendant's perception of the probability of ultimate conviction. The defendant's perception of the case's likely outcome is important because the efficacy of threats and innuendoes are largely premised on his conviction. As will be seen in the next chapter, the court's sentencing structure is designed to induce guilty pleas by penalizing defendants who resist expeditious processing. But the threat of a more severe sanction after a trial may be ineffective against a defendant who knows that the state's only eyewitness just died, and likewise in the case of a defendant who had made an out-of-court settlement with the victim.

Because of the nature of the screening process in the preliminary hearing courts, the likelihood of conviction in most trial court cases is high, but there is some variation. Tapping this variation, however, presented unique and troublesome measurement problems. An accurate reflection of the defendant's perception of his chances for ultimate conviction would require, at a minimum, extensive interviews with him and perhaps even with his defense counsel and members of his family. This type of information was not available. Fortunately, however, a rough surrogate was available—the defendant's request for a formal plea bargaining session with the prosecutor.

Such a request is an adequate though by no means wholly acceptable surrogate for the defendant's perception of his chances for ultimate conviction. A defendant who foresees a substantial probability of ultimate conviction would be apt to request a bargaining session because it is a first step toward securing concessions from the state. It also provides him some information with which to evaluate the costs of going to trial and being convicted. A defendant who did not foresee a significant likelihood of conviction would not be apt to request a formal plea bargaining session; for him such a session entails certain costs. If he requests a session and then persists in his demand for a trial, he sacrifices credibility in the eyes of the judge and prosecutor. Moreover, at the meeting his defense counsel will be pressured into disclosing much of the defendant's defense. Both occurrences could have an adverse effect on the defendant at later stages of the process.

Data Analysis

To examine these various expectations, multiple regression was used with guilty plea coded as a dummy variable (plea = 1, no plea = 0).[7] The following equation explained 40 percent of the variance in 429 cases in the merged trial court sample.[8]

$$Y = -.16 - .06X_1 + .009X_2 + .27X_3 + .10X_4 + .08X_5 + .51X_6, \quad (7.1)$$

where

Y = Guilty plea
X_1 = Defendant's SES
X_2 = Defendant's arrest record
X_3 = Indictments variable (dichotomous version)
X_4 = Judge's responsiveness[a]
X_5 = Prosecutor's responsiveness
X_6 = Defendant's request for a plea bargaining session.

Table 7-1 contains the approximate proportion of variance attributable to each of the variables,[9] the beta weights, and the F values (all significant beyond the .01 level, using a two-tailed test of significance).

In terms of the implications of this analysis for the utility of the organizational perspective developed here, the results were somewhat mixed. As expected, the session variable, a crude indicator of the defendant's perceptions of his ultimate chances of conviction, had a

---

[a]This is a dichotomized version of the judge responsiveness scale. The continuous variable had no significant effect so judges were categorized as more responsive (1), less responsive (0).

188 The Empirical Analysis

Table 7-1. Essential Data on the Guilty Plea Regression Analysis

Variable	Approximate Percentage of the Variance Accounted for	Beta Weight	F Value
X_1	1.0	−.10	7.0
X_2	3.0	.13	10.9
X_3	13.5	.24	35.6
X_4	1.0	.11	7.2
X_5	3.0	.17	20.1
X_6	18.5	.46	138.9

very strong impact. Indeed, an examination of its B coefficient (.51) reveals that the probability of a plea was over fifty points higher for defendants who requested a plea than for those who did not, if all other factors in the equation are held constant. To the extent that the session variable is a good indicator of the defendant's perceptions of his chance for conviction, these findings lend support to the arguments made earlier.[10]

With regard to susceptibility and responsiveness, although most of the indicators significantly affected plea in the hypothesized manner, the indictments variable was the only measure to have a truly strong effect in the analysis. While this variable accounted for more than 13 percent of the variance in the plea variable, none of the others accounted for more than 3 percent. Indeed, the SES variable and a dichotomized version of the judge responsiveness scale each accounted for only 1 percent of the variance, while a modified version of the defense counsel responsiveness measure had no direct effects upon plea.

These figures may be an accurate reflection of the relative importance of the various factors in the courtroom elite's efforts to obtain convictions expeditiously. However, they may also reflect the fact that, of all the susceptibility and responsiveness indicators used in this analysis, the derivation of the indictments variable was the most straightforward. Each of the others, as noted earlier, was a rather crude measure of the underlying concept. Moreover, beyond these rather obvious measurement problems, it may be that the rather meager impact of these variables is due to more fundamental theoretical problems. That is, their role in the plea attainment process may be more complicated than thought initially. Before a real assessment of the effects of susceptibility and responsiveness upon plea bargaining can be made, it may well be necessary to develop a more refined understanding of the conditions under which these factors affect the plea attainment process. For instance, perhaps certain aspects of the defendant's susceptibility affect the plea process only in certain types of cases. Moreover, the impact of the responsiveness measures may vary with the characteristics of the defendant or some other aspects of the case. Before such judgments can be made, however, much more refined measures of the various concepts must be developed and a much deeper understanding of the dispositional process must be obtained.

Before leaving this aspect of the analysis, a few comments are in order concerning the defense counsel responsiveness scale. Neither the continuous nor the discrete version of this measure had a significant impact on the plea variable when all of the other variables were in the regression equation. This is true despite the fact that the bivariate correlation (r) between the discrete version of this scale and the plea variable was .18, not significantly different from the correlation between the prosecutor responsiveness variable and plea ($r = .21$).[11] This hypothesized position relationship was not reflected in the guilty plea equation because clients of more responsive defense counsel tended to have longer arrest records ($r = .14$) and additional indictments pending against them ($r = .12$), and were more apt to request a bargaining session ($r = .16$) than clients of less responsive defense counsel. These correlations eliminated the initially significant relationship between defense counsel responsiveness and plea.[12]

From a technical perspective, these correlations account for the failure of the defense counsel variable to have a statistically significant effect upon the plea variable. If the plea bargaining process is viewed in light of the sentencing process, however, a substantive explanation for this finding also becomes clear. It will be demonstrated in Chapter 8 that, to induce pleas from clients of less responsive defense counsel, they were given substantially lower sentences than clients of more responsive defense counsel. For example, the predicted sentence in an armed robbery case involving a defense counsel with the lowest score on the responsiveness scale was 32.5 months, while for a public defender it was 40.3 months. The predicted sentence for a private defense counsel with a scale score of 4.00 was 56.3 months. These sentencing differentials may well act to mitigate the differences in guilty plea rates among different types of attorneys. While clients of highly responsive defense counsel may be under more pressure from their attorney to plead guilty than clients of less responsive attorneys, apparently the latter defendants are provided with an added incentive.

THE DECISION TO PURSUE A CASE TO TRIAL

Many issues in the study of criminal courts have been subjected to much heated debate and extended discussion, with little empirical base for either. The decision to pursue a case to trial, however, is one facet of the dispositional process that has not been extensively debated, discussed, or subjected to much empirical research. This is unfortunate because, especially in guilty-plea-oriented systems like that in Chicago, what happens to cases once negotiations fail is quite important.[13] Despite the fact that 80 percent of all convictions in Chicago trial courts during the time of this study were the result of guilty pleas, about 44 percent of trial court defendants did not plead guilty. In such a case the decision had to be made to pursue a case to trial (and allow the defendant to decide whether he wanted a jury trial) or to dismiss it. Like other decisions analyzed here, this one had important consequences for individual defendants as well as the community at large. It presents another opportunity to examine how various considerations are blended into decisions affecting "who gets what, when, and how" in the criminal court context.

The organizational perspective being developed here has several direct implications for the types of factors expected to be embodied in this decision. Clearly a case's dispositional value is expected to be a major criterion in the decision to pursue a case to trial. It is hypothesized that, the greater a case's dispositional value, the greater the probability of its being pursued to trial. Second, the responsiveness of the participants is thought to be relevant. All other things being equal, more responsive judges and prosecutors would be expected to be less inclined to pursue a case to trial than less responsive judges and prosecutors. This expectation is put forward because it is believed that more responsive judges and prosecutors pursue different dispositional strategies than less responsive ones. The former are expected to be more disposition minded.

There is an abundance of cases to choose from, convictions cannot be obtained in all of them, and different strategies for handling work loads will produce different results. With a given expenditure of energy and time, resources devoted to obtaining guilty pleas will produce more convictions than resources devoted to conducting trials. Because more responsive judges and prosecutors, by definition, are expected to be more concerned with what *can* be done in a given situation than with what *ought* to be done, it is expected that they are less inclined to devote their energies to trial related functions than are less responsive judges and prosecutors. They are expected to use whatever influence they can to dissuade others from engaging in resource-consuming dispositions. When they fail they are expected to be more inclined to use their dismissal power than their less responsive counterparts.

Opposite expectations hold for defense counsel responsiveness: cases involving more responsive defense counsel are expected to be pursued more frequently than those involving less responsive ones, other factors held constant. Underlying this hypothesis is the belief that cases involving more responsive defense counsel are expected to be easier to handle at trial than those involving other types of defense attorneys. Trials involving regular, cooperative defense counsel tend to be less involved and easier to schedule than others. Moreover, there are less apt to be "surprises" during the trial and the probability of arranging a slow plea is greater. Because such considerations are expected to be relevant to judges and prosecutors, who largely determine whether a case is pursued, they are expected to be reflected in the decision to pursue a case to trial.

One last set of expectations concerning the decision to pursue a case to trial concerns cases in which informal trial court norms and understandings have been violated flagrantly.[14] It is one thing for a defendant to refuse steadfastly to plead guilty; it is another for him (or his attorney) to take positive actions to disrupt the cordial trial court atmosphere. Cases in which such positive actions are taken are expected to be pursued more vigorously than other cases. Given what has been said about the tendency of trial court personnel to avoid conflictual interactions, this expectation may seem incongruous: one might expect that cases involving such recalcitrance are avoided at all costs. If looked at in a larger sense, however, one would not expect such cases to be dismissed. To dismiss them would be to reward, and in the long run encourage, violations of informal understandings. Hence, despite the fact that such cases are apt to result in highly adversary trials, they are expected to be pursued more vigorously than other types of cases.

Several indicators of resistance to cordiality norms were developed in this study, but not all are relevant for the present analysis (resistance indicators are also important for the sentencing analysis). The two that are relevant here are the number of legal motions raised by the defendant (motions variable) and the amount of time elapsing between arrest and final disposition (delay variable).[15] The motions variable is an indicator of resistance because, while a minimal number of legal motions might be acceptable, an extensive number is inconsistent with the maintenance of a cordial atmosphere conducive to the informal handling of cases.[16] Extensive motions are viewed as impediments to conviction procurement because usually they focus resources on tangential legal issues as opposed to the ascertainment of culpability and appropriate disposition. Also, legal motions often entail a good deal of preparatory work as well as a formal presentation. Finally, they are undesirable because the use of such legal devices introduces an element of uncertainty into the handling of a case. Since rulings on motions can be appealed, control over the ultimate disposition of a case is removed from the courtroom elite and placed in the hands of an outside body.[17]

A somewhat similar argument can be made for viewing the delay variable as an indicator of resistance. Some delay is acceptable and even functional. It gives the state time to assemble its case, allows private defense attorneys time to collect their fee, and permits continuing informal discussion of the case. But extreme delays are evidence of stalling tactics by the defense and are dysfunctional. After an extended period of time the prosecution's case begins to stale. Witnesses forget or move away, victims lose interest, and so forth. Stalling can have the same ultimate impact as legal motions and jury trials. As stalling has its intended impact upon victims and witnesses, the courtroom elite loses control over the ultimate disposition of the case. This inhibits the trial court's performance of its conviction procurement function and is inconsistent with cordiality norms. When stalling tactics are successful, a substantial amount of preparatory work can be for naught.

Before the data analysis is presented, it should be noted that some problems arise in using the delay variable as an indicator of stalling tactics. One is an analytical problem that can be handled without undue difficulty: delay figures are not meaningfully comparable between confined defendants and released defendants. Under the statutory term provisions noted earlier, prosecutors must bring confined defendants to trial more quickly than released defendants. Because of this, prosecutors make concerted efforts to bring cases involving confined defendants to trial more quickly than cases involving released defendants. Thus, while a 300-day delay in a case involving a confined defendant may be "long" for confined defendants, it may not be unusual for released defendants. More important, however, the different scheduling priorities of the prosecutor may mean that the *responsibility* for delay in released cases is not as clear-cut as in confined cases. This raises the possibility that the impact of the delay variable may be different for confined and released cases. Hence, a technique suggested by Wright for handling conditional relationships was used in analyzing the impact of delay.[18]

The second problem with using the delay variable as an indicator of resistance is substantive, peculiar to this analysis, and cannot be resolved with the available data: stalling may have worked in some cases but not in others, and it is not possible to distinguish between the two sets of cases. Where it did work and irreparable damage was done, the case is not expected to be pursued, despite the undesirable consequences. This is expected to obscure the hypothesized relationship in this analysis.[19] This problem will not affect the expected relationship between delay and sentence, which will be examined in the next chapter. There only cases where stalling tactics failed will be examined.

Data Analysis

To analyze these expectations multiple regression analysis was again used in conjunction with a dummy pursued variable (0 = dismissed; 1 = pursued).[20] The following equation explained slightly more than 11 percent of the variance in the pursued variable ($R^2 = .116$) in 241 cases.[21]

$$Y = 1.44 - 1.20X_1 - .28X_2 + .40X_1X_2 + .19X_3, \qquad (7.2)$$

where

Y = Pursued variable (0 = dismissed; 1 = pursued)
X_1 = Strength of the state's case
X_2 = Case seriousness
X_3 = Motions variable.

Table 7-2 contains other relevant data on the regression analysis.

In terms of the theoretical perspective being elaborated here, the results of the pursued analysis were rather discouraging. Neither the seriousness evidence variable had any significant linear effect upon the pursued variable, and the interaction term accounted for only a little over 3 percent of the variance.[22] None of the responsiveness measures had any significant impact. Moreover, while the legal motions variable proved to have the expected effect, the delay variables were insignificant. Some, but not all, of these dismal results can be attributed to the statistical and measurement problems discussed earlier. Subsequent analyses revealed that the role played by some of the participants was more complex than thought originally.

Table 7-2. Essential Data on the Pursued Regression Analysis

Variable	Approximate Percentage of the Variance Accounted for	Beta Weight	F Value
X_1	0	−.30 (.00)*	4.0 (.01)*
X_2	0	−.73 (−.02)*	4.4 (.09)*
$X_1 X_2$	3.3	.63	3.7
X_3	8.3	.30	22.1

*The figures in parentheses are the corresponding values before the interaction term was entered into the equation.

Judges. Like the defense counsel and prosecutor measures of responsiveness, the judge responsiveness variable had no impact in the pursued analysis. Some reasons for the failure of judge responsiveness to have its hypothesized effect become clear if differences in the types of trials conducted by different types of judges are considered. The relative frequency of jury trials was much lower among more responsive judges than their less responsive counterparts. Using the dichotomized version of the judge responsiveness scale employed in the guilty plea analysis, it was found that while 40 percent of all trials conducted by less responsive judges were jury trials, such trials made up only 20 percent of all trials conducted by more responsive judges. Thus, responsive judges' concern for expeditious dispositional procedures was not manifested in higher guilty plea rates and higher dismissal rates, but in higher guilty plea rates and higher bench trial rates.

This result was unanticipated because the defense, not the judge, makes the decision to request a bench trial. Evidently, however, the judge plays some indirect role in this decision. For example, the informal, clubby atmosphere in the courtrooms of more responsive judges may lead to less adversary trials. Whatever the cause, the judge's role in post-negotiation matters was more complex than anticipated initially, and this caused problems in the pursued analysis. More responsive judges appear to be faced more frequently with situations where the choice is between a dismissal or a bench trial, while less responsive judges are more frequently faced with the choice between a dismissal and a jury trial.[23] This situation obscured the relationship hypothesized initially between judge responsiveness and the decision to pursue. While the initial hypothesis may be overly simplistic (or even wrong), a more meaningful analysis of the role of judge responsiveness in the decision to pursue a case to trial would have to take into consideration the type of choice embodied in a case (i.e., is the decision between a dismissal and a bench trial or a dismissal and a jury trial?).[24]

Defense Attorneys. Subsequent analyses revealed that the initial hypothesis concerning the role of defense counsel responsiveness in the decision to pursue also was overly simplistic. A better understanding of the role that defense counsel responsiveness plays in the post-negotiation phases of the dispositional process can be obtained by examining its role in the preliminary stages of trial court operations. While the defense counsel responsiveness scale had no direct effect upon the dummy plea variable analyzed earlier, markedly different guilty plea rates were observed across the four categories of the discrete version of this scale (see Note 11). For example, defense counsel in the lowest category had a guilty plea rate of .43, while those in the highest category had a guilty plea rate of .86. This has important implications for the pursued analysis because the residue of cases in the post-negotiation stages of the dispositional process is likely to be quite different across categories of defense counsel responsiveness.

Despite the extensive screening process at the preliminary hearing level, it is likely that some unconvictable or problem cases seep through to the trial court. These cases may simply be "junk" cases or cases where something has occurred in the interval between the lower court stage and the trial court stage to make them unconvictable or undesirable to pursue. If these problem cases are somewhat evenly distributed across defense attorneys, it is likely that a significant proportion of the residue of highly responsive defense attorneys' cases are problem cases. For example, if just 5 percent of all trial cases are problem cases and *none* result in guilty pleas, then almost one-third of the residue of highly responsive defense counsel cases would be problem cases (.05/.16). Only about 10 percent of the residue of highly unresponsive defense counsel cases would be problem cases (.05/.57). Such complexities could obscure the hypothesized impact of the defense counsel variable in the present analysis.

Examining this possibility, needless to say, presented some problems. A rough test was devised, however, using the session variable (employed in the guilty plea analysis), a dichotomized version of the defense counsel responsiveness variable (0 = nonregular; 1 = regular),[25] and an interaction term involving each. The session variable was used because it was thought to be the best available indicator of whether a case had some type of problem at the trial level. If a case had a problem, it is doubtful that negotiations would have reached a formal stage. Rather, probably nothing beyond informal discussion would have taken place. A dichotomized version of the defense counsel scale was used to simplify the analysis and the interpretation of the results. An interaction term was employed because it is expected that the impact of the defense counsel variable would be different depending upon whether a formal session was held. More specifically, it was expected that where a session was held, cases involving regular defense counsel would be pursued with greater frequency than those involving nonregulars.

Adding these three terms to the regression analysis reported in Equation 7.2 nearly doubled the proportion of variance explained ($R^2 = .21$), and produced the following equation:

$$Y = 1.57 - 1.33X_1 - .28X_2 + .39X_1 X_2 + .14X_3 + .06X_4 - .35X_5 + .37X_4 X_5, \qquad (7.3)$$

where

Y = Pursued variable (0 = dismissal; 1 = pursued)
X_1 = Strength of the state's case
X_2 = Case seriousness
X_3 = Motions variable
X_4 = Session variable (0 = no session; 1 = session)
X_5 = Dichotomized defense counsel responsiveness variable (0 = nonregular; 1 = regular).

Table 7-3 reports other relevant information on the regression analysis.

Despite the fact that the addition of these variables significantly enhanced the explanatory power of the pursued equation, the expected results were not realized. Where formal plea bargaining sessions were held, cases involving regular defense counsel were not pursued with any greater frequency that those involving nonregulars. Some other unanticipated insights did emerge, however, from the refined analysis reported in Equation 7.3. An example will illustrate. Assume a burglary case with values on variables X_1, X_2, and X_3 such that Equation 7.3 produced a predicted probability of .70 (the mean), without considering variables X_4 and X_5. Table 7-4 reports the various predicted probabilities of such a case for each of the four possible combinations of the session and defense counsel variables (X_4, X_5).

The results reported in Table 7-4 make obvious what was reported above: there was no real difference across attorney types in the probability that a case would be pursued when a formal plea bargain-

Table 7-3. Essential Data on Second Pursued Regression Analysis

Variable	Approximate Percentage of the Variance Accounted for	Beta Weight	F Value
X_1	0	−.33 (.00)*	5.3 (.01)*
X_2	0	−.70 (−.02)*	4.5 (.09)*
$X_1 X_2$	3.3	.61	3.8
X_3	8.3	.23	13.5
X_4	3.5	.07 (.19)*	.7 (9.8)*
X_5	2.5	−.38 (−.17)*	18.0 (7.2)*
$X_4 X_5$	3.5	.36	10.6

*Figures in parentheses are values before the interaction term was entered.

Table 7-4. Predicted Probabilities for Various Combinations of Session and Defense Counsel Variables

	No Session and Nonregular	No Session and Regular	Session and Nonregular	Session and Regular
Predicted probability of a case being pursued	.70	.35	.76	.78

ing session was held. What does emerge, however, are very different predicted probabilities in cases where no session was held: cases involving regulars were much less apt to be pursued than others. What these findings suggest is that regular defense counsel's perceptions of what constitutes a problem or unconvictable case are more in line with those of other courtroom regulars (judges and prosecutors) than nonregular attorneys. While this was unanticipated, it should not have been surprising given the socialization effects of continuing interactions within the courtroom setting.[26]

NOTES

1. It should be emphasized that not all judges condoned such activities in their chambers. A few judges (perhaps three at most) were very selective as to whom entered their chambers and for what purposes. The atmosphere in these courtrooms was significantly more formal than in others.

2. It appeared during the observational phase of this study that trial courts were usually in session between two and three hours per day. A Chicago newspaper did a quantitative study of the time that judges in these courts spent on the bench, which confirmed this estimate. The estimate was that court was in session 2.75 hours per day and that judges spent another 1.5 hours a day in chambers (*Chicago Sun Times*, January 20, 1974). Although these estimates are

fairly accurate, court time really varies throughout the year. Around the Christmas holidays activity slackens considerably, as it does during the summer months (most of the courtrooms were not air-conditioned). Also, activity frequently picks up toward the end of the month, right before the clerk must forward monthly data on dispositions to the presiding judge.

3. These figures were computed from official reports compiled by and furnished by the clerk of the circuit court's office (criminal division).

4. Proceedings involving more than just continuances usually took place after the continuances were disposed of. Frequently an agreed-upon time was set for more involved proceedings and the defense attorney merely showed up at that time.

5. When an attorney arrived to obtain a continuance while the court was in the midst of a formal proceeding, it was not unusual for the judge to call a recess to grant the continuance. When that was not feasible the junior assistant state's attorney often took the defense attorney into the judge's chambers and arranged the continuance.

6. Guilty pleas are considered to be satisficing dispositional modes in Chicago's trial courts because they are consistent with the trial court's conviction procurement function, can be obtained with a relatively low expenditure of resources, and fall clearly within established notions of due process. One should be very cautious in generalizing this statement beyond the present context (the trial courts of Chicago) because the term "satisficing dispositional mode" is a relative concept. What is considered a satisficing dispositional mode may vary from court system to court system. For example, in systems where extensive screening does not take place prior to the trial court stage (such as in Baltimore) there may be different satisficing dispositional modes for different types of cases (for instance, dismissals—one form of an expeditious disposition—might be appropriate in one category of cases, while guilty pleas—another form of an expeditious disposition—may be appropriate in another). Other systems, where screening does not take place, may employ slow pleas extensively. Hence, both slow pleas and guilty pleas may be considered satisficing dispositional modes. Such complexities could introduce considerable analytic difficulties. In Chicago they do not, at least not to any great extent. Slow pleas were used in Chicago, but only rarely. Moreover, screening was extensive. Hence, in this context the term satisficing dispositional mode will be used synonymously with guilty plea. While this will introduce some measurement error in the dependent variable (where a slow plea was used or where a dismissal was considered appropriate) the data do not provide any viable alternatives.

7. The use of multiple regression analysis here again violated certain formal assumptions. But, as before, the cost of such violations is considered minimal. The breakdown of the plea variable was 56-44 (56 percent guilty pleas, 44 percent not guilty pleas)—very close to the ideal 50-50 split mentioned by Cox (see Note 11, Chapter 6).

8. Of the 816 cases in the two merged trial court samples described in Chapter 5 information on the final disposition was available for only 674. Of these, 254 had missing information on one or more of the variables used in the regression analysis. For 164 of these cases missing information was on the session variable. A procedure was developed to predict whether a session would

be requested, and it worked quite well. Unfortunately, because the information on sessions and the information on the defendant's arrest record generally come from the same source (the prosecutor's file), estimated arrest records would have been required in a large number of cases. Moreover, an examination of the two subsamples (the 429 cases with information on the session variable and the 593 cases with information on all other variables) revealed that there were only miniscule changes in the relationships of the susceptibility and responsiveness variables with plea. Indeed, for the 429 cases the five susceptibility and responsiveness variables explain 17.8 percent of the variance in plea, while for the 593 cases they explain 17 percent of the variance. Given this, it was decided to proceed using the smaller sample and the more reliable set of indicators.

9. There was a mild amount of intercorrelation among the independent variables, making an exact determination of the importance of a variable impossible. This is, of course, one of the inherent difficulties with multiple regression. The only variables for which the proportion of variance explained varied significantly (more than one-half of a percentage point) were the indictments variable and the session variable. Depending upon when it was entered into the equation (before or after the session variable), 5 percent or 13.5 percent of the variance could be attributed to the indictments variable. Anywhere from 25 to 18.5 percent of the variance could be attributed to the session variable. The indictments variable was entered before the session variable because it was considered prior to it temporally and causally.

10. A question that cannot be answered is, How meaningful an indicator is the session variable? There is some basis for thinking that a defendant's decision to request a plea bargaining session is grounded in fact. This decision has, for example, a .30 correlation with the strength of the state's evidence measure. On the other hand, it has a .16 correlation with the discrete version of the defense counsel responsiveness scale, which indicates that the defense counsel had some impact upon the defendant's decision. Beyond this, however, a more significant question concerns the role of the psychological dimension of the defendant's susceptibility in the decision to request a plea bargaining session. It would seem that defendants who had a great deal of difficulty dealing with uncertainty would be more apt to request a session. Without some indicator of this dimension of susceptibility, however, it is impossible to assess its role in this analysis.

11. A breakdown of guilty plea rates by the discrete version of the defense counsel responsiveness scale reveals marked and expected differences in guilty plea rates:

Defense Counsel Code	Guilty Plea Rate
1	.43($n = 163$)
2	.56($n = 147$)
3 (public defender)	.61($n = 303$)
4	.86($n = 42$).

12. These results should not be construed to mean that defense counsel responsiveness has only a spurious relationship to the guilty plea variable. In a strictly temporal sense it can be said that the defense counsel variable is prior

only to the request for a bargaining session. A path analysis would show that the defense counsel has an indirect effect upon plea through the session variable. This notwithstanding, much more needs to be known about the dynamics of client recruitment and attorney selection in criminal courts before the defense counsel can be incorporated in a causal model of the plea process that meaningfully allocates the variance shared by the defense counsel and his client. For example, it has been known since the 1920s that private courtroom regulars receive a part of their caseloads through referrals by bailiffs, clerks, policemen, and so forth. What is not known, however, is whether these private attorneys recruit certain types of defendants (e.g., those who are amenable to manipulation). If they do, then part of the variation in guilty pleas attributed to defendant characteristics is in fact attributable to the defense counsel. Until these matters are clarified, a more precise view of the defense counsel's role in the plea process is not possible.

13. This discussion is based upon the premise that, in all cases coming into trial courts, efforts are made to negotiate a guilty plea. It is believed that enough resources are expended on a case by the time it reaches a trial court that, usually, a decision will not immediately be made to dismiss it. Rather, efforts will be made to negotiate a bargain. Any problems or deficiencies that may have arisen during the interval between the preliminary hearing court and the trial court are expected to be reflected in the state's bargaining position, in most instances. If negotiations fail, then the decision is made whether to pursue or dismiss the case. Courtroom observations lent support to this view.

This rather subtle point is emphasized here because it has analytical implications. The analysis of the decision to pursue will be done only on cases that were *not* plea bargained. The latter were simply excluded from the analysis. This procedure is the opposite of what was done in an analogous analysis on the same data base by James Eisenstein and Herbert Jacob in *Felony Justice: An Organizational Analysis of Criminal Courts* (Boston: Little, Brown, 1976), Chapter 9. They first attempted to discriminate between dismissed and pursued cases and then, eliminating dismissed cases, attempted to discriminate between guilty plea and trial cases.

14. It should be noted that the concept of the defendant's susceptibility is not expected to be relevant to the decision to pursue. This concept was considered relevant in the screening decision at the preliminary hearing level because it was expected that, once cases involving more susceptible defendants reached the trial courts, they would be easier to dispose of expeditiously through plea negotiations. The guilty plea analysis lent some support to this expectation. In this analysis, however, the decision is to dismiss the case or pursue it to trial. The expectation of an expeditious disposition has largely been lost, slow pleas playing a relatively minor role in Chicago. Hence, the relevance of the defendant's susceptibility becomes marginal. Empirical analyses confirmed this.

15. A third resistance indicator is the invocation of a jury trial, which will be used in the sentencing analysis. This indicator is inappropriate here because it is a component of the dependent variable.

16. In the preliminary hearing court analysis a variable depicting the existence of a legal motion was used as a dispute indicator. Here, information on the number of legal motions is considered a resistance indicator. The justification for the different interpretations given to similar phenomena lies with the differences in the setting of the two types of courts. It was argued earlier that general court cases not involving legal motions were more apt to be dismissed than others because they were more apt to involve personal disputes. This expectation was verified. In light of what has been said in this chapter, however, one might reinterpret that finding. That is, one could contend that preliminary hearing court judges are less apt to dismiss cases involving legal motions merely to discourage such types of activity. While this reinterpretation might have some validity, it is not believed to account for the findings reported in Chapter 6. At the preliminary hearing level, legal motions are not regarded with the disdain they are accorded at the trial level: they provide lower court participants with valuable information at an early stage of the proceedings. By the time a case reaches the trial courts a good deal about the case is already known *and* a preliminary decision has been made that a conviction is worth pursuing. Moreover, a good deal of resources has already been devoted to that end. Legal motions at the trial level can only impede efforts to secure convictions. Hence, they are viewed as violations of cordiality norms.

One last point needs to be made about the motions variable used in the trial court analysis. Because of its initially skewed distribution it was coded as follows: 0 or 1 motions were scored 0; 2 through 5 were scored 1; more than 5 were scored 2.

17. It should be mentioned that the same arguments made with regard to the motions variable can be made for the third indicator of resistance to cordiality norms—the invocation of a jury trial. The use of a jury trial is an indicator of resistance because of the amount of work it entails and the uncertainty it introduces.

18. Gerald C. Wright, Jr., "Linear Models for Evaluating Conditional Relationships," *American Journal of Political Science* 20 (March 1976):349-73. In this article Wright advocates introducing three variables into the regression equation. One (X_0) is a dummy variable reflecting group membership—in this case the confined variable (confined = 1, not confined = 0). The other two variables $(X_1$ and $X_2)$ are modified versions of the independent variable of interest, in this case the delay variable. The delay variable is modified as follows: X_1 is scored zero if the defendant is released and is given the score on the delay variable if the defendant is confined. X_2 is scored zero if the defendant is confined and is given the score on the delay variable if the defendant is released. The interpretation of the B coefficient for the three variables is as follows: the B coefficient for X_1 is the slope of the regression line for delay in confined cases; the B coefficient for X_2 is the slope of the regression line for delay in released cases; and the B coefficient for X_0 is the difference in the intercepts of the two regression lines.

19. The motions variable is not plagued by similar problems because the *immediate* outcome of motions is controlled by the judge. Courtroom regulars

cannot, however, control the consequences of stalling, although in some instances they may be able to put an end to stalling tactics.

20. Here, as in the preliminary hearing court analyses, the breakdown of the dependent variable was 30–70 (30 percent dismissed, 70 percent pursued) and was within the limits discussed by Cox (see Chapter 6, Note 11).

It should also be pointed out that, in addition to the technical problems involved with the use of a dummy pursued variable, conceptual problems exist. Most of the hypotheses with regard to the decision to pursue are phrased in terms of "apt to be pursued more vigorously," yet the pursued variable has only two categories. This equates a slow plea involving very little preparation with a jury trial requiring extensive preparation. Undoubtedly such measurement problems introduce considerable error into the analysis. Given the available data, however, there was no real alternative to the dummy variable approach. A trichotomous dependent variable was contemplated (0 = dismissal, 1 = bench trial, 2 = jury trial) but was considered inappropriate for the purposes of the analysis. It would have confused the state's decision to pursue the case with the defendant's decision to demand a jury trial.

21. All guilty plea cases were eliminated from the merged trial court samples.

22. Some intercorrelation was found between the interaction term and the motions variable ($r = .20$), which detracted somewhat from the strength of the interaction term. Before the motions variable was entered the F value of $X_1 X_2$ was 7.9 (significant beyond the .01 level) and its B coefficient was .60 (as opposed to the .40 reported in Equation 7.2). With the motions variable in the equation, $X_1 X_2$ is barely significant at the .05 level.

23. It should be emphasized that the choice of a bench or jury trial is not something sprung on the judge and prosecutor on the day of the trial. It is usually known well in advance of the trial's beginning.

24. As an aside, it should be mentioned that while the delay variables had no effect upon the pursued variable they were, like the dichotomized judge responsive variable, related to the decision to choose a jury trial over a bench trial. Defendants who employed stalling tactics were more likely to choose jury trials than bench trials, especially confined defendants. The motions variable was also positively related to the decision to request a jury trial ($r = .48$). These findings add strength to the interpretation of the motion and delay variables as resistance indicators. Together with the dichotomized version of the judge responsiveness variable, the motion and delay variables explained almost 38 percent of the variance in the decision to choose a jury trial over a bench trial ($R^2 = .376$, $n = 120$).

25. The two lowest categories in the discrete version of the defense counsel responsiveness scale were scored 0; the two highest categories, 1.

26. One consequence of the greater overall propensity to pursue cases involving nonregular defense attorneys is that the disparities in overall conviction rates across types of defense counsel, due to disproportionately high guilty plea rates in regular attorney cases, are mitigated. Despite this, there were still significant differences in the proportion of expeditious dispositions (guilty pleas +

dismissals) across the various categories of the discrete defense counsel responsiveness scale. These data are reported in the following table:

Types of Dispositions across Discrete Categories of Defense Counsel Responsiveness

	Defense Counsel Responsiveness			
	1	2	3	4
Proportion of guilty pleas	.43	.56	.61	.86
Conviction rate	.60	.69	.77	.88
Proportion of expeditious disposition (guilty pleas + dismissals)	.60	.76	.76	.95

❊ *Chapter 8*

Sentencing in the Trial Courts

When viewed in light of the entire felony disposition process in Chicago, the sentencing decision in the trial courts affects relatively few defendants.[1] Only about 12 percent of all defendants are sent to a trial court and only 60 percent of them are convicted. This decision is nonetheless a crucial one; it is a judgment that allocates one of the most basic political values—freedom. It is also a decision that important elements of the court's environment perceive to have significant implications for the protection of community values. The sentencing decision symbolizes, more than any other decision made by local criminal courts, the extent to which the community disapproves of the specific actions of a defendant.

Given the significance of sentencing decisions it is not surprising that most sentencing researchers have attempted to evaluate the types of interests and values reflected in them. Sociological studies of sentencing, for instance, have focused upon the role of class interests. Perhaps the primary question raised in these studies is: Does the dominant class in American society utilize the criminal process as a tool to oppress the lower classes?[2] Race and rather crude indicators of financial status have been used, quite unsuccessfully, to examine these notions as applied to disparities in sentencing. While political scientists have not done as much work on sentencing as have sociologists, the research they have done evidences a markedly different concern with the interests and values reflected in sentencing decisions. Political scientists tend to view criminal courts as extensions of the local political system; they have examined the effects of such things as elections, political culture, and the recruitment process upon the interests reflected in sentencing and other criminal court outputs.[3]

While scholars from different disciplines have approached the study of sentencing from fundamentally different perspectives, sentencing studies do share one basic feature. In their analyses of the various considerations reflected in sentencing decisions, sentencing researchers have consistently failed to include the interests of those who control the dispositional process, the courtroom elite. This has left a considerable void in our understanding of the sentencing decision because the court's sentencing power is an integral part of the dispositional strategy employed by the courtroom elite to process their work loads. Indeed, it is perhaps their most potent tool in their efforts to expeditiously perform the trial court's conviction procurement function. One cannot truly understand the sentencing decision independent of its role in this larger strategy.

SENTENCING: AN ORGANIZATIONAL PERSPECTIVE

The theoretical perspective being developed here can contribute much to our understanding of the sentencing decision. Several implications become clear if sentencing is viewed in light of its role within the courtroom elite's dispositional strategy. The most basic of these implications is that, in Chicago, the context of the sentencing decision in a guilty plea case is significantly different from that in a trial case.[4] Guilty plea cases represent situations where, from the perspective of the courtroom elite, the system has worked; trial cases largely represent situations where the system has not work.[5] For this reason it is expected that factors affecting sentencing in guilty plea cases will be fundamentally different from those affecting sentencing in trial cases, and must be treated separately.

Factors Affecting Sentencing After a Guilty Plea

Guilty plea cases represent situations in which the system worked, a satisficing disposition was achieved. In such cases the sentence is, in part, a reflection of the factors that make the system work. In the negotiation process there are certain realities that must be dealt with in order for a guilty plea to be obtained. Succinctly stated, these realities are that, in certain types of cases, one must be prepared to more readily grant concessions or exert more pressure than in others.

Also, it must be recognized that there are some criminal justice officials who are more inclined than others to utilize the powers under their control to achieve organizationally satisficing outcomes. Hence, here again the notions of organizational responsiveness and organizational susceptibility are expected to be relevant.

With regard to judges and prosecutors, it hypothesized that responsiveness will be negatively related to sentence in guilty plea cases. In an effort to induce guilty pleas, most judges and prosecutors in most cases will agree to give a defendant pleading guilty a significantly lighter sentence than that given a defendant convicted of a similar offense after a trial. However, because more responsive judges and prosecutors are more attuned to the desirability of expeditious dispositions than are less responsive judges and prosecutors, the former would be expected to offer more concessions more easily. The opposite expectation, however, holds for defense counsel responsiveness. While all defense counsel may value expeditious dispositional procedures to dispose of their cases, less responsive defense counsel are less dependent upon such procedures than are more responsive defense counsel. An occasional trial will not jeopardize the economic livelihood of a nonregular defense attorney. His ties are normally stronger to his clients than to members of the court organization. He usually does not share in, nor is he dependent upon, scheduling and other benefits enjoyed by regular defense counsel. Hence, he needs special inducements to persuade him to advise his clients to plead guilty. These inducements are expected to take the form of sentencing concessions, and it is hypothesized that defense counsel responsiveness will be positively related to sentence in guilty plea cases.

The expectations with regard to the defendant's organizational susceptibility are more straightforward. More susceptible defendants are generally in weaker bargaining positions than less susceptible defendants. A defendant with a long criminal record, for example, must take prosecutor threats of a long sentence after a trial much more seriously than a defendant with no criminal record. The latter can rely upon the leniency of a parole board, whereas the former cannot. A defendant who can afford an adequate defense at trial is in a better bargaining position than is a defendant who must deal with monetary pressures in addition to those emanating from the courtroom elite. Thus, it is expected that a defendant's susceptibility will be positively related to sentence after a guilty plea.

Organizational responsiveness and susceptibility are hypothesized to affect sentences in guilty plea cases in the manner outlined above because of the nature of the interest and power structure within the court organization. It is in the interest of the courtroom elite to expeditiously perform the trial court's conviction procurement functions; the factors outlined above are a reflection of the realities involved in the pursuit of that end. But, while these factors are thought to significantly affect sentencing after a guilty plea, to posit that the interests of the courtroom elite are the only, or even the primary, determinant of sentencing would be nonsensical. As is the case with most other organizations, the manner in which the court organization operates is significantly affected by external constraints.

At the sentencing stage, the greatest impact of external considerations is upon levels of sentencing for different offenses. Serious offenses must be dealt with more harshly than more trivial offenses. For example, a case involving a policeman murdered in the midst of an armed robbery must be dealt with more severely than one involving the theft of a dozen television sets from a local retailer; the latter case must be dealt with more severely than a case involving the theft of some necessities by a welfare mother. If the courtroom elite were to ignore these considerations, it would be courting external intervention. Sentencing patterns that are markedly and consistently irrational, from an external perspective, would lead to media exposés, public indignation, and, ultimately, legislative action curtailing judicial sentencing powers (flat-term sentences) or eliminating them completely (administrative sentencing boards). Any curtailment of judicial sentencing powers would drastically alter the ability of the elite to pursue its self-interests through the expeditious handling of cases. Hence, while the interests of the courtroom elite affect sentencing, the primary determinant of sentencing must be the seriousness of the case. To pursue any other strategy would, in the long run, lead to severe repercussions.

Before outlining the factors affecting sentencing after a trial, one last point needs to be made. While the factors discussed above are thought to affect sentencing after a guilty plea, they are not the only important factors. In addition, when dealing with complex situations, one must often control for the effects of certain factors in order to understand the real effects of other variables. Such is the case in the present situation. While differences in judges' concerns for the expeditious handling of cases may affect sentencing in guilty plea cases, so do other aspects of judges' psyches. In the observational phase of this study it was very evident that judges differed in their perceptions of the appropriate sentence for a given crime. This was confirmed in the empirical analysis. It also became clear, however, that the real effects of differences in judges' responsiveness could not be gauged without controlling for differences in their punitiveness.[6]

Hence, while judicial punitiveness is not an integral part of the theory being delineated here, an indicator of it will be used in the empirical examination of the theory.[7]

Factors Affecting Sentence After a Trial

The only factor thought to affect sentencing both after a trial and a guilty plea is the seriousness of the crime involved in the case. However, the impact of this factor is expected to be significantly different in each situation. The seriousness of the crime affects sentencing after a trial for the same reason it affects sentencing after a guilty plea—the need for decision making that is roughly rational from an external perspective. The form of the relationship between seriousness and sentencing in the two situations is expected to be different, however, because of internal factors. As was mentioned earlier, trials generally represent situations in which the interests of the courtroom elite were frustrated. To discourage such situations, costs—in the form of longer sentences for similar offenses—are imposed upon defendants who assert their right to a trial and are convicted. From an internal perspective this differential sentencing policy is necessary. If the decision to invoke a trial were costless, there would be little incentive for the defendant to plead guilty. This, in turn, would make it very difficult for the trial court work groups to expeditiously perform their conviction procurement function.

The other factors that were hypothesized to affect sentencing after a guilty plea are not relevant after a trial. They reflected certain realities that must be dealt with in the negotiation process to resolve the case in a satisficing manner. After a trial nothing remains to be negotiated. What is important at this stage, however, is the extent of the defendant's resistance to the courtroom elite's desires to expeditiously process cases. Some bench trials are merely "slow pleas"—make-believe trials with predetermined outcomes, performed merely to placate a recalcitrant defendant. They do little violence to the cordiality norms that usually prevail in trial courts. Sentences after these types of trials are not much more severe than those after a guilty plea. Other trials, however, are prolonged adversary affairs involving juries, legal motions, delaying tactics, and the like. These trials involve a great deal of preparation and uncertainty, and do violate cordiality norms. Thus, if convicted after a trial, defendants who frustrate the desires of the courtroom elite by invoking their right to a jury trial, making legal motions, or engaging in delaying tactics are expected to be sentenced more severely than other defendants.[8]

DATA ANALYSIS

To examine the various expectations just presented, convicted cases were separated into two groups—those pleading guilty and those convicted after a trial. Multiple regression, with sentence as the dependent variable, was then employed in conjunction with the relevant measures to test the relevant hypotheses in each set of cases.[9]

Sentencing in Guilty Plea Cases

The following equation explained 60 percent of the variance ($R^2 = .6003$) in 295 guilty plea cases.[10]

$$Y = -18.4 + X_1 + 5.8X_2 + 3.6X_3 - 4.2X_4 + 7.8X_5, \quad (8.1)$$

where

Y = Sentence in a guilty plea case
X_1 = Seriousness of the case
X_2 = Indictments variable
X_3 = Punitiveness of the judge
X_4 = Responsiveness of the judge (continuous version)
X_5 = Responsiveness of defense attorney (continuous version).

Table 8-1 contains other relevant data from the regression analysis.

Despite the fact that most of the variables used in the regression analysis were measured only crudely, the model does a fairly good job of explaining sentencing in guilty plea cases. All of the variables that had a significant effect upon sentence affected it in the predicted manner, and, as expected, case seriousness was the most important variable.[11] But, the above notwithstanding, neither the arrest record variable nor the prosecutor responsiveness variable had

Table 8-1. Essential Data on the Guilty Plea Sentencing Regression Analysis

Variable	Approximate Percentage of the Variance Accounted for	Beta Weight	F Value
X_1	46.0	.65	288.4
X_2	10.0	.22	33.5
X_3	1.0	.11	7.6
X_4	1.0	.10	6.0
X_5	2.0	.15	15.4

a significant effect upon sentencing, and the trichotomized SES variable had only indirect effects. To explore the implications of these results for the theoretical perspective espoused here, the impact, or lack thereof, of the susceptibility and responsiveness measures will be discussed at greater length.

The Susceptibility Measures. The indictments variable was the only susceptibility measure to have a direct impact upon sentencing, and its impact was quite strong. In a modal armed robbery case, for example, the guilty plea equation would predict a sentence of 39 months if there were no other indictments resolved in the plea, and if all other variables in the equation are accorded the mean.[12] If there were one other indictment, the predicted sentence would be about 45 months, and so on. While neither the arrest record nor the SES variable had a direct effect upon sentencing, the SES variable originally had a weak, but significant, association with sentencing ($r = -.13$, $F = 4.5$). Mild correlations between SES and case seriousness ($r = -.14$), as well as the judge punitiveness variable ($r = -.19$), however, wiped out the weak relationship between SES and sentence.

The failure of the arrest record and SES variables to directly affect sentencing is discouraging, although not as discouraging as it appears at first glance. First, as mentioned earlier, these two variables were much cruder indicators of their corresponding concepts than the indictments variable. Second, if these results are examined in light of the guilty plea analysis in Chapter 7, the failure of the arrest record and SES variables to affect sentencing is not inconsistent with the organizational perspective outlined earlier. As reported, with the attainment of a guilty plea conceptualized as a dummy variable (plea, no plea), the indictments and arrest record variables were positively related to the attainment of a plea, while the SES variable was negatively related to plea. Given these findings, it might well be the case that the effects of the defendant's susceptibility are more pronounced at an earlier stage of the dispositional process, which, in turn, mitigates its impact at the sentencing level. That is, it may not be possible to obtain higher guilty plea rates *and* substantially more severe sentences in cases involving defendants who are more susceptible to organizational pressures than are other defendants. It appears from the available data that tradeoffs are more likely to be made in favor of higher guilty plea rates than higher sentences—an outcome that is not surprising in light of the interest that the courtroom elite has in expeditiously processing cases. In any event, the crudity of the arrest record and SES measures, combined with the mitigating effects of actions taken at earlier stages of the dispositional process, appear to account for the failure of these variables to affect sentencing in guilty plea cases.

The Responsiveness Measures. While the prosecutor responsiveness variable had no effect upon the sentence in a guilty plea case, the judge and defense counsel responsiveness variables did.[13] Tables 8-2 and 8-3 contain predicted sentences in modal armed robbery cases for judges and defense counsel with different scores on their respective responsiveness scales.[14] As expected, more responsive judges were more apt to give lower sentences than were their less responsive colleagues. Moreover, less responsive defense counsel were more able to obtain lower sentences for their clients than were more responsive defense counsel, who are as dependent upon expeditious dispositional procedures as are judges and prosecutors.[15]

As in the case of the arrest record and SES variables, the failure of the prosecutor responsiveness variable to affect sentencing in guilty plea cases can be explained with reference to its impact upon the attainment of a plea. Although all three responsiveness variables were positively related to the attainment of a guilty plea, it was found that the prosecutor had a much stronger impact on the attainment of a plea than either the judge or defense counsel. The finding that the prosecutor responsiveness variable is strongly related to the attainment of a plea, while not related to sentencing after a plea, leads to a

Table 8-2. Impact of Judge's Responsiveness upon Predicted Sentence in Modal Armed Robbery Cases (in months)

	Judge Responsiveness Scores						
	1.00	1.69	2.16	2.95	3.30	3.63	4.81
Predicted armed robbery sentence	47.6	44.7	42.8	39.4	38.0	36.6	31.6

Table 8-3. Impact of Defense Counsel's Responsiveness upon Predicted Sentence in Modal Armed Robbery Cases (in months)

	Defense Counsel Responsiveness Scores				
	1.00	1.37	2.00*	2.24	4.00
Predicted armed robbery sentence	32.5	35.4	40.3	43.3	56.3

*Public defender cases

view of Chicago prosecutors as accommodators in the plea bargaining process. In Chicago, judges generally take a very active role in plea negotiations; defense counsel often bargain directly with them for sentencing concessions. This notwithstanding, however, most Chicago judges will not agree to a plea bargain opposed by the prosecutor. Hence, it appears that the role performed by highly responsive prosecutors is to create an environment conducive to expeditious bargaining by making "reasonable" offers and by agreeing to reasonable modifications of them proposed by judges and defense counsel. Less responsive prosecutors, on the other hand, make "unreasonable" offers and, apparently, are less inclined to agree to modifications of them. This type of accommodative role would account for the higher guilty plea rates of more responsive prosecutors and the failure of the prosecutor responsive variable to significantly affect sentence.

Sentencing in Trial Cases

The following equation explained 73 percent of the variance in 103 trial cases ($R^2 = .729$).[16]

$$Y = -13.3 + .68X_1 - 84.8X_2* + 3.1X_1X_2 + 38.6X_3 + .0007X_4^2, \qquad (8.2)$$

where

Y = Sentence in a trial case
X_1 = Seriousness of the first offense
X_2 = Type of trial (bench = 0; jury = 1)
X_3 = Number of legal motions (0, 1, 2)
X_4 = Delay variable for confined defendants only.[17]

Table 8-4 contains other relevant data for the regression analysis.

Seriousness of the First Offense and the Type of Trial Variable. The seriousness of the first offense variable was the central factor in the determination of sentence at the trial level. Like the case seriousness variable in Equation 8.1, this variable is a measure of the seriousness of the crime for which the defendant was convicted.

*This coefficient is negative only because of the presence of the interaction term, the trial variable's bivariate and net impact is positive.

Table 8-4. Essential Data on the Trial Sentencing Regression Analysis

Variable	Approximate Percentage of the Variance Account for	Beta Weight	F Value
X_1	30.0	.14	4.5 (41.2)*
X_2	17.0	−.25	5.6 (32.5)*
$X_1 X_2$	14.0	.64	29.7
X_3	2.0	.18	8.9
X_4^2	10.0	.35	34.5

*Figures in parentheses are F values before the interaction term was entered.

Although both variables play a similar role in the two equations, two crucial differences between them are important to note for analytical and theoretical reasons. First, it will be remembered that the case seriousness measure is nothing more than the seriousness of the first offense variable adjusted for various situational factors that also affect sentencing in guilty plea cases. In both guilty plea and trial cases, the seriousness of the first offense accounted for almost an identical proportion of the variance explained—30 percent. But if the offense seriousness variable was to be replaced by the case seriousness variable in the trial equation (Equation 8.2), the R^2 would drop by more than 10 percentage points. The reason for the drop is quite clear: none of the situational factors used in the computation of case seriousness significantly affect sentence after a trial. The value of situational variables as mitigating factors obviously diminishes when nothing remains to be negotiated.

An examination of the role played by the seriousness of the first offense in Equation 8.2 reveals a second important difference. In trial cases the determination of sentence takes place at significantly higher levels, for similar types of offenses, than in guilty plea cases. While the variance explained by the offense seriousness variable is similar in both types of cases, the B coefficient (slope) is markedly different. In guilty plea cases the B coefficient for the seriousness of the first offense is .8, while in trial cases it is about 2.7. Hence, if one were to predict a sentence solely upon the basis of offense, one would predict a significantly greater sentence in trial cases than in guilty plea cases.

Because trial cases were analyzed separately from guilty plea cases and the analysis produced markedly different results, the exact "cost" imposed upon defendants for asserting their right to trial is difficult to determine. The comparison of B coefficients for the seriousness of the first offense was useful for heuristic purposes, but it cannot validly be used to estimate sentencing differentials. Many other factors affect sentencing after a trial, and some modify the impact of the offense seriousness variable. To obtain a more accurate estimate of the cost differentials associated with trials, the following technique was employed: Predicted guilty plea sentences for each of the three modal types of offenses discussed earlier (Note 12) were computed by assigning the mean to all factors which affect sentencing in plea bargains. Predicted sentences in trial cases for *released* defendants were then computed by assigning the mean to the legal motions variable and letting the type of trial variable vary for each offense. This produced a conservative estimate of sentence (see Table 8-5) for each of the three offenses when, at the relevant stage, all factors affecting sentence (except mode of disposition) were controlled.[19] The resulting differences are then attributable to differences in the mode of disposition; they can be interpreted as reasonable estimates of the cost assessed by the courtroom elite for the extra expenditure of resources required in nonexpeditious dispositions.[20]

An examination of Table 8-5 reveals that the sentence differentials between bench trials and jury trials are generally greater than the differentials between guilty pleas and bench trials. In addition, the size of the differential varies directly with the seriousness of the offense. The differential between bench trials and jury trials is generally greater than the differential between guilty pleas and bench trials because of internal considerations discussed earlier. Jury trials are much more exacting than bench trials. They require much more preparation and entail much more risk. Moreover, many bench trials are merely slow pleas that require little more preparation than a guilty plea.

The costs of exercising the right to trial, especially a jury trial, vary with the seriousness of the offense because of both external and internal considerations. There are limits—legal and otherwise—to the sanctions that can be imposed upon a defendant convicted of a given crime. These constraints are much more stringent for less serious

Table 8-5. Impact of Mode of Disposition upon Predicted Sentences in Modal Cases for Released Defendants (in months)

	Guilty Plea	Bench Trial	Jury Trial
Predicted murder sentence	86.6	109.3	407.7
Predicted armed robbery sentence	39.2	63.7	154.6
Predicted sale of heroin sentence	26.5	49.3	72.8

offenses like burglary, theft, and robbery (where legal ranges may vary from probation to four years) than for more serious offenses such as murder (where the legal range may vary from probation to life imprisonment). Internal considerations also lead to a costing strategy that varies with the seriousness of the offense. For purposes of organizational maintenance, offenses most threatening to the community must be pursued most vigorously. To stave off external criticism and interference, high conviction rates for armed robbery, rape, and murder cases are far more important than high conviction rates for theft, forgery, and marijuana cases. To ensure high conviction rates in important categories of offenses, the differential costing strategy, captured in Table 8-5, is used to induce less risky and more expeditious dispositional modes (guilty pleas and bench trials) in more serious cases.

The Legal Motions Variable. The motions variable had a bivariate correlation with sentence in trial cases of almost .5 ($r = .49$). However, substantial correlations between it and the offense seriousness variable ($r = .30$) and the type of trial variable ($r = .43$) considerably reduced its net contributions to the analysis. Despite this, the size of the B coefficient ($B = 38.6$) of the motions variable indicates that even after controlling for these other factors, the defendant's decision to assert legal defenses in his behalf is a costly one. A released defendant who was convicted of a modal armed robbery case after a bench trial, and who made one or no legal motions, would receive a sentence of 25.1 months on the basis of Equation 8.2.[20] The same defendant would receive about 64 months if he made between two to five motions and about 102 months if he made more than five motions.

The Delay Variable. The B coefficient for the delay variable in Equation 8.2 (.0007) is deceptively low because a quadratic term was used to capture the effects of delay upon sentence. Its very significant impact upon sentence (especially in cases involving long delays) is better conveyed in Table 8-6. An examination of Table 8-6 reveals a second important point: confined defendants whose cases are disposed of quickly do not receive substantially longer sentences than released defendants. One last point should be made with regard to delay. Despite the fact that cases involving released defendants generally took longer to dispose of than cases involving confined defendants, the delay variable in released cases had no effect upon sentence. This is because, as alluded to earlier, the responsibility for the delay in released cases is not as clear-cut as it is in confined cases. However, it is also important to note that the findings reported here

Table 8-6. Impact of Confined Delay Variable upon Predicted Sentence in Modal Armed Robbery Cases (in months)

	Delay					
	0 (Released Defendants)	108 Days	147 Days	194 Days	239 Days	362 Days
Predicted armed robbery sentence	63.7	71.8	78.8	90.0	103.6	155.4

do not mean that released defendants do not engage in stalling tactics or that they are not sanctioned for employing such tactics. Rather, the findings merely reflect the fact that before these phenomena can be captured in a regression equation, the responsibility for delay in released cases must be partitioned between the defense and the prosecution.

Trial Sentencing Reexamined

The picture painted by the trial regression analysis is quite grim. Defendants who resist efforts by the courtroom elite to maintain a cordial atmosphere and expeditiously process cases appear to be sanctioned quite severely. Because of the rather negative connotations of this analysis, an effort was made to reexamine the analysis from a somewhat different perspective. It was believed that if the impact of various resistance indicators (especially the jury trial and motions variable) upon the sentence variable was really reflective of informal sanctioning, their impact would vary with courtroom work loads. During periods when the judge and prosecutor are under pressure due to increased caseloads, the problems associated with the invocation of jury trials and the use of legal motions are enhanced. Hence, it is expected that defendants who resist expeditious processing would be more severely sanctioned during periods when caseloads are high than when they are low. What is expected then is an interactive relationship between work loads and the jury trial and motions variable.[21]

Fortunately some quite reliable data on courtroom work loads were available.[22] In the judge-oriented data base with the judge-month as the unit of analysis (see Chapter 5), data on the number of cases on a judge's docket in each of the eighteen months spanned in this study were available. There was a good deal of variance in these caseloads. They ranged from a low of 109 cases to a high of 559 (mean = 282). For the purpose of this analysis the work load variable was trichotomized.[23]

Equation 8.3 and Table 8-7 report the results of the reexamination ($R^2 = .77$, $n = 95$).[24]

Table 8-7. Essential Data on the Second Trial Sentencing Regression Analysis

Variable	Approximate Percentage of the Variance Accounted for	Beta Weight	F Value	
X_1	30.0	.12	3.5	(40.2)*
X_2	19.0	−.19	3.5	(34.8)*
$X_1 X_2$	13.0	.61	27.4	
X_3	2.0	−.15	1.1	(9.6)*
X_4	10.0	.34	31.5	
X_5	1.0	−.07	.62	(4.6)*
$X_3 X_5$	2.0	.42	7.0	

*Figures in parentheses are F values before the interaction term was entered.

$$Y = 12.6 + 59X_1 - 70.8X_2* + 3.0X_1 X_2 - 33.6X_3* + .0007X_4^2 - 15.5X_5* + 41.5X_3 X_5, \quad (8.3)$$

where

Y = Sentence in a trial case
X_1 = Seriousness of the first offense
X_2 = Type of trial (bench = 0; jury = 1)
X_3 = Number of legal motions (0, 1, 2)
X_4 = Delay variable for confined defendants only
X_5 = Trichotomous caseload variable.

As is evident, the expectations were only partially realized. While the interaction term involving the caseloads variable and the jury trial variable was not significant, the interaction term involving the caseload variable and the motions variable was well beyond the .01 level. Table 8-8 reports predicted sentences (in a modal armed robbery case involving a released defendant convicted after a jury trial) for the three categories of the motions variable in each of the three categories of the caseload variable. As documented in Table 8-8, the impact of the motions variable upon sentence is much greater when caseloads are high then when they are low. The predicted differential in sentence due to variations the motions variable (between 0 and 2) is 57.4 months when caseloads are low, but 181.8 months when

*These B coefficients are negative only because of the presence of the interaction term, the bivariate and net impact of the variables is positive.

Table 8-8. Impact of Motions Variable upon Predicted Sentence in Modal Armed Robbery Cases Across Categories of the Caseload Variable (in months)

Motions Variable =	Caseload = Low			Caseload = Medium			Caseload = High		
	0	1	2	0	1	2	0	1	2
Predicted armed robbery sentence	129.1	137.1	186.5	113.7	163.1	212.5	98.7	189.5	280.5

caseloads are high. Thus it appears that when work loads are more pressing, defendants are sanctioned more severely for violating cordiality norms. The results reported in Equation 8.3 and Table 8-8 lend strong support to the initial interpretation of the trial sentencing analysis.

NOTES

1. It should be emphasized that, while sentencing decisions are also made by the preliminary hearing court judges when a defendant pleads guilty to an information, this chapter will deal exclusively with the trial courts. While the 144 cases in the information sample provided enough cases to analyze sentencing in "information" cases, not enough was known about the types of cases disposed of by informations to meaningfully utilize this sample. We were not permitted to observe plea bargaining sessions in the lower level courts. Moreover, the preliminary hearing court samples yield too few informations to meaningfully distinguish them from other types of cases.

2. This conflict-oriented perspective is delineated most elaborately in Richard Quinney, *The Social Reality of Crime* (Boston: Little, Brown, 1970).

3. Two of the most interesting political analyses of sentencing are Herbert Jacob, "Politics and Criminal Prosecution in New Orleans," *Tulane Studies in Political Science* 8 (1963): 77-98, and Martin Levin, *Urban Politics and the Criminal Courts* (Chicago: University of Chicago Press, 1977). Jacob compares sentences as well as other criminal court outputs in the administration of a machine-oriented state's attorney with those of a reform-minded state's attorney. Levin compares sentences in Minneapolis (a good government city with a reformed judicial recruitment process) with those in Pittsburgh (a traditional city with a politicized recruitment process).

4. See Chapter 3 for the treatment of the sentencing decision in a more complex, slow plea system.

5. One cannot say, without qualification, that all trial cases represent instances in which the system has failed. Occasional trials serve symbolic functions. In highly publicized cases a formal trial may be the most desirable form of disposition. No one has to take responsibility for the outcome of the case, and

220   The Empirical Analysis

the system appears to be working properly when under public scrutiny. Occasional trials also reinforce the virtues of cordiality in the minds of the participants. Aside from these exceptional situations, however, real trial cases (i.e., not slow pleas) are generally viewed as undesirable and dysfunctional by most participants most of the time.

6. The reason for this appears to be that younger judges in the sample tended to be more punitive as well as more responsive than older judges.

7. The derivation of the judge punitiveness scale was quite involved and, because it is only tangentially related to the thrust of this analysis, will only be dealt with in this note.

No attitudinal data were available to construct this scale, so several of the output indicators in the judge-oriented data bases were employed in a multistep procedure. First, four output indicators were used to compute an unadjusted punitiveness scale—the average conviction rate of a judge over the twenty-four month period $\left(\text{conviction variable} = \dfrac{\text{average number of convictions}}{\text{average number of dispositions}} \right)$; the average proportion of convicted defendants a judge sent to the penitentiary $\left(\text{penitentiary variable} = \dfrac{\text{average number of defendants sent to penitentiary}}{\text{average number of convictions}} \right)$; the average dismissal rate $\left(\text{dismissal variable} = \dfrac{\text{average number of dismissals}}{\text{average number of dispositions}} \right)$; and the average probation rate $\left(\text{probation variable} = \dfrac{\text{average given probation}}{\text{average number of convictions}} \right)$. An examination of the distribution of the variables used to construct each of these mean score variables, in the file of data where judge-month was the unit of analysis, indicated that for the most judges the four mean score variables employed here were, in fact, reasonable indicators of central tendency (i.e., there was not a good deal of variation in these variables for most judges over the twenty-four month period). The unadjusted punitiveness scores were then computed in the following manner:

Unadjusted Punitiveness Scores = Z (conviction variable * penitentiary variable) − Z (dismissal variable * probation variable) (Z indicates variables are in standard form).

While the above procedure may appear somewhat confusing, it makes sense when two factors are considered. First, it must be recognized that there are three major types of sentences given by trial court judges in Chicago: penitentiary commitments (for defendants confined over a year), detention in county-level facilities (for defendants confined for a period not exceeding a year), and probation. It must also be recognized that some judges will acquit or dismiss a case involving a defendant whom they consider undeserving of punishment. This makes it necessary to include dismissal and conviction rates in calculations of punitiveness scores when using the types of data employed here. Judges who convict a high proportion of cases *and* send a high proportion of convicted defendants to the penitentiary are considered to be the most punitive. This is reflected in the first term of the unadjusted punitiveness algorithm. Judges who dismiss a high proportion of cases *and* who have high probation rates are considered to be less punitive judges. This is reflected in the second term of the algorithm. Either of these terms could be used individually as an indicator of punitiveness, were it not for the fact that some judges send a considerable proportion of convicted defendants to county-level detention centers for short periods of confinement. This procedure used here takes this into account, as illustrated by the following example.

Consider two judges with identical conviction rates, penitentiary rates, and dismissal rates, but different probation rates. Under these circumstances, the only way for the two judges to have different probation rates is if they send different proportions of convicted defendants to county-level detention centers. The judge who sends a *higher* proportion of convicted defendants to county-level detention centers will receive a *lower* score in the second term in the algorithm used to compute the unadjusted punitiveness score. This, in turn, will be reflected in a *higher* unadjusted punitiveness score. This is appropriate because county-level detention is considered to be a more severe form of punishment than probation.

One last step was used in the derivation of the judge punitiveness scores. The unadjusted punitiveness scores were adjusted for differences in the average seriousness of cases assigned to different judges. To estimate these differences, the case seriousness variable was broken down by trial judge in the merged trial court sample. This sample, it will be remembered, is a sample of cases processed by trial court judges during the same time frame in which the information used to compute the unadjusted punitiveness scores was compiled. The average case seriousness scores, derived from the trial court sample, were then added to the judge file. The following procedure was then used to adjust the punitiveness scores for differences in the average seriousness of cases:

Judge Punitiveness Score = Z (unadjusted punitiveness variable) $-$ Z (average case seriousness variable).

In this way, judges scoring above the mean on the adjusted punitiveness variable and above the mean on the average case seriousness variable had their scores reduced, and so on.

    8. Each of these three resistance indicators was discussed more thoroughly in Chapter 7.

    9. In Illinois, sentences must be given in ranges (two to four years, three to nine years, etc.). Thus, the dependent variable was measured by taking the average of the maximum and minimum. Probation cases were scored zero, since no time is actually spent in jail.

    10. Initially there were 378 trial cases that resulted in guilty pleas. Of these 378, 73 had missing data—largely because responsiveness and punitiveness scores were available only for regular judges, not standins or new judges. Also, 9 extreme guilty plea cases were eliminated—3 were extremely low, 6 were extremely high. The elimination of the 9 cases did not have much effect upon the R^2, but with the extremes removed the B coefficients were much more stable.

11. There are some problems related to using the case seriousness measure in the guilty plea sentencing analysis because the sentence in these cases was used to assign weights to the variables used to compute case seriousness. But, it should be emphasized, the problems are merely interpretational. Despite initial impressions the use of the case seriousness variable in this analysis is not circular and it does not inflate the proportion of variance explained. The same results could have been obtained if a "set" approach had been used to control for factors related to the crime involved in the case. In other words, the offense variables and the situational indicators could have been defined as variables related to the crime with which the defendant had been charged. If this "set" of variables had been entered on the first step of a stepwise multiple regression analysis (with the sentence as the dependent variable), it would have explained exactly the same proportion of variance as the case serious variable. Moreover, the residuals would have been identical. Instead of controlling for case seriousness, the latter approach might more aptly be described as controlling for factors relevant to the commission of the crime. It is, in effect, the approach used by Eisenstein and Jacob in *Felony Justice*. The case seriousness variable was used here because it was more consistent with the earlier analyses and was more straightforward.

One last point should be made with regard to the use of this measure in the sentencing analysis. Because crime-related factors were allowed to explain as much variance in sentencing as they could before other factors were entered into the analysis, and because the crime-related factors were then combined into a very powerful composite-variable, this procedure may well inflate the amount of explained variance *attributable* to the case seriousness variable. If, for example, some of the variance explained by the defendant's sex could also be attributed to the defense counsel, this procedure, by allowing case-related variables to enter first, will attribute that variance to case seriousness. This is, of course, wholly justifiable. It is a statistically conservative approach in light of the analysis undertaken. For any of the judge or defense counsel or prosecutor variables to be statistically significant, it must explain variance beyond what can be accounted for by case-related characteristics.

12. By a modal armed robbery case is meant a case where, in the indictment sampled, a male was charged with committing one count of armed robbery against another male while sober. These cases are referred to as modal armed robbery cases because, when all factors affecting case seriousness are considered (see Chapter 5), there were more armed robberies with the above-mentioned characteristics than any other combination of characteristics. Modal armed robbery cases, along with modal murder and sale of heroin cases (which were defined in the same manner as modal armed robbery cases), will be used at several points in the analysis to demonstrate the predicted impact of various variables. Modal case categories are useful devices for displaying predicted differences in sentences because they allow one to control for relevant case characteristics without extrapolating too far beyond the actual data base—a real danger when using regression equations to predict outcomes.

13. Because of the manner in which public defenders were included in the sentencing analysis, one might argue that part of the variance attributed to the

defense counsel responsiveness variable is more appropriately attributable to the indigent nature of public defenders' clients. In other words, one might argue that public defender cases get longer sentences than some other types of cases because of the indigent status of their clients, not because of the public defender's relationship to the court organization. All that can be said to such a criticism is that, while this might be the case, when the SES variable is introduced into the analysis the impact of public defenders is not substantially affected.

14. These predicted sentences, like all others in this analysis, are computed using Equation 8.1 with all variables assigned the mean, except the variable being examined. It should be noted, however, that the differences attributed to judge responsiveness scores in Table 8-2 are slightly inflated. This is because there was a mild positive correlation ($r = .19$) between the punitiveness scale (which was positively related to sentence) and the responsiveness scale (which was negatively related to sentence).

15. In light of these findings and the predicted sentences in Tables 8-2 and 8-3, it would seem that some of the claims made by Eisenstein and Jacob in *Felony Justice* are questionable. After noting that their judge variables (a set of dummy variables representing each judge in each sample) and a dummy defense counsel variable (public defender, private) significantly affected sentence length only in Baltimore, they state, "Thus much of the sentencing disparity that other studies emphasize was apparently absent from these cities [Baltimore, Chicago, and Detroit]. These findings also conflict with the beliefs of courtroom participants," (p.285). Using their Chicago data base, it can be said that in Chicago guilty plea cases the judge and defense counsel handling a case did make a significant difference in sentencing and disparities did exist.

Two differences in our analyses apparently explain these different conclusions. First, by focusing upon those attributes of the judge and defense counsel that concern their relationship to the court organization, this study provides a more refined approach than the dummy variable approach adopted by Eisenstein and Jacob. Because some of the judges' outlooks are very similar to those of other judges, the dummy variable approach suppresses the amount of variance actually attributed to the judge. Moreover, much explanatory power is lost when all private attorneys are lumped into one category, as Table 8-3 demonstrates. A second important difference in our analyses lies in the fact that here guilty plea cases were separated from trial cases. This was done because, as was argued earlier, different types of factors are relevant for sentencing decisions made after a trial than for those made in the context of a bargain. The payoff of this strategy is evident when the results of the guilty plea analysis are compared with the results reported by Eisenstein and Jacob. Because bargaining positions are so much more important in guilty plea cases than in trial cases (where nothing remains to be bargained), factors related to relative bargaining positions more readily emerge when the extraneous trial cases are removed from the analysis.

16. There were 110 convictions at the trial level in the sample, but seven were eliminated because of missing values.

17. It should be noted that, using Wright's technique for analyzing conditional relationships (see Note 18, Chapter 7), the only delay variable which had a

significant impact upon sentence was the delay variable for confined defendants (X_1). The delay variable for released defendants (X_2) and the dummy variable depicting the difference between the intercepts (X_0) were not statistically significant. Because these two variables were insignificant *and* because their exclusion did *not* affect the B coefficient of X_1 or its interpretation, they were excluded from the analysis and are not reported in Equation 8-2. The diagram below depicts the relationship between the delay variables and sentence.

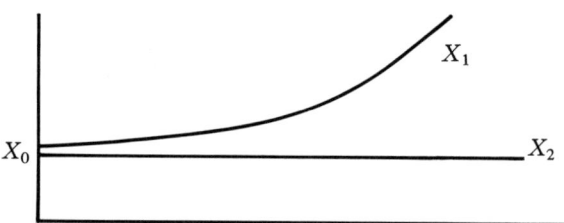

X_0 = Difference between the intercepts of the two regression lines
X_1 = Regression line for delay in confined cases
X_2 = Regression line for delay in released cases.

18. A different approach could have been used to compute predicted trial sentences by employing the mean delay score for confined defendants. This would have added about thirty months to each of the predicted trial sentences reported in Table 8-5.

19. These results again conflict with those obtained in *Felony Justice* by Eisenstein and Jacob, who state, "Disposition mode—the manner in which a defendant was convicted—makes little difference when other characteristics of the case are taken into account. Apparently, in these three cities, defendants convicted by a bench or jury trial were not given longer prison sentences than those who pleaded guilty," (p. 282). This is wholly inconsistent with the results reported here and displayed in Table 8-5. Moreover, the reasons for the differences again appear to be largely methodological. First, Eisenstein and Jacob analyze sentence length by eliminating all probation cases; in this analysis they were included and coded as 0 because no time was to be spent in prison. Their approach suppresses the impact of the disposition mode variable in the analysis because probation is rarely given after a jury trial. Twenty-five percent of all defendants pleading guilty were given probation; 22 percent convicted after a bench trial; and only 5 percent after a jury trial.

Second, besides eliminating the least severe sentences from their analysis of sentence length, Eisenstein and Jacob also perform a natural log transformation upon the dependent variable. While this linearizes the relationship, it also has the effect of "pulling down" the extreme cases. This has significant implications for the disposition mode variable because, in the Chicago instance at least, most of these extreme cases were trial cases. The dependent variable used here ranged from 0 to 720. In guilty plea cases, however, the range was only from 0 to 174. The sixteen extreme cases (which ranged from 210 to 720) were all trial cases and constituted about 15 percent of all trial cases analyzed. An example will clarify the implications of using a natural log transformation in such a situation. The natural log of 50 is 3.9, the natural log of 100 is 4.6, and the natural log of 150 is 5.0. But the natural log of 220 is only 5.5, and the natural log of 500 is only 6.2. Clearly one of the effects of Eisenstein and Jacob's use of the natural log transformation, in the Chicago case at least, was to rob the disposition mode variable of much of its explanatory power.

A final methodological difference is that while Eisentstein and Jacob assume a linear relationship between disposition mode and sentence, this analysis employs a nonlinear model. Moreover, it is very clear, for reasons outlined in the text, that the real impact of disposition mode cannot be understood independent of the seriousness of the case. The interaction term involving seriousness and type of trial contributed an additional 14 percent of explained variance to the analysis. (Parenthetically, it should be noted that this analysis emphasizes an advantage which the composite offense seriousness variable has over the approach used by Eisenstein and Jacob to control for offense. Only one interaction term was required to capture the joint effect of offense seriousness and type of trial. If a set of dummy offense variables had been employed, an interaction term for every dummy variable would have been required).

On a substantive level it should be noted that Eisenstein and Jacob admit that there are differences in sentences after a trial and after a guilty plea; they attribute these differences to differences in the characteristics of cases. I would agree with this position to a point. But where they would argue that the important differences relate to the types of offenses and circumstances surrounding the offenses, I would argue that the basic differences between the two sets of convicted cases (those convicted after a trial and those pleading guilty) relate to differences in the defendant's and defense counsel's orientation to the process. Those inclined to buck the system are more apt to go to trial, while others are more inclined to plead guilty. Those that buck the system and are convicted are sanctioned.

These individuals' orientations are not, of course, the only important determinants of the decision to request a trial. This is not, however, the place for an extensive treatment of the question. What is important to note is that the position taken here is that the differences between the two sets of convicted cases are not such that the sentencing differentials reported in Table 8-5 can be legitimized by reference to them, and that disposition mode does make a difference in sentencing.

20. It is important to note that this figure is actually lower than the predicted sentence of a modal armed robbery guilty plea case (Table 8-5). This, of course, indicates that a released defendant who requests a bench trial, and engages in no other form of resistance, is sentenced at about the same level, or lower than, a defendant who pleads guilty. The same is not true, however, for most confined defendants. What this finding may reflect, of course, is that many bench trials involving no other form of resistance are merely "slow pleas."

21. These hypotheses exclude the delay variable because defendant stalling tactics do not entail additional work for prosecutors and judges to the extent that jury trials and legal motions do. Stalling tactics endanger the courtroom

226 The Empirical Analysis

elite's control over the ultimate outcome of a case but do not require the formal preparation which the other forms of resistance do.

22. It should be noted that the role of workloads in other facets of the felony disposition process in Chicago are examined elsewhere. See Peter F. Nardulli with Kathleen Proch, "The Caseload Controversy and the Study of Criminal Courts" (unpublished mimeograph). This paper reviews the role of work loads in the study of criminal courts and empirically examines the "work load hypothesis" in a number of different ways. The failure of variations in work loads to have the significant effects that are traditionally attributed to them is analyzed in light of the general arguments developed in this work.

23. Cases sentenced in months when caseloads ranged from 109 to 239 were scored 1; cases sentenced in months when caseloads ranged from 240 to 313 were scored 2. Those higher than *313* were scored 3.

24. Eight cases were lost due to missing values on the caseload variable, but the B coefficients and other important facets of the regression analysis remained quite stable, as a comparison with Equation 8.2 and Table 8-4 will demonstrate.

Postscript

This book has tried to develop the thesis that certain institutional characteristics of criminal courts—their elitist power structure and closely knit interest structure—have important implications for how they process their work loads. Earlier traditions in the study of criminal courts did not recognize these implications and, in different ways, their analyses suffered. Chapter 3 argued that one consequence of these institutional characteristics is that there are important parallels between how criminal courts process their work loads and how other organizations handle theirs. Several relevant notions in the literature on organizational behavior were integrated into a mode of analysis thought to be applicable to the study of criminal courts, and some hypothetical examples were used to demonstrate its potential contributions.

The organizational mode of analysis was then used to examine the operations of the felony court system in Chicago during 1972-73. Chapter 4 discussed some of the problems involved in extending the rather abstract, macro-level ideas discussed in Chapter 3 to a micro-level study of one system at one point in time. It outlined the structure of the felony court system in Chicago and discussed some of the organizationally relevant dimensions of its inputs, personnel, and dispositional tools. Chapter 5 described the data collected during the observational phase of this project and the approaches used to measure some of the concepts introduced in Chapter 4.

The empirical chapters (6, 7, and 8) outlined the types of tasks performed by the different courtroom workgroups—degradation ceremonies, informal sanctioning, socialization and training, defense counsel placement, screening, conviction procurement, and sentencing—as well as how they were performed and how they related to one another. In some instances, using the samples and measures described in Chapter 5, quantitative analyses of certain facets of courtroom operations were undertaken. These analyses were limited by the crudeness of the available measures as well as certain statistical problems encountered (heteroscedasticity). But, where the heteroscedasticity problem was minimal (the guilty plea analysis) and where the data conformed more closely to other assumptions (e.g., interval-level measures) underlying multiple regression (the sentencing analyses), the predictive power of the model was moderate to strong.

Despite the statistical problems encountered in the screening analysis, it is clear that the dispositional value of a case is an important screening criterion. It appeared, however, to be more important in the general courts than in the drug courts. The nature of the dispute invovled also appeared to be an important screening criterion in the general felony courts, although the dispute indicators were quite crude. In the drug courts the defendant's susceptibility and the defense counsel's responsiveness played a much more significant role than in the general courts. It was argued that the differences in the screening criteria employed in the two types of courts arose from differences in their immediate setting. These differences led to a less open system in the drug courts, which permitted drug court personnel greater flexibility in manipulating internal processes.

An example of this flexibility was documented empirically. It was demonstrated that drug court personnel attempt to use bail as a tool to manage caseloads. Confined defendants—especially those represented by regular defense counsel—are often persuaded to plead guilty to a misdemeanor in exchange for a sentence equal to the time they have already spent in jail. Some defendants resist such bargains and ultimately have their cases dismissed, but only after an extended stay in a local detention center. The period of incarceration in these cases often exceeded the normal sentence given in exchange for a misdemeanor guilty plea, and this was viewed as an integral part of the informal sanctioning process in the preliminary hearing courts.

At the trial level it was found that all the responsiveness and susceptibility measures were related, directly or indirectly, to the attainment of a plea, although none but the indictments variable had a particularly strong effect. More significant problems were encountered in the analysis of the decision to pursue a case to trial. Of the expected relationships, only those relating to the case's dispositional value and the legal motions variable were verified empirically. Extended analyses of the role of the judge and defense counsel indicated much work needs to be done on the post-negotiation phases of the dispositional process. The sentencing analysis, however, provided some of the most valuable empirical insights of the study. It demonstrated not only that sentences were generally lower after a guilty plea than after a trial, but also that different criteria were used in each type of sentencing situation. After a guilty plea, factors related to bargaining positions were important. What was important after a trial conviction, however, was the extent of the defendant's resistance to cordiality norms. Like incarcerated drug court defendants, trial court defendants who resisted the courtroom elite's efforts to manage caseloads effectively were sanctioned severely.

It should be remembered, and emphasized, that these results were the product of a study of one criminal court system at one point in time; their generalizability is subject to the provisos discussed in Chapter 4. Nonetheless, the empirical chapters demonstrate that the application of the mode of analysis developed in Chapter 3 can produce valuable insights into the operations of criminal courts. It is believed that the extension of this perspective to other court systems can contribute to a more generalized understanding of how criminal courts handle their work loads (i.e., dispense justice). It can also lead to a better understanding of how these institutions can be made more responsive to the ideals embodied in due process of the law, the expectations of the communities they serve, and the needs of the defendants they process. The concluding sections below discuss the implications of the perspective developed here for the direction of future research and the structure of criminal court reform.

IMPLICATIONS FOR THE DIRECTION OF FUTURE RESEARCH

If Chapter 3 is viewed in light of the empirical chapters in this work and other organizationally oriented studies of criminal courts, several implications for the direction of future criminal court research emerge. First, it is clear that there is a need for comparative inquiry into the operations of criminal courts. Case studies such as this cannot examine many of the lines of inquiry suggested in the last section of Chapter 3. Just as clear as the need for comparative inquiry, however, is that before meaningful comparative inquiry can be undertaken, a well-planned series of intensive case studies is needed. Such case studies are important because before this mode of analysis can be used in a truly comparative, broadly based analysis of criminal courts, certain extensions and refinements are necessary.

Case Studies

The contemplated series of case studies should be conducted in jurisdictions that vary significantly in terms of their setting. While a good deal of thought needs to be given to the important dimensions of setting, some of the most obvious include: type of indigent defense system, nature of complaint-initiation mechanism (prosecutor initiated versus police initiated), structure of the relationship between lower courts and trial courts (integrated versus separate systems), case assignment procedures (stable versus unstable), personnel assignment procedures, and types of jurisdiction (felony, misdemeanor, quasi-criminal, mixed). Indeed, at this point in the study of criminal courts, a comprehensive overview of variations in criminal court settings would be an important contribution in itself.

Case studies like these could lead to many refinements in the organizational perspective proposed here. Some are essential to the comparative study of courts; others are not. The greatest contribution these studies could make to the comparative study of courts would be a better understanding of the notion of dispositional strategy. They could provide more comprehensive and systematic analyses of the types of tasks performed in the processing of criminal cases than was provided here, as well as of the types of factors affecting the performance of those tasks. These case studies could shed considerable light on how dispositional strategies differ in various settings and the implications of these differences for the processing of criminal cases, as well as for the study of criminal court operations. A typology of dispositional strategies might even emerge.

Another contribution would be conceptual and methodological refinements in the framework used here. Others would not only offer more refined definitions of such concepts as dispositional value, susceptibility, and responsiveness, but would introduce other concepts that, from an organizational perspective, are meaningful for various aspects of courtroom operations. In turn, these refinements and supplements could lead to a clearer specification of the role of organizational considerations in the performance of various tasks.

In addition, the thoughtful integration of observational, file, questionnaire, and interview data could lead to more refined measures of various concepts. For example, systematic observations of the behavior of judges, prosecutors, and public defenders, if combined with loosely structured interviews and some questionnaire data, could lead to more refined responsiveness measures for these individuals. In many court systems, the clerk of the circuit court keeps a file of appearances. Data culled from this file on the frequency of appearances of private defense attorneys could provide a sounder base for a participation scale than the data used here. This information could be supplemented by questionnaire data. Complete access to prosecutor and probation files would be necessary before truly refined measures of case level attributes such as dispositional value and susceptibility could be developed. The use of these refined measures in conjunction with more advanced and sophisticated methods of data analysis could lead to a better assessment of the power of the proposed organizational mode of analysis.

One last contribution of these case studies could be the integration of this perspective with other theoretical frameworks. Theoretical approaches to the study of criminal courts have been scarce. But approaches focusing upon the role of judicial backgrounds, attitudes, and role perceptions offer promise. The integration of these various bodies of thought, roughly along the lines suggested in Chapter 3, could enhance our understanding of criminal court phenomena, leading to insights that no single approach can produce independently.

Comparative Studies

Comparative studies of the operation of criminal courts are essential to the development of a systematic, generalized understanding of how these entities process criminal cases, as well as how they respond to the environments within which they operate. Such studies could, for example, lead to a better understanding of the linkages between local political culture and the performance of various criminal court tasks such as screening, conviction procurement, and sentencing. They could also be used to assess the impact of the various environmental control devices (such as the media and the appellate courts) upon the processing of criminal cases in different settings, perhaps clarifying the interaction between setting and environment.

Such analyses, however, must await a more refined understanding of the notion of dispositional strategy. While some limited types of valid comparative inquiry are possible at present, the validity of many such inquiries requires that, in a sense, dispositional strategy be controlled. A valid assessment of the impact of various environmental factors upon different courtroom tasks (such as screening and sentencing) cannot be made if the tasks being compared do not perform similar roles within each system. Ignoring these different roles would obscure findings and lead to misleading and unfounded conclusions. Thus, many comparisons between guilty plea and slow plea systems would be unsound, as would some comparisons between systems where prosecutors prescreen cases and systems where the police initiate complaints.

An example of how insensitivity to such considerations can obscure findings was cited in Chapter 1. It was noted that there were marked differences in the conviction rates of St. Louis (where prosecutors prescreen cases) and Kansas City (where police largely control the complaint-initiation process). These differences were reduced considerably when convictions were examined in light of warrants applied for by the police. Eisenstein and Jacob's study of Baltimore, Chicago, and Detroit provides a more recent and detailed analysis of how misleading comparisons of similar measures of criminal court operations can be across different systems.[1] They report that conviction statistics at the trial level reveal similar conviction rates in all three systems, but that considerable differences in sentencing structure were apparent. Chicago appeared to be the harshest as almost all convicted defendants received prison sentences, compared to only one-third of convicted defendants in Detroit. Eisenstein and Jacob go on to note, however, that:

> Quite different outcome patterns emerge when we take preliminary hearing results into account. We find that Detroit convicted more than half of its felony defendants; Baltimore convicted substantially less than half; and Chicago convicted only a quarter. However, the range of convicted defendants sent to prison did not vary greatly. The reason for these differences—when we take preliminary hearing results into account—is shown in the last line of [the table]. Chicago had a low overall conviction rate because its preliminary hearing workgroups screened out most cases, as we showed [earlier]. Only 12.7 percent of all defendants were sent forward to trial; preliminary hearing workgroups convicted a few and took some guilty pleas; the rest were dismissed. Baltimore preliminary hearing workgroups convicted more and dismissed fewer. Finally, in Detroit most defendants went to a trial court if they got as far as the preliminary exam, but substantial screening occurred before that stage through the work of the prosecutor's warrant office.[2]

Thus it is clear that examining the effect of differences in such factors as environmental influences upon the performance of various courtroom tasks without considering differences in overall dispositional strategies would be largely futile.

IMPLICATIONS FOR THE DIRECTION OF CRIMINAL COURT REFORM

An examination of Chapter 3 in light of the analyses reported in the three empirical chapters led to several suggestions for future criminal court research. A similar examination leads to recommendations for the direction of criminal court reform. The organizational perspective developed in Chapter 3 viewed criminal court operations as the result of the tension between two kinds of factors—internal and external. Internal factors relate to the interests of the courtroom elite; external factors concern community expectations of quantitative and qualitative aspects of courtroom operations. These two types of factors were expected to interact differently in different settings, but within a given setting, they are expected to be largely determinative of how cases are processed. External considerations are reflected in the structure of dispositional strategies because of the existence of various environmental control devices which exercise some influence within the court organization, while internal factors are reflected because of the nature of the court's interest and power structure. The impact of the latter upon operating procedures is enhanced by the severe limitations upon the ability of environmental control devices to monitor courtroom operations effectively.

In the empirical analyses it was not really possible to gauge the impact of environmental factors. However, the importance of the evidentiary and case seriousness measures in some of the analyses demonstrated that, to a certain extent, decisions were made in an externally rational manner. For example, the very strong correlation between the case seriousness measure and sentence in guilty plea cases demonstrated that there was a good deal of consistency in the sentences given to defendants who were charged with similar types of offenses and pleaded guilty. But, while the roles of the case seriousness and evidentiary measures were important in some decisions, the impact of various internal considerations was also considerable. This impact was demonstrated in the decision to dismiss in the drug courts, the factors affecting the attainment of a guilty plea, and especially in the sentencing analyses. The results of these analyses lend a good deal of support, at least in Chicago, to the assertion made earlier: While there are certain external constraints upon the operations of criminal courts, these operations are affected significantly by the interests of the courtroom elite.

This conclusion—to the extent it can be supported in other systems—suggests that what is happening in criminal courts is not dissimilar from what transpires in other bureaucracies. What is being maximized in the day-to-day operations of criminal courts is not the interests of its clientele (defendants) or society, but the interests of those who control courtroom operations. Tasks are not structured predominantly to meet the needs of defendants, to protect the community from dangerous felons, or to conform to contemporary notions of due process. Rather, within limits, they are structured in a manner that allows the courtroom elite to dispose of its work load expeditiously and to maximize personal interests. Stated more succinctly, this perspective leads to the view that the fundamental problem with criminal courts is that a small cadre of individuals—charged with the responsibility for performing a given task, vested with the power to perform it, and subjected to few external constraints—has utilized the resources under its control for its own self-interest.

This view has direct implications for what will and will not constitute effective criminal court reform. It suggests that simple increases in criminal court resources will not bring about meaningful change in courtroom operations. Increased flows of resources into the present system would merely make it easier for all concerned to pursue personal interests, under more comfortable conditions. Proposals aimed at enhancing the information available to the various participants and providing them with regular training sessions are also not apt to remedy the problems suggested by the empirical analyses. Observations have indicated that, in most situations, the participants have most of the information they deem relevant and understand the complexities of the system quite well. Formalized bargaining sessions and self-reports of bargaining activity are also bound to be futile; they do nothing to change the realities of the bargaining process. A defendant in a weak bargaining position in a hallway conference will be in just as weak a position in a judge's chambers.

Rather than these somewhat cosmetic reforms, the perspective elaborated upon here leads to the view that before criminal courts can be made responsive to the needs of defendants, community expectations, and the dictates of due process, fundamental modifications must be made in their interest and power structure. In addition, efforts must be made to enhance external monitoring of criminal court operations.

Modification of Interest and Power Structures

Although the notion of modifying the interest and power structures in criminal courts seems somewhat abstract, several very straightforward, concrete steps could be taken to achieve such modifications. For example, to modify the power structure it is recommended that the charging, dismissal, and sentencing powers be stripped from courtroom workgroups. An independent charging board could be set up to evaluate cases referred by the police. The board could refuse to initiate charges in some cases, utilize diversionary programs or mediation boards in other cases, and send others into the felony court system.[3] Cases sent to the court system would then be assigned to a criminal court. The sole function of these courts would be to decide the guilt or innocence of the defendant. If guilt were determined, the case would be sent to an independent sentencing board that would then impose sentence in accordance with set, though flexible, criteria.

This arrangement would have several benefits. First, it would substantially reduce the undesirable consequences of discretion without eliminating it. It was argued that the discretionary nature of the power enjoyed by judges, prosecutors, and defense counsel enabled them to forge a coalition that dominated the operations of criminal courts; the empirical analyses documented some of the manifestations of this dominance. However, eliminating discretion from the system would be self-defeating. Inflexible rules would lead to many injustices. They would also lead to attempts to circumvent the occurrence of certain injustices, resulting in confusion, irrationality, and further inequities.

The approach advocated here maintains the discretion necessary for the meaningful application of the criminal law. By vesting this discretion in separate, independent entities, however, it negates the potential for the types of abuses documented earlier. It would virtually eliminate plea *bargaining* because those concerned with the adjudicative phase of the process would have little with which to bargain. There would be little incentive for overcharging by the charging board and, in any event, the adjudicative team would not be empowered to dismiss charges in exchange for pleas or for any other reason.[4] Since the adjudicative team would have no control over sentencing and could not recommend sentences, it could not be used as a tool to induce expeditious dispositions or sanction recalcitrants.

A second benefit of this arrangement is that it assigns to lawyers—judges, prosecutors, and defense counsel—tasks that their formal training prepares them to perform: applying the law to a given set of facts, determining legal issues, implementing formal procedures, and so forth. Indeed, the transformation of the practice of criminal law to a "true" trial practice could well attract a new breed of lawyers into the criminal courts. Moreover, the realization that every case had to be adjudicated would eliminate many of the tactical maneuvers and foot dragging designed to facilitate guilty pleas. This, in turn, might lead to the application of sophisticated management practices by those in charge of adjudication.

A third advantage is that this arrangement would reaffirm the fact that the charge-initiation and sentencing aspects of the dispositional process are fundamentally different from the adjudicative phase. Wholly different criteria are relevant to the performance of these tasks. But, in the present system, these distinctions all too often became blurred in efforts to "handle the case." Insufficient attention is given to what types of cases ought to be processed in the criminal court system and to the best type of alternate forums to handle disputes and personal problems deemed inappropriate for the criminal justice system. Such neglect gives rise to community dissatisfaction with the operations of criminal courts as well as to later situations that, by their increased gravity, are appropriate for the court system. Perhaps an independent charging agency could devote more consideration to such issues than the present multifaceted court system has in the past. Likewise, a separate sentencing board, unconcerned with adjudicative problems, could be more concerned with meeting the needs of the defendants as well as the community in making the sentencing decision. Such an agency, being system-wide, could eliminate many of the inequities in the sentencing process. This arrangement would also foster discussion as to the type of people (criminologists, lawyers, psychologists, laypeople, or some combination thereof) who should be responsible for the performance of nonadjudicative tasks such as charge initiation and sentencing, as well as the criteria that should be embodied in these decisions.

There is one final advantage to this proposed rearrangement of tasks: By separating largely legal facets of criminal court operations (adjudication) from those with political and social components (charge initiation and sentencing), this arrangement provides for identifiable agencies that could be held accountable for charge initiation and sentencing policies. This might make these agencies more attuned to the consequences of their actions. In addition to being better motivated, these agencies would be better equipped to evaluate their policies than any single component of the present court system. They would also be able to effectuate systemwide policy modifications.

More difficult problems would be involved in any attempt to modify the interest structure within criminal courts. Even if the above recommendations were adopted and the courtroom elite had only adjudicative responsibilities, certain problems would still exist. That is, it would still be in the interests of these individuals to handle cases in an informal, expeditious manner. A modified slow plea system might well emerge in which courtroom regulars performed largely ceremonial trials, and merely shifted responsibility "upstairs" to the sentencing board. While such tendencies might be hard to neutralize, one approach would be to use financial incentives to ensure adversary adjudications. That is, bonuses might be given to prosecutors and public defenders (perhaps even to private attorneys) for the successful handling of cases. There are a number of ways such a system might be implemented—a case-by-case basis, monthly, an annual bonus, or some combination of each. These incentives would, of course, be in addition to regular salaries or fees. Also, they might have to be weighted and based upon deviations from average conviction or acquittal rates. Such difficulties could be worked out in practice. The important thing would be to reintroduce a sense of adversariness into the adjudicative phase of the process.

Enhancement of External Monitoring

What is suggested to enhance the monitoring capabilities of relevant environmental control devices is the development, collection, and use of a set of quantitative indicators of various facets of courtroom operations. Millions of dollars have been spent on crime reporting systems and victimization surveys to gauge and analyze crime. But, to the best of the author's knowledge, virtually nothing has been spent on monitoring the agencies that process those charged with crimes. Various administrative offices regularly produce some aggregate figures on courtroom outputs, but not the type of information necessary for a meaningful evaluation of how cases are being processed. This is a serious oversight. If the operations of criminal courts are examined in light of the perspective outlined in Chapter 3, it can be seen that one of the fundamental problems is the significant limitations on the ability of the court organization's environment to monitor and control its operations. These limitations are related to the rather unique institutional nature of criminal courts: it is not subjected to the forces of competition, its function is too important to eliminate, and its outputs are difficult to evaluate. Consequently, vis-à-vis other types of organizations, criminal courts are relatively closed systems.

The body of indicators suggested here could be collected, analyzed, and distributed by an independent monitoring agency and would be modeled upon the system of indicators used to monitor the state of the national economy. As economic measures gauge such diverse phenomena as unemployment rates, building starts, and wholesale prices, the court measures would focus upon such things as sentencing structures, delays, charge initiation policies, and relevant conviction measures. These measures could be used to gauge not only the performance of the system, but also the performance of individuals and the different components of the system, thereby fostering accountability. Moreover, the information could be used by individual components within the system (such as a charge initiation or sentencing board) to evaluate the impact of their policies, as well as by elements in the court's environment.

The implementation of such a monitoring board would present formidable problems. The appropriate computer technology and methodological sophistication exist, but collecting, analyzing, and distributing the data would be costly. More important, deciding what criteria should be used in evaluating various criminal court operations could cause serious problems. One of the basic problems in criminal justice administration has always been the conflict over the values to be embodied in criminal court decisions such as sentencing and charge initiation. But these conflicts may not be any more troublesome than those in the economic sector. After all, there is much dispute over which economic trends are healthy or unhealthy. An advantage of trying to implement the monitoring system proposed here would be that these conflicts could be addressed on a very practical level. While their resolution may involve a good deal of time and compromise, an ultimate outcome could be the development of a set of fairly concrete criteria to guide criminal court decision makers.

As a concluding note, it should be stressed that this agenda is not meant to be a comprehensive package of reforms that will cure all the ills plaguing criminal courts. Rather, it is proposed as a foundation upon which more extensive and specific suggestions can build. It is viewed as a foundation because, during the period of this study, it became very apparent that the greatest impediments to change in criminal courts are, first, the vested interests that criminal justice practitioners have in the present structure and, second, their power to resist external interference. Nothing less than a fundamental restructuring of the power and interest structure within criminal courts, supplemented by an effective monitoring system, will bring about a criminal court system that can be made responsive to the needs of individual defendants, the expectations of the community, and the dictates of due process.

NOTES

1. James Eisenstein and Herbert Jacob, *Felony Justice: An Organizational Analysis of Criminal Courts*, (Boston: Little, Brown, 1976).
2. Ibid., p. 290.
3. This board would also be responsible for setting bail and, in effect, would replace the preliminary hearing courts. Unlike the preliminary hearing courts, however, its task would not be to determine probable cause. Rather it would be

to determine whether the case, as then constituted, merited criminal adjudication. The board would have the power to effectuate noncriminal resolutions in appropriate cases. It would have its own counsel to advise it on legal aspects of charge initiation in cases deemed appropriate for criminal processing.

4. Exceptional cases in which dismissals were warranted (perhaps because of an occurrence that took place after charges were initiated) would have to be referred to the charging board.

Index

American Bar Association, 5
American Bar Federation, 41
Analysis, organizational mode of, 66-67, 77-78; environmental considerations, 71-77; internal considerations, 67-71; setting, 77
Averments, negative, 19

Bailiffs, 4
Bail studies, 45-49
Baltimore, 153
Barrett, Jessee W., 18
Berlin, 10
Bettman, Alfred, 5, 7-8, 15, 16, 18, 22
Blumberg, Abraham, 152-153
Bond court, in Chicago, 106

Case, seriousness of, 129-130
Case studies, 230-231
Chicago, 153; dismissal rate in, 153; environment, 119-121; felony courts, dispositional tools, 116-119; felony courts, inputs, 109-113; felony courts, personnel, 113-117; felony courts, structure of, 106-109; municipal court, 16; police commissioners in, 10; trial courts, 182-183
Civic Center (Chicago), 109
Clerks, 4
Cleveland, 18; court of common pleas, 13, 16; municipal court, 16, 17
Cleveland crime survey, 3, 5, 11-12; report, 6
Cleveland Foundation, 3

Comparative studies, 231-232
Cook County, 29-32; judgeships in, 119, 135
Cordiality, 183-185
Coughlin, John "Bathhouse," 4
Courtroom elite, 67-71
Crime survey: empirical evidence, 21-32; tradition, 3, 4-5, 15-19; paradigm, 5-8, 19-21
Criminal cases, disposition of, 24-25, 26-27, 28
Criminal Court Building (Chicago), 109
Criminal court reform, 232-238
Criminal lawyers. See Defense attorneys
Criminal procedure, 7, 18-19

Daley, Richard, 119
Data bases: defendent-oriented, 126-127; judge-oriented, 127-128; private defense council, 128
Defendent: degradation ceremonies, 152-153; susceptibility, 112-113, 133-135
Defense attorneys: and decision to pursue case to trial, 195-197; political connections, 4; and preliminary hearing court, 157-158; professional criminal, 12-13; responsiveness of, 137, 169-172
Degradation ceremonies, 152-153
Delays, 22-23
Delay variable, 216-217
Dependent variable, 163

241

242 Index

Detroit, 15, 153
Dismissal, 153-154, 165-169
Dispositional value, 110-112, 133
Dispositional strategy, 44
Dispositions: and crime survey paradigm, 22-23
Drug courts: in Chicago, 108; decisions to dismiss, 167-169; operations of, 169-172

Eisenstein, James, 153
Elite, courtroom, 67-71
England, 18
Environment, and study of criminal courts, 71-77
Evidence, weight of, 130-133

Felony courts, Chicago, 108; dispositional tools, 116-119; inputs, 109-113, 161; personnel, 113-117; structure of, 106-109
Felony courts, decision to dismiss, 165
First offense, and sentencing, 213-216
Foote, Caleb, 45, 48
Frankfurter, Felix, 3
Franklin County (Illinois), 29-32
"Fundamental Trouble, The," 6

Gehlke, C.E., 29-32
"Gentlemanly behavior," 179-185
Gibson, James L., 92
Goffman, Erving, 152-153
Graft, 17
Green, Edward, 55-56
Guilty plea: and sentencing, 206-209, 210-213; in trial courts, 185-190

Hadley, Herbert S., 18
Harrison Street court, 16
Healy, 9-10, 11

Illinois, 3, 5, 10

Jackson, Robert H., 41
Jacob, Herbert, 153
Journal of the American Judicature Society, 15
Judges: competency of, 13; and decision to pursue case to trial, 194-195; and media, 14-15; political connections, 4, 13-14; responsiveness, 135-137
Judicial Attitudes in Sentencing, 54-56
Jury, instructions to, 19

Kansas City, 23
Kenna, Michael "Hinky Dink," 4

Lashley, Arthur, 16
League of Women Voters, 3
"Legal man," 20-21
Legal motions variable, 216
Levin, Martin, 92, 93-97
Line personnel, activity of, 78-81

Manhattan Bail Project, 45
Measurement. *See* Organizations
Minneapolis, 93-94
Missouri, 3, 16
Missouri crime survey, 18
Mohr, Lawrence, 91
Moley, Raymond, 7-8, 12, 13-14, 16, 17
Monitering, external, 237-238
Municipal administration, 5
Municipal reform movement, 4, 6
Murder court, Chicago, 108

Newman, Donald, 50-52
New York, 3
Nonurban systems, 21-22

Organizations, measurement of phenomena: data bases, 126-128; defendent susceptibility, 133-135; dispositional value of case, 133; key concepts, 128-129; responsiveness of participants, 135-143; seriousness of case, 129-130; weight of evidence, 130-133
Organized crime, 4-5

Personnel, 6-7; line, 78-81; and municipal reform, 6-8; and politics, 9-15
Pittsburgh, 93-94
Pleading, defective, 19
"Pleading Guilty for Consideration: A Study of Bargain Justice," 50-52
Pleas: plea bargaining studies, 49-54; guilty, 29, 285-290, 206-209, 210-213
Police Court Ring, 12
Politics, and personnel, 9-15
Pound, Roscoe, 3
Power structure, 234-237
Preemptory challenges, 19
Preliminary hearing courts: in Chicago, 106; defense attorney placement, 157-158; degradation ceremonies, 152-153; informal sanctioning in, 153-156; screening, 160-161; screening, decision to dismiss, 165-169; screening, and drug courts, 169-172; screening, and organiza-

tional considerations, 161-162; screening, problems, 163-165; socialization in, 156-157; time constraints, 158-160
President's Commission on Law Enforcement and Administration of Criminal Justice, 52-54
"Pretrial Detention and Ultimate Freedom," 48
Probation, 29
Probation department, 17
Procedure, rules of criminal, 7
Prohibition, 4-5
Prosecutor: facilities, 17; and "legal man" assumption, 21; offices of, 18; responsiveness of, 142-143; and scheduling, 17
Public defenders, responsiveness of, 140-142

Records, 17
Research, future, 229-232
Responsiveness: of defense council, 137-142; of judges, 135-137; measures of, 212-213; of prosecutors, 142-143

St. Louis, 23
Sanctioning, informal, 153-156
Scheduling privilege, 180-182
Scotland Yard, 10
Screening, 160-161; analytical problems, 163-165; decisions to dismiss, 165-169; organizational considerations, 161-162
Sentencing: hypothetical decision, 81-91; studies of, 54-56; in trial courts, 205-206, 217-219; in trial courts, and guilty plea, 206-209, 210-213; in trial courts, after trial, 209, 213-217

Simon, Herbert, 91
Skogan, Wesley, 119
Smith, Reginald Heber, 6, 9-10, 11-13, 17, 18
Socialization, in preliminary court, 156-157
Studies, 230-232. *See also* Crime surveys
Susceptibility measures, 211-212. *See also* Defend susceptibility

Time constraints, in preliminary hearing court, 158-160
Topical tradition: bail studies, 45-49; paradigm, 41-45; plea bargaining studies, 49-54; sentencing studies, 54-56
Training, in preliminary hearing court, 156-157
Trial courts, 179-180; within court organization, 83-85; decision to pursue a case to trial, 190-197; guilty pleas in, 185-190; operations, 180-185; sentencing in, 205-206, 217-219; sentencing in, and guilty plea, 206-209, 210-213; sentencing in, after trial, 209, 213-217

"Ungentlemanly behavior," 182-183
Urban studies, 21-22

Variables, 163-165
Vetri, Dominick, 53

Wald, Patricia, 48-49
Wickersham Commission report, 10-11, 15
Wigmore, John Henry, 5
Williamson County (Illinois), 29-32

About the Author

PETER F. NARDULLI is Assistant Professor in the Institute of Government and Public Affairs and the Department of Political Science, University of Illinois, Champaign-Urbana. He received a J.D. (1973) and a Ph.D. (1975) from Northwestern University. His broad interests in law, urban politics, and organization theory are joined in the study of criminal justice at the local level. He is currently editing a collection of original essays on the study of criminal courts and working on a study of the delivery of public services.

TEXAS A&M UNIVERSITY-TEXARKANA